NATCHITOCHES CHURCH MARRIAGES
1818–1850

Marriages 379–381, Register 12

NATCHITOCHES CHURCH MARRIAGES 1818-1850

Translated Abstracts
from the
Registers of
St. François des Natchitoches
Louisiana

Elizabeth Shown Mills

HERITAGE BOOKS
2007

HERITAGE BOOKS
AN IMPRINT OF HERITAGE BOOKS, INC.

Books, CDs, and more—Worldwide

For our listing of thousands of titles see our website
at
www.HeritageBooks.com

Published 2007 by
HERITAGE BOOKS, INC.
Publishing Division
65 East Main Street
Westminster, Maryland 21157-5026

Other books by the author:

Natchitoches, 1729-1803

Natchitoches: Translated Abstracts of Register Number Five of the Catholic Church Parish of St. Francois des Natchitoches in Louisiana: 1800-1826

Tales of Old Natchitoches
Elizabeth Shown Mills and Gary B. Mills

International Standard Book Number: 978-1-58549-924-3

To
PIERRE RACHAL, JR.
and his newest 9th great-grandson
PHILIP DANIEL MILLS

Other Books in This Series

Vol. 1
CHAUVIN dit CHARLEVILLE

Vol. 2
NATCHITOCHES, 1729–1803:
Abstracts of the Catholic Church Registers
of the French and Spanish Post of
St. Jean Baptiste des Natchitoches in Louisiana

Vol. 3
TALES OF OLD NATCHITOCHES

Vol. 4
NATCHITOCHES, 1800–1826
Translated Abstracts of Register Number Five
of the Catholic Church Parish of
St. François des Natchitoches in Louisiana

Vol. 5
NATCHITOCHES COLONIALS:
Censuses, Military Rolls, and Tax Lists, 1722–1803

CONTENTS

Preface viii

Register 11 3

Register 12 89

Appendix A 161

Appendix B 162

Index 163

TABLE

Ethnic Distribution - Natchitoches Church Marriages xiv

PREFACE

Marriage registers in the civil parish (county) of Natchitoches, from which all of Northwest Louisiana was carved, do not begin until 1855. As the student of Louisiana history is aware, no civil marriages were performed in the colonial period, since marital unions were *holy* contracts between the spouses and their God; as such, vows had to be exchanged before the Mother Church, and records of such marriages were necessarily entered into the registers of that church. In the ecclesiastical parish of Natchitoches, that authority was the Church of St. François, presently, the Church of the Immaculate Conception within the town of Natchitoches.

After the legal "Americanization" of Louisiana, which began in 1804, civil marriages were permitted. Eventually, state legislation mandated the issuance of civil licenses by the parish judge, the signing of bonds by the groom and his surety as a "guarantee" that the forthcoming union met the requirements of law, and the filing of returns by officiating ministers, judges or justices of the peace. Officials who were already laboring to adapt traditional Creole record keeping practices to new American expectations, and who still viewed marriage more as a religious institution than a state one, were both inconsistent and negligent in the recording and preserving of marriage bonds, licenses, and returns. In the years 1804-1818 a *rare few* such documents were recorded intermittently among the "notarial records" (now bound into 40 volumes termed French Archives) in the parish courthouse; a greater concentration of "loose" marriage papers for the years 1816-1819 have been collected into a single volume labelled "Books 2 & 3, Marriages and Miscellaneous." Between 1819 and 1855, a somewhat larger *but seriously incomplete* number were randomly scattered in conveyances volumes; and another fifty or so unrecorded bonds and licenses from 1830-1831 have been found in the process of remodeling the older courthouse building at Natchitoches. These were published in *The Natchitoches Genealogist*, Vol. 5, October 1980. Still, it is obvious that many (perhaps most) of the civil marriages for the parish of Natchitoches prior to 1855 are completely missing -- making the extant religious records of extreme value to genealogists.

By far the bulk of ecclesiastical marriage entries to be found for the old civil parish of Natchitoches are within the registers of St. François. *NO PROTESTANT RECORDS FOR THIS ERA*

ARE KNOWN TO EXIST aside from the records of Trinity Episcopal church which begin in 1841 and have been very briefly abstracted in *The Natchitoches Genealogist* (Vol. 2, October 1977 and Vol. 4, October 1979). Several small Catholic chapels came into being throughout the civil parish in the period covered by the present volume: St. Jean Baptiste de Cloutierville in 1816, St. Augustine de l'Isle Brevelle in 1829; Nativity of the Blessed Virgin at Campti in 1831; but the bulk of the sacraments administered in these mission chapels were recorded at Natchitoches. Two exceptions existed. Between 1825 and 1829 a separate register was kept for Cloutierville, duplicating entries in the St. François registers; in the latter year, with the formation of St. Augustine, the Cloutierville Church appears to have disbanded or at least lost most of its worshippers. The church was reorganized as a separate parish circa 1845, and ecclesiastical sacraments administered there after 1847 are maintained in the separate registers of that church rather than at St. François. Separate registers for Isle Brevelle and Campti were not begun until 1856 and 1851 respectively.

The years spanned by *Natchitoches Church Marriages: 1818-1850* were tumultous ones in the history of Northwest Louisiana. "Anglo" migrants poured into the region from older states to the east -- Winters, Cables, Smiths, Hickmans, Knotts, and others -- bringing with them a different culture that sometimes clashed with and sometimes meshed with traditional Creole ways. Political unrest in Texas drove many Spaniards or Indio-Spaniards eastward across the Sabine. Such families as the de la Garzas, Moras, Basques, Padillas, and y Barbo had roots already grounded in and around the old Spanish post of Los Adaës near present Robeline, Louisiana, and they became the nucleus of the broad community known even today as Spanish Lake. Myriad conditions across the European continent and British Isles impelled a variety of other men and women to emigrate. Some merely paused at Natchitoches before moving to more remote areas, while such others as Michel Boyce, Joseph Henry, and William Payne became leaders of Natchitoches business, society, and politics. In an ironic quirk of fate, which reflects the extent to which diverse cultures blended, when Natchitochians gathered in 1848 to celebrate the establishmen of the new French Republic, only one Creole (Antoine Prudhomme) was noted among the leaders of the festivity -- the other *confrères* at the podium were of decidedly Anglo or British origins: C. A. Bullard, William L. Tuomey, J. G. Campbell, and the previously mentioned Judge Michel Boyce. (*Red River Republican*, 29 April 1848)

The marriage registers which have been translated, abstracted and indexed within *Natchitoches Church Marriages: 1818-1850* reflect both this cultural diversity and this cultural homogenization. Of the 681 marriages recorded therein, 103 (15%) involved at least one Anglo-American party -- the twelve states from which they hailed ranged widely from Illinois to Vermont to South Carolina, with more New Englanders being represented than any other geographical group. Another 115 marriages (17%) involved at least one Spanish Creole, almost always a Texan, although a few natives of Mexico or New Orleans were represented. While European immigrants to this "traditionally French" settlement might be expected to be French also, that ethnic group actually accounted for only one-half (n=38) of all the foreign-born men and women who were wed in the Church of St. François. The remaining half (n=38) came from such diverse regions as England, Ireland, Belgium, Switzerland, Italy, and Canada. Nearly 15% (n=101) of the marriages involved free people of color, usually in-group marriages although 5 cases of "racial crossover" are documentable (all involved individuals whose African ancestry was several generations removed and, in two of the five cases, can be found only by tracing the families involved back through a prior residence at the Ouachita Post to their origins in a northern English colony). Two of the marriages within this Catholic church (.2%) involved Jewish migrants from the Carolinas. Cross-cultural marriages accounted for roughly half of all unions. (See Table 1.) Some distinctive features or preferences do appear in out-group marriages; for example, Anglo-Americans were more prone to marry French Creoles than Spanish Creoles, and they were more apt to choose French Creoles who already possessed some Anglo or British ancestry.

Marriages from four of the St. François registers have been translated for *Natchitoches Church Marriages, 1818-1850*: Registers 7, 8, 11, and 12. The latter two volumes comprise the main marriage series for the period and are the framework upon which the published volume is compiled. Some of the entries recorded in Registers 11 and 12 are "originals," containing actual signatures of the parties involved, while other entries are "recorded copies" for which originals *sometimes* can be found in Register 8. Within Register 7, a volume set aside by church authorities for the baptisms of nonwhite children, one marriage (white) has been found; it is published as Appendix A. Register 8 is not actually a "register" for the "recording" of marriages, but a bound and unpaginated collection of random loose sheets representing "originals" of *some* of the marriage entries for the period. Many chronological gaps appear in Register 8's collection; for example, there are no entries at all for the years 1842-1844 although *copies* of records for these years are to be found in Register 12. In every case in which Registers 11-12 contain a recording for which the original may be found in Register 8, both versions have been minutely compared before the translated abstract was made, and a cross-reference appears in the abstract. Two Register 8 entries are not to be found in either Register 11 or 12. These are presented in Appendix B.

In using Registers 11 and 12 as the framework of *Natchitoches Church Marriages, 1818-1850*, problems with both organization and numbering have to be reconciled. Apparently these two volumes were once combined but were later split and rebound. Therefore, the first entry for 1837 appears in Register 11 and all subsequent entries for 1837 are in Register 12. Through 1837 the pastors numbered entries consecutively *each year*, beginning with #1 at the start of each new year, but in 1838 this numbering system was abandoned. Where annual numbers appear in Registers 11 and 12, the numbers are included in the translated abstracts and appear on the second line of the marginal notation (for example: #1-1818). Meanwhile, in January 1837, a new system of consecutive numbering was adopted. The pastor or clerk responsible for recording entries appears to have counted all previous entries and then began numbering from that point; however, he miscounted the number of prior entries and began with #348 instead of #351. In presenting this volume of translated abstracts, the editor has inserted the numbers 1-347 on the earlier entries. In order to cope with the miscalculation of numbers by the original clerk, three entries at the end of Register 11 have been assigned the "bis": [i.e.: the last six entries are 345, 345 (bis), 346, 346 (bis), and 347, 347 (bis)]. In this manner, #348 falls into line with the numbers recorded in Register 12.

In writing the parish church to order photocopies of desired entries, *the researcher should use the annual number whenever one appears*. The parish clerk cannot readily locate Register 11 entries from the overall number. If the researcher wishes, he may secondarily identify Register 11 entries according to the added overall number (i.e.: Mills, *Natchitoches Church Marriages, 1818-1850*, #250), which would assist the secretary in the event that she desires to consult the translated abstract. If no annual number appears beside the published abstract, then the overall number should be used. It is regrettable that users of these records must be inconvenienced by the inconsistent numbering of the originals, but it is also understood that parish priests of the early 19th century did not anticipate their registers being used by a legion of genealogical researchers!

The careful genealogist also will note one other "discrepancy" in the records covered by this volume. *Numerous* marriages occurred between cousins (a trait common to most societies). For some such unions as remote as third cousins once-removed, dispensations from the impediment of consanguinity were requested and obtained, while in other cases in which the spouses were first cousins there is no reference to a marital dispensation at all. In at least one of the latter cases, as noted in the registers, the marriage was "rectified" decades later. When notations of marital dispensations are included in the entries, the thorough researcher will want to locate a copy of that dispensation to glean additional detail. However, *these are not maintained by the parish church*. Requests for dispensations were forwarded to the bishop and remained in the diocesan office. Bishopric files containing requests for dispensations from

Natchitoches during this period are now housed in the Archives of the University of Notre Dame, *but must be personally consulted by the researcher or by someone in his employ. Letters of request should NOT be sent to the university archives.*

By and large the dispensations issued for Natchitoches couples covered four types of impediments: 1) consanguinity (i.e.: a blood relationship); 2) affinity (i.e.: a relationship created by marriage; the union of a man and his sister-in-law, for example, would be prohibited unless special circumstances justified the granting of a dispensation); 3) disparity of faiths (i.e.: parties are of differing religions); and 4) marriage during a prohibited period of the Church calendar. Within the published abstracts, researchers will note several instances of disparity of faith in which it is stated that the non-Catholic party has met the requirements for marriage to a Catholic within the latter's church. Very generally, these requirements were: 1) that no legal or moral impediment exists; 2) that the non-Catholic party agrees not to interfere with the freedom of the Catholic party to worship with the Church; and 3) that the non-Catholic party agrees to the rearing, within the Church, of all children born of the union.

A final word must be directed especially to researchers whose family resided at Natchitoches but who have no knowledge of a Catholic connection: the identification of one's ancestors as Protestants should not lead the researcher to ignore the Catholic registers. Migrants into Louisiana from other states usually did not move alone. Censuses, for example, may indicate that one's Protestant ancestor migrated from Tennessee, and auxiliary research may indicate a connection between him and a fellow Tennesean in Natchitoches, Julius C. Saunders. While extant courthouse records may never indicate a place of origins in Tennessee for either, the record of Saunder's marriage in the Catholic Church reveals that he was born in the county of Davidson. The use of Catholic records can be even more important in cases in which one's own direct ancestor remained Protestant while that ancestor's sibling married a Catholic. Again, for example, descendants of Miller Dendy of Sabine Parish once expressed a failure to identify his mother's maiden name in any records of the area, although through a variety of records they had reconstructed his birth family. The only known area record which identifies the birth name of the mother is the Catholic marriage of Miller's sister Elizabeth to Theodore Buvens in 1845 (Reg. 12, #613).

Used thoroughly, but with due caution, the Catholic records of the Parish of St. François have much to offer genealogists of all ethnic backgrounds. As always, the editor of this series recommends that users go beyond the limitations of the published work. Photocopies of all documents vital to one's lineage should be acquired, studied, and carefully compared to all other known records, rather than relying upon a translated abstract. All humans err. Despite sincere efforts otherwise, the compiler of this volume undoubtedly has incorporated some mistakes into her work in the process of translating, typing, and indexing. The original clerks or priests who recorded the entries definitely made their own mistakes; in some cases the editor has caught and noted these within the publication, and thorough family researchers undoubtedly will uncover others. Above all, the researcher should remember that one record, alone, cannot be considered an absolute authority -- not even a church record.

E.S.M.

TABLE 1

Natchitoches Church Marriages, 1818-1850
Ethnic Distribution

Ethnicity of Spouses	# of Marriages in this Category	% of All Marriages
French Creole - French Creole	307	45.1
Free Nonwhite - Free Nonwhite	96	14.1
Spanish Creole - Spanish Creole	77	11.3
Anglo American - French Creole	65	9.5
French - French Creole	38	5.6
Spanish Creole - French Creole	31	4.5
Anglo American - Anglo American	19	2.8
European - European	8	1.1
Anglo American - European	6	.9
Italian (or Swiss Italian) - French Creole	6	.9
British - French Creole	5	.8
Anglo American - Spanish Creole	5	.8
Anglo American - Free Nonwhite	2:	
Spanish Creole - Free Nonwhite	2:	.8
French Creole - Free Nonwhite	1:	
Anglo American - British	4	.4*
Canadian - French Creole	3	.4*
German - French Creole	3	.4*
Anglo American - Italian	1	.1
Anglo American - Jewish	1	.1
French Creole - Jewish	1	.1
Totals	681	100.0*

----

*Slight variations exist in fractional points due to necessity of rounding off percentages.

Sincere appreciation is extended to the past and present pastors and secretaries of the Church of the Immaculate Conception at Natchitoches for the generous assistance which they have rendered to the editor, for the courteousness they extend to a seemingly endless stream of genealogists, and for their concern for the preservation of the priceless records which document the lives of the humble as well as the great men who settled Northwest Louisiana.

NATCHITOCHES CHURCH MARRIAGES
1818-1850

REGISTER 11

1818: Registre de mariages des Blancs et Libres de Natchitoches, comienza en 13 de Octubre 1818

1.
#1-1818

ANDRES GALINDO (s)
MARIA CONCEPCION CARMONA (x)
13 October 1818. 3 bans.
Groom: 25, native of Saltillo, legitimate son of Francisco Galindo and Maria Getrudis de Cuellar. Bride: 22, native of San Antonio de Bexar, legitimate daughter of Francisco Carmona and Catalina Estrada, all of the Kingdom of Mexico. Witnesses: Francº Ruiz (s); Pedro Procela (s); Juan Mora (s); Patricio de Torres (s); Encarnasion Chirino (s). Priest: Francisco Magnes.

2.
#2-1818

PIERRE WALLET [WALLACE] (x)
MARIE BASILIA GRANDE (x)
13 October 1818. 3 bans.
Groom: 19, native of Bayoupier, legitimate son of James Wallet and [blank] Gagne. Bride: 14, native of Nacogdoches, legitimate daughter of Julien Grande and Maria Trinidad Flores. Witnesses: Francº Ruiz (s); Pedro Procela (s); Juan Mora (s); Patricio de Torres (s); Encarnasion Chirino (s). Priest: Francisco Magnes.

3.
#3-1818

JOSE AGUINO BARRON (x)
MARIA CESARIA DE LA CRUX (s)
19 October 1818. 3 bans.
Groom: 19, legitimate son of José Antonio Barron and Maria Antonio Hernandez, all natives of San Antonio de Bexar. Bride: 16, legitimate daughter of Pedro Cruz and Juana Amador, all natives of San Antonio de Bexar. Witnesses: Ml Prevot Dupré (s); Manuel Rodrigue (x); Joseph Castro (x); Juan José Medina (s). Priest: Francisco Magnes.

4.
#4-1818

LOUIS TOMASIN (x)
MARIE CEDALISSE RACHAL (x)
19 October 1818. 3 bans.
Groom: 23, legitimate son of Louis Tomasin and Chatarine Lattier, a bachelor and native of this parish. Bride: [illegible], native of this post, legitimate daughter of Bmy. Rachal and Françoise Laprery [La Berry]. Witnesses: Ml Prevot Dupré (s); Pierre Baudouin (x);

Louis Julien Rachal (x); Nicola Gracia (s); Priest: Francisco Magnes.

5. JUAN BAPTISTA ISAC FREDIEU (s)
#5-1818 MARIE LOUISE LISSE LAFFITTE (x)
28 October 1818. 3 bans.
Groom: 21, bachelor, native of this post, legitimate son of Augustin Fredieu and Maria Juana Sorel, already deceased. Bride: 14, native of this post, legitimate daughter of Pablo Laffitte already deceased, and Mariana Soto. Witnesses: Athanasse Poissot (s); Honoré Fredieu (s); Jean Bte. Fontenau (s); François Serpentini (s); Dominiqe. Sorel (x); Antoin Fredieu (x). Priest: Francisco Magnes.

6. CHARLES NERESTANT ROQUES (s)
#6-1818 MARIE POMPOSSE METOYER (x)
3 November 1818. 3 bans.
Groom: native of Nueva Orleans, natural son of Pedro Roques and Lisette Glaplion, a free woman of color. Bride: 17, native of this parish, legitimate daughter of Agustin Metoyer and Marie Añes, all free people of color. Witnesses: Pierre Metoyé (s); J. Btte. Conan (s); M. Llorens (s); J. Bte. Metoyer, fils Augtin. (s); Agustin Metoyer (x); Btte. Adlé (s); Maxlle. Metoyer (s); Jn. Bte. Metoyer, fils Louis (s). Priest: Francisco Magnes.

7. CEZER BOSSIER (s)
#7-1818 MARIE MODESTE GONIN (x)
9 November 1818. 3 bans.
Groom: 22, native of this post, legitimate son of Sulans Bossier and Leonor Himel. Bride: 16, native of this post, legitimate daughter of Francisco Gonin, already deceased, and Marie Barbara Federic. Witnesses: Me. Barbara Federic. J. Bte. Lestage (x); Barthelemy Lestage (x); A. L. Deblieux (s); Ae. Chamard (s); Samuel [illegible] (s); J. B. Trezinni (s). Priest: Francisco Magnes.

8. LOUIS EMMANUEL GALLIEN (x)
#8-1818 MARIE FRANÇOISE TOMASIN (x)
19 November 1818. 3 bans.
Groom: 22, native of this post, legitimate son of Nicolas Gallien and Marie Le Cour. Bride: 16, native of this post, legitimate daughter of Louis Tomasin and Catarine Lattier. Witnesses: Joseph Lattier, fils (s) Louis Thomassin (x); Louis Galien (x); Me. Franç. Dupré (s); [Le] Comte, fils (s); Fs. Rambin (s). Priest: Francisco Magnes.

9. JOSEPH LATTIER (s)
#9-1818 MARIE ADELINNE GALIEN (x)
23 November 1818. 3 bans
Groom: 18, legitimate son of J^{n} Baptista Lattier and Marie Pelagie Federic, native of this post. Bride: 19, native of this post, legitimate daughter of Nicolas Galien and Marie Le Cour, already deceased. Witnesses: Baptiste Latier, pere (x); Neville Galien, fils (x); [Le] Conte, fils (s); Mc Sompayrac (s); M^{l} Prevost Dupré (s); J^{h} Lattier (s); J^{n} B^{te} Lattier, fils (s). Priest: Francisco Magnes.

10. AGUSTIN CLOUTTIER (x)
#10-1818 MARIA TERESA METOYER (x)
12 December 1818.
Groom: 30, free man of color, native of this jurisdiction, natural son of Françoise, now deceased. Bride: 18, native of this jurisdiction, natural daughter of Magdeleine Grappe, a free woman of color. Witnesses: J. B^{te} Metoyer, fils Aug^{tin} (s); J^{n} B^{te} Metoyer, fils de Louis (s); Auguste Metoyer (s). Priest: Francisco Magnes.

[Ed. note: The above entry does not appear on the microfilm that has been made of this register by Northwestern State University of Natchitoches.]

11. LUCAS S. HAZELTON (s)
#11-1818 CARMELITA CHAVUS (s)
12 December 1818. No bans.
Groom: 25, from New York, legitimate son of Samuel Hazelton and Rachel Shattuck. Bride: 16, native of this post, legitimate daughter of Francisco Chavus and Marie Jean Manet Malege. Priest has been informed that no blood relationship exists between parties. Witnesses: Julia (s) [No last name; appears to be same as Julia J. Slocum, below]; Marianne Bardon (s); François Chabus (s); John Sibley (s); B. Leonard (s); Marcelitte Cortes (s); Julia J. Slocum (s); W. T.(?) Cobbs (s); Margaret Sibley (s). Priest: Francisco Magnes.

12. CHARLES NOYRIT (s)
#12-1818 MARIE ASELY LAMBRE (s)
23 December 1818. No bans.
Groom: 34, native of Libos, department of Lot- [et]-Garonne, Kingdom of France; legitimate son of Graciano Noyrit and Teresa Campy. Bride: native of this post, legitimate daughter of Remy Lambre and Susanna Proudhomme, already deceased. Priest has been informed that no blood relationship exists between parties. Witnesses: Benjamin Metoyer (s); Aurore Lambre (s); Lambre (s); Prudhomme (s); J. W. Cortes (s); G. Robertson (s); A^{re} Ponthieu (s). [One illegible signature]. Priest: Francisco Magnes.

13. JEAN BTTE. TREZZINI (s)
#1-1819 MARIE ARTHEMISE CHAMARD (s)
6 January 1819. 3 bans.
Groom: 22, native of Milan, Italy, legitimate son of Pier Celestin Trezzini and Marie Camadi. Bride: 16, native of this post, legitimate daighter of Michel Chamard and Marie Euphrosine Rambin. Witnesses: Michel Chamard (s); Luis Trezzini (s); Catharine Chamard (s); Rozamond Chamard (s); A^{e} Chamard (s); A^{d} Lauve (s); Deblieux (s); Jh. Tauzin (s); A. Sompayrac (s); A. L. Deblieux (s). Priest: Francisco Magnes.

14. JOSEPH MANUEL SANCHEZ (x)
#2-1819 JUANA BAPTISTA BARELA (x)
17 January 1819
[Entry badly blurred]
Groom: 23, native of San Antonio de Bexar; son of Joseph Sanchez and [illegible] Coronado [Casanova?]. Bride: [age illegible], native of Nacogdoches, legitimate daughter of Antonio Barela and Maria Josepha Caro. Witnesses: José Sanches (s); José Ant^{o} Sepulvedo (s); José Noriss(?) (s); José Aco ___ [illegible] (s); Manuel B[ustamente?] (s). Priest: Francisco Magnes.

15. CHARLES MANANSON (x)
#3-1819 MARIE LOUISE BOUDOIN (x)
1 February 1819. 3 bans.
Groom: 26, bachelor, native of Malmel, Isle of St^{o} Domingo, legitimate son of Pier Mananson and Magdalenne Dupré. Bride: 19, native of this post, legitimate daughter of Pierr Bouduoin and Anne Rovin. Witnesses: Pier Boudouin (x); J^{n} B^{te} Cazenave (s); Athanas Brosset (s); B. Chenat (s); Rocheto (s). Priest: Francisco Magnes.

16. ANTONIO SOLIS (x)
#4-1819 MARIA DEL PILAR SARNAC (x)
8 February 1819. 3 bans.
Groom: 23, native of Alamo de Parrai, legitimate son of Estevan Solis and Juana Oliveros. Bride: 17, legitimate daughter of Luis Sarnac and Ana Maria de la Cerda. Witnesses: Guillom Veve (x); François Serpentini (s); Louis Saucier (s); Domingo Losoya (x); Ignacio de los Santos Coy (s). Priest: Francisco Magnes.

17. FIRMIN POISSOT (s)
#5-1819 JULIANA JOSEPHA SLOCUM (s)
11 February 1819. 3 bans.
Groom: 17 years, 16 months, native of this post, a bachelor, legitimate son of Athanas Poissot and Elenne Pavie. Bride: 14 years, native of New York, New Durham; legitimate daughter of Charles Slocum and Dame

Thanks Mills. Witnesses: Charles Slocum (s); Athanase Poissot (s); Thankful Slocum (s); Hélène Pavie (s); Aaron Coe (s); B. Leonard (s); B. Dranguet (s); Bauvard St. Amans (s); John C. Carr (s); Pavie (s); Prudhomme, fils (s). Priest: Francisco Magnes

18. #6-1819 LOUIS ARCOIT (s)
MARIE ASPASYE DUVOIS (x)
17 February 1819. 3 bans.
Groom: 26, single, native of St. Louis in Illinois, legitimate son of Francisco Arcoit and Marie Sueyos. Bride: 24, native of this post, legitimate daughter of François Duvois and Leonor J.[n] Ris of this post. Witnesses: François Duvois (x); Remy Perot (x); Henry Triche (s); P.[re] Ternié (s); P.[re] Elie (x). Priest: Francisco Magnes.

[Ed. note: This entry does not appear on NSU's microfilm.]

19. #7-1819 HONORÉ FREDIEU (s)
SUSANNE PLESANS (s)
27 February 1819. 3 bans.
Groom: 19, native of this post, bachelor, legitimate son of Augustin Fredieu and Susanne Plesans*. Bride: 20, native of this post. legitimate daughter of Bertrand Plaisans and Marie Barbe Grillet. Witnesses: Bertrand Plaisance (x); Marie Barbe Grillet (x); Manuel Rachal (s); A.[d] Lauve (s); B. Vienne (s); C. Noyrit (s); Germaine (s); Rouquier, fils (s); Isaac Plaisance (s); A. Sompayrac (s). Priest: Francisco Magnes.

[Ed. note: *This name is in error. The groom's mother did not have the same name as his bride. According to Honore's baptismalentry, he was son of Augustin Fredieu and Marie Jeanne Sorel. See E. S. Mills, *Natchitoches, 1800-1826* (New Orleans: Polyanthos, 1980), No. 6.]

20. #8-1819 JOSEPH FELIX VARELA (x)
MARIA JULIANA QUIÑONES (x)
9 March 1819. 3 bans.
Groom: 17, bachelor, native of Nacogdoches, legitimate son of Feliciano Antonio Varela and Maria Josefa Caro. Bride: 18. Legitimate daughter of Joseph Quiñones and Maria Ynes Cruz, native of Bexar. Witnesses: Concepcion Ybarbo (x); [illegible] Varela (x); Rouzet (s), John Brown (s), Phillip [illegible] (s); Ygnacio de los Santos Coy (s). Priest: Francisco Magnes.

21. #9-1819 JEAN JACQUE LAMBRE (s)
MARIE LISE CLOUTTIER (s)
1 April 1819. 3 bans.
Groom: 23, native of this post, legitimate son of Remy

Lambre and Susanne Prudhomme, already deceased. Bride: 14, native of this post, legitimate daughter of Pierre Clouttier and Marie Salvant, already deceased. Witnesses: Prudhomme (s); Bmin. Metoyer (s); J. F. Hertzog (s); Mc. Sompayrac (s); Ml. Prevost Dupré (s); Jn. Pre. Me. Dubois (s). Priest: Francisco Magnes.

22. FRANÇOIS DERVAN (x)
#10-1819 MARIE LOUISE CARMELITE LANGLOIS (x)
15 April 1819. 3 bans.
Groom: 20, native of this jurisdiction, bachelor, legitimate son of deceased Jean Baptiste Dervan and Marie Elenne Brevel. Bride: 22, native of this jurisdiction, legitimate daughter of Agustin Langlois and Marie Celeste Vercher [Verger]. Witnesses: Lavespère (s); P. S. Compère (s); Fçois Frederic (s); Jn. Bte. Lattier, fils (s); Augustin Langlois (s). Priest: Francisco Magnes.

23. JOSEPH FRANÇOIS LATTIER (x)
#11-1819 MARIE HORRORE [AURORE] DUPRE (x)
17 April 1819. 3 bans.
Groom: 23, native of the parish of Rapides, legitimate son of Joseph Lattier and Françoise Slecttre, now deceased. Bride: 17, native of this parish, legitimate daughter of Pier Dupré, already deceased, and Marie Françoise Lecour. Witnesses: Françoise, Widow Dupré (x); Ml. Prevost Dupré (s); Fs. Lattier (s); A. Baillio (s); Fs. Perot, fils (s); Nicola Gracia (s); Julien Delouche (s). Priest: Francisco Magnes.

24. CEZER TOMASIN (x)
#12-1819 MARIE DENIS DERVAN (x)
20 April 1819. 3 bans.
Groom: 21, bachelor, legitimate son of Louis Tomasin and Chatarine Lattier, already deceased. Bride: 19, legitimate daughter of Jean Bte. Dervan and Marie Elenne Brevel, all residents and natives of this jurisdiction. Dispensation given for impediment of third grade consanguinity existing between spouses through the mother of the groom and the father of the bride. Witnesses: Louis Tomasin (x); Marie Elenne Brevel (x); Ls. Derbanne (s); Btte. Adlé (s); Jh. Lattier, fils (s): Julien Delouche (s). Priest: Francisco Magnes.

25. JUAN MARIA LASARINO (s)
#13-1819 MARIA JOSEPHA LA VEGA FLORES (x)
28 April 1819. 3 bans.
Groom: 23, bachelor, native of Alamo de Porrai, legitimate son of Joseph Lasarino and Juana Maria Rivas. Bride: 16, native of Nacogdoches, natural daughter of Maria Antonia Flores. Witnesses: Jos. Lasarino (x); Juan Mora (s); José Maria Capelo (s); Jossé Maria (s);

Ignacio de los Santos Coy (s); José Luis de la Bega (s). Priest: Francisco Magnes.

26. THEODORO QUINTERO (x)
#14-1819 MARIA IGNACIA ROSALES (x)
28 April 1819. 3 bans.
Groom: 20, bachelor, native of the Mission of Pegotes in the province of Coaguila, legitimate son of Domingo Quintero and Felipa Hernandes. Bride: 16, native of Nacogdoches, legitimate daughter of Julian Rosales and Agustina Alamillo. Witnesses: "Ignacio de los Santos Coy for Rosales," (s); José de la Bega (s); Juan Mora (s); José Maria Capela (s); Juan Maria Lazarin (s). Priest: Francisco Magnes.

27. JEAN BTTE. ZENOR RAMBIN (x)
#15-1819 MARIE AGENLA PALVADO (x)
28 April 1819. 3 bans.
Groom: 21, bachelor, native of this parish, legitimate son of Michel Rambin and Marie Thérèse Malloud, already deceased. Bride: 16, native of this jurisdiction, legitimate daughter of Jean Palvado and Leonor Tessier, all inhabitants of this parish. Witnesses: Michel Rambin (x); Jean Palvado (x); Juan Mora (s); José de la Bega (s); Lauran Maillioux, fils (s); Bte. Charleville (s). Priest: Francisco Magnes.

28. JEAN LOUIS CRISOSTOM PERAUT (x)
#16-1819 MARIE ARSISE TERNIER (x)
29 April 1819. 3 bans.
Groom: 20, bachelor, native of this parish, legitimate son of Jean Crisostom Peraut and Marie Louisse Salvant, already deceased. Bride: 13, legitimate daughter of Pierre Ternier and Marie Rosse Gagne, all inhabitants of this jurisdiction. Witnesses: Crisostom Peraut (x); Remy Perot (s); Bauvard St. Amans (s); Jn. B. Perot (s); Fs. Perot, fils (s); Hre. Fredieu (s); Marie Françoise Gagne (x). Priest: Francisco Magnes.

29. ONEZIME ST. ANDRÉ (s)
#17-1819 MARIE HERZILE ADLÉ (x)
20 May 1819. 3 bans.
Groom: 26 years and 1 month, native of this jurisdiction, legitimate son of Andres St. Andres and Marie Jacob Rachal. Bride: 13, legitimate daughter of Jn. Bte. Adlé the elder, and of Marie Victoir Brevel. Witnesses: Btte. Adlé (s); André St. André (x); Jh. Vercher (s); Baltazard Brevel (s); Pre. Michel (s); J. F. Hertzog (s); Silvestre Rachal(?) (s). Priest: Francisco Magnes.

30. JOSEPH MIGUEL DELGADO (x)
#18-1819 MARIA NICOLASA LONGORIA (x)
21 June 1819. 3 bans.

Groom: 36, native of San Antonio de Bexar, bachelor, legitimate son of Manuel Delgado and Angela Arocha. Bride: 22, native of town of San Fernando de Aguaverde. Legitimate daughter of Ignacio Longoria and Maria Antonia Cortina. Bride is widow of Francisco Sn. [illegible], by whom she had no children. Witnesses: Rowzee? (s); Domingo Losoya (x); Ignacio de los Santos Coy (s); Agustin Dunois?. Priest: Francisco Magnes.

31. #19-1819 GAVRIEL JUAN DUVOIS (s)
MARIE ADELLE RACHAL (x)
1 July 1819. 3 bans.
Groom: 39, bachelor, legitimate son of Nicolas Duvois, already deceased, and Catharina Bouvai, natives of Neyrac in the province of Lot-et-Garont. Bride: 19, native of this town, legitimate daughter of Louis Rachal and Maria Lavery, already deceased. Witnesses: Jn. Bte. Rachal (x); Bmy. Rachal (x); José Rachal, fils (x); Fs. Perot, fils (s); Antoine Coindet (s); Jas. F. Porter (s); Chas. Slocum (s). Priest: Francisco Magnes.

32. #20-1819 JOSEPH MIGUEL YVARBO (x)
MARIA JETRUDIS PROCELA (x)
19 July 1819. 3 bans.
Groom: 29, native of Nacogdoches, bachelor, legitimate son of Joseph yBarbo and Maria Anastasia Mansolo, already deceased. Bride: 14, native of Nacogdoches, legitimate daughter of José Maria Procela and Maria Manuela Cerda. Witnesses: José Maria Procela (x); Josef Ybarbo (x); Ignacio de los Santos Coy (s); Cassenava (s); José Ignacio Acosta (s); Agustin Dunois? (s). Priest: Francisco Magnes.

33. #21-1819 JOSEPH CRISOSTOMO CORDOVA (s)
MARIA MANUELA SANCHES (x)
30 July 1819. 3 bans.
Groom: 20, bachelor, native of Nacogdoches, legitimate son of Joseph Cordova and Maria Tivurcia Ybarbo. Bride: 18, native of Nacogdoches, legitimate daughter of Mariano Sanches and Maria Paula Ruis. Witnesses: Mariano Sanchez (x); Ignacio de los Santos Coy (s); Calletano Villareal (s); Juan Varrera (s); José Cordova (x); Hermasilla (s); [one illegible signature]. Priest: Francisco Magnes.

34. #22-1819 JUAN JOSEPH DE LUNA (x)
MARIA JETRUDIS CORDOVA (x)
16 September 1819. 3 bans.
Groom: 17, native of Havahia [La Bahia?], legitimate son of Faustino de Luna and Maria Josefa Herrera, already deceased. Bride: [age blank]; native of Nacogdoches

Legitimate daughter of Joseph Cordova and Tiburcia Ybarvo. Witnesses: José Cordova (x); Antonio Trevino (x); Ignacio de Santos Coy (s); Ramon de los Santos Coy (s); Rafl. Gonz. de Hermosillo (s). Priest: Francisco Magnes.

35.
#23-1819

VALENTIN DUBOIS (s)
MARIE ZELINE DUPRE (x)
23 September 1819. 3 bans.
Groom: 21, native of the parish of Rapides, legitimate son of Juan Baptista Dubois and Rosa Slecttre. Bride: 18, native of Natchitoches, legitimate daughter of Athanase Dupré and Cecile LeCour. Witnesses: Athanase Dupre (x); Jn. Bte. Duvois (x); Ylario Carrasco (x); Antoin Lemoin (x); Thos. Graham (s); Jean Baptiste Dubois, fils (s). Priest: Francisco Magnes.

36.
#24-1819

ANDRÉ MICHEL RAMBIN (s)
MARIE EMÉ [AIMÉE] CASANOUVE (x)
30 September 1819. 3 bans.
Groom: 24, legitimate son of Michel Rambin and Teresa Mailloud. Bride: 14, native of Natchitoches, legitimate daughter of Michel Denis Casaneuve of the town of La Rochelle, parish of St. Jean du Perot, and Marie Ris. Witnesses: Cazenave (s); Bernot, aine (s); Fçois Rouquier (s); Ml. Barberoux (s); Paul Cazenave (s); "Geo. McTier for Michal Rambine" (s); Marie Ris (s); Bauvard St. Amans (s); Mailloud (s). Priest: Francisco Magnes.

37.
#25-1819

JOSEPH ANDRES TORRES (x)
MARIA DE JESUS (DE) LEON (x)
3 October 1819. 3 bans.
Groom: "about 28," native of the city of Lima in the parish of la Merced, legitimate son of Bernardo Torres and Rosa Espinosa. Bride: "about 20," native of San Antonio de Bexar, legitimate daughter of Valentin de Leon, already deceased, and Maria Isavel Flores. Witnesses: Juan José Medina (s); Juan Rrera [Herrera?] (s); Manuel Bustamente (s). Priest: Francisco Magnes.

38.
#26-1819

LOUIS GERONIMO RACHAL (s)
MARIE LOUISE CELINE PLAISANCE (s)
27 December 1819. 3 bans.
Groom: 19 years, bachelor, native of this parish, legitimate son of Dominique Rachal and Rosalie Vorchor. Bride: 14, native of this parish, legitimate daughter of Bertrand Plaisance and Marie Barbare Grillet. Witnesses: D. Rachal (s); Arnaud Lauve (s); S. Davenport (s) A. G. N___ [illegible] (s); Julio Estrada (s); Honoré Fredieu (s); Barbe Grillet (x); [one illegible signature]. Priest: Francisco Magnes.

39. JOSEPH ENCARNACION CHIRINO (s)
#1-1820 MARIA JOSEFA CANDIDA DELGADO (s)
20 January 1820. 3 bans.
Groom: 32, bachelor, native of Nacogdoches. Legitimate son of Bartolo Chirino, already deceased, and of Maria Josefa Arriola. Bride: 25, native of San Antonio de Bexar, single, legitimate daughter of Manuel Delgado and Angela Arocha, already deceased. Witnesses: Mª Josefa Arriola (x); José Miguel Delgado (x); Martin Ybarbo (x); James Long (x); Manuel Bustamte. (s). Priest: Francisco Magnes.

40. MANUEL RACHAL (s)
#2-1820 MARIE LOUISSE LECOUR (x)
24 January 1820. 3 bans.
Groom: 20, single, native of this jurisdiction, legitimate son of Mr. Antoine Rachal, already deceased, and Mde. Marie Louisse Lemoin. Bride: 14, native of this jurisdiction, legitimate daughter of Mr. Gaspar LaCour and Mde. Marie Felicité Brevel. Witnesses: Gaspar Lacour (x); Me. Felicité Brevel (x); Silvestre Rachal (s); [Le] Conte, fils (s); Will. A. Dromgoole; Ls. Gme. Rachal (s); Narcisse Rachal (s); Nicola Gracia (s); Ls. Derbanne (s). Priest: Francisco Magnes.

41. FRANÇOIS PERAUT (s)
#3-1820 MARIE MANNET FELIS FONTANEAU (s)
27 January 1820, 3 bans.
Groom: 23, native of this parish, single, legitimate son of Francisco Peraut and Marie Agat Lavery, already deceased. Bride: 19, native of this parish, legitimate daughter of Louis Fonteneau, already deceased, and Marie Pelagie Grappe. Witnesses: "Le. Fonteno, for my father" (s); Manuel Rachal (s); Jean Bte. Fontenau (s); H. Bossier (s); Chevalier (s). Bride signed as "Manette Fontenau." Priest: Francisco Magnes.

42. HILAIRE LAVESPÈRE (x)
#4-1820 MARIE AGATHE RACHAL (s)
7 February 1820, 3 bans.
Groom: 26, native of this parish, legitimate son of François Lavespère and Marie Louise Dervan. Bride: 21, native of this jurisdiction, legitimate daughter of Louis Bertelemy Rachal and Marie Françoise Grillet. Witnesses: Ls. Bertelemis Rachal (s); Lavespere (s); Compère (s); Prudhomme, fils (s); Prudhomme (s); Ls. Gme. Rachal (s); Clement Rachal (s). Priest: Francisco Magnes.

43. PIERRE RACHAL (x)
#5-1820 MARIE PERINE METOYER (x)
8 February 1820. 3 bans.
Groom: 18 years, native of this parish, free man of color, natural son of Juan Baptista Rachal and Marie

Françoise Lecomte, a free woman of color. Bride: 17 years, native of this parish, free woman of color, legitimate daughter of Dominique Metoyer and Marguerite Le Compte, both free people of color. Witnesses: Dominique Metoyer (x); L^{s} Derbanne (s); Jerome Sarpy (s); Elisé Roques (s); J. B^{te} Metoyer, fils Aug^{tin} (s); C. N. Roques (s); Pierre Metoyer (s); Mr. J. B^{te} [Louis] Rachal (x); Max^{lle} Metoyer (s). Priest: Francisco Magnes.

44. ANDRES FORT (s)
#6-1820 MARIE LOCODITE HIMEL (x)
12 February 1820. 3 bans.
Groom: 22, native of this jurisdiction, legitimate son of Jacques Fort and Marie Françoise Malver, already deceased. Bride: 14, native of this post, natural daughter of Mr. J. Baptiste Buard and Marie Françoise Himel. WItnesses: Me Françoise Himel (x); H. Bossier (s); Louis Fort (s); Antoine Himel (x); D. Bossier (s). Priest: Francisco Magnes.

45. NARCISSE RACHAL (s)
#7-1820 MARIE LOUISE DESIRE RACHAL (x)
14 February 1820. 3 bans.
Groom: 21, native of this jurisdiction, bachelor, legitimate son of L^{s} B^{my} Rachal and Marie Françoise Grillet. Bride: 14, native of this jurisdiction, legitimate daughter of J^{n} B^{te} B^{my} Rachal and Marie Pelagie Brevel, already deceased. Groom signed as Narcisse Bertolmie Rachal; bride as Marie Louise Rachal. Witnesses: Jean B^{te} Rachal (s); L^{s} Bertelmis Rachal (s); Clement Rachal (s); Hilaire Rachal (s); B^{min} Metoyer (s); L^{s} G^{me} Rachal (s); Jh. Latiere, fils (s); Honoré Fredieu (s); J^{n} B^{te} Lattier?, fils (s). Priest: Francisco Magnes.

46. LOUIS LASTY DERVAN (X)
#8-1820 MARIE ELENNE LEMOIN (x)
5 June 1820. 3 bans.
Groom: 22, native of this jurisdiction, bachelor, legitimate son of Jean B^{te} Dervan, already deceased, and Marie Elenne Brevel. Bride: [no age given], legitimate daughter of Charles Lemoin, already deceased, and Jeanne elbron [Le Brun]. Witnesses: M^{de} Ve Lemoin (x); H^{ré} Fredieu (s); A. Sompayrac (s); Bertran Plaisance (x); Jh. Derbanne (s). Priest: Francisco Magnes.

47. ELISÉ ROQUES (s)
#9-1820 MARIE SUSET METOYER (x)
26 June 1820. 3 bans.
Groom: 23, native of New Orleans, natural son of Louise Glapion and [no first name] Roques, a bachelor. Bride: 14, native of this jurisdiction, legitimate

daughter of Agustin Metoyer and Marie Agnes Poissot, free people of color. Witnesses: Agustin Metoyer (x); Me Agnes Poissot (x); Manuel Llorens (s); Jerome Sarpy (s); J. B^{te} Metoyer, fils Aug^{tin} (s); Pierre Metoyé (s); Max^{ille} Metoyer (s); [one illegible signature]. Priest: Francisco Magnes.

48. JEROME SARPY (s)
#10-1820 MARIE ADELAYDE METOYER (x)
27 June 1820. 3 bans.
Groom: 24, native of the town of New Orleans, single, natural son of Barton Beler and [no first name] Sarpy. Bride: 16, native of this jurisdiction, legitimate daughter of François Metoyer and Margarite Lafantasy, already deceased, all free people of color. Witnesses: François Metoyer (x); Agustin Metoyer (x); J^{n} B^{te} Metoyer fils Aug^{tin} (s); Manuel Llorens (s); E. Roques (s); Pierre Metoyé (s); Aug^{te} Metoyer (s); [one illegible signature; same as in previous entry]. Priest: Francisco Magnes.

49. REMY MARCEL SOTO (x)
#13-1820 MARIE ADELAYDE CHAMARD (x)
6 July 1820. 3 bans.
Groom: 22, bachelor, native of this parish, legitimate son of Jose Antonio Marcel Soto and Maria Bailloud. Bride: 16, native of this parish, legitimate daughter of Michel Chamard and Marie Euphrosine Rambin. Witnesses: "Athanasse Poissot, for Marcel de Soto" (s); A^{e} Chamard (s); Jh. Tauzin (s); Deblieux (s); B. Dranguet (s); Luis Procela (s); J. B. Trezzini (s). Priest: Francisco Magnes.

50. JEAN ANDRES VALENTINE (x)
#14-1820 MARIE LOUCOUVICHE (x)
11 July 1820. 3 bans.
Groom: 49, native of this parish; widower of Marie Louis Malegs, by whom he had a son, Joseph Valentin, already married. Bride: 16, native of Nacogdoches, legitimate daughter of Joseph Loucouvichi, already deceased, and Mauricia Mora. Witnesses: Michel Bensan [Vicente] (x); José Antonio Bega (x).

51. ZERAPHIN LLORANS (s)
#15-1820 MARIE ASPASY METOYER (x)
3 August 1820. 3 bans.
Groom: 23, native of New Orleans, bachelor, natural son of Francisca Nivet. Bride: 16, native of this parish, legitimate daughter of José Metoyer and Marie Pelagie LeCour. All are free persons of color. Witnesses: Joseph Metoyer (x); Me Pelagie Le Cour (x); Manuel Llorens (s); J^{n} B^{te} D^{que} Metoyer (s); E. Roques (s); J^{n} B^{te} Metoyer, fils de Louis (s); Aug^{te} Metoyer (s). Priest: Francisco Magnes.

52.
#16-1820 JOHN BAKER (x)
MARIE DENISE (x)
25 October 1820. 3 bans.
Groom: 32. "Native of Virginia in Broneston," son of John Baker, a man of color, and of Nancy, a white woman. Bride: 14 years, 6 mos., daughter of Marianne Baden, a free Negro. Witnesses: Marianne Baden (x); Louis Lamatt, free man of color (x); Antoin Badin, free man of color (x); Faustino del Rio (s); [two illegible signatures]. Priest: Francisco Magnes.

53.
#17-1820 ANTOIN LE MOINE, JR. (x)
ISAVEL SIDRE (x)
7 December 1820.
Groom: 25, native of the parish of Rapides, legitimate son of Antoin Lemoin and Genoveva Bergard. Bride: 21, native of the parish of Rapides, legitimate daughter of Jean Sidre and Marie Bergard. All are residents of the jurisdiction of Rapides. Dispensation granted from the impediment on consanguinity resulting from the relationship of the 2 mothers. Witnesses: Antoine Lemoin, Sr. (x); Jean Sidre (x); Felix St. André (x); Ths. Graham (s); Valentin Dubois (s); Jean Baptiste Dubois (s). Priest: Francisco Magnes.

54.
#1-1821 ANTOIN CRISTIN HESSER (x)
MARIE LOUISE GAGNE (x)
1 January 1821. 3 bans.
Groom: 20 years and 3 months, bachelor, legitimate son of Christin Hesser and Marie Adelayde Rambin. Bride: 16 years, native of this jurisdiction, legitimate daughter of Mr. Louis Basil Gagne, already deceased, and Marie Denise Lafitte. Witnesses: Marie Denis Lafitte (x); François Prudhomme (x); Ls. Ternié (s); Cesaire Fontenau (s); Jean Batis Fredieu? (s); Henry Trichel (s); Michel Chamard (s). Priest: Francisco Magnes.

55.
#2-1821 PLACIDE DERVAN (x)
MARIE ROSSE SOPHRONIE GRAPPE (x)
2 January 1821. 3 bans.
Groom: 25, native of this jurisdiction, bachelor, legitimate son of Gaspar Dervan and Maria Josefa Peraut, already deceased. Bride: [age not given], native of this jurisdiction, legitimate daughter of Jeann Btte. Grappe, already deceased, and Genoveva Sorel. Witnesses: "Jn Pre. Grappe, for my mother," (s); Fçois Grappe (s); Henry Trichel (s); Athanasse Trichel (s); Cesaire Fontenau (s); Louis Perot (s); Samuel Fagot (s); Onesime Grappe (x). Priest: Francisco Magnes.

56.
#3-1821 BERNARD MERICQ (s)
MARIE PALMIER CELESTE GOTTIER (s)
8 January 1821. No bans.
Groom: 32, native of the Canton de la Ricolle, depart-

ment of La Gironde, legitimate son of Bernardo Mericq, now deceased, and Marie Bourg. Bride: 15, native of New Orleans; legitimate daughter of René Gothier, now deceased, and Emelye? Victoire Local. Dispensation from bans since family has informed priest that there is no blood relationship between the parties. Witnesses: Leonard Gauttier (s); Lafon (s); B^{min} Metoyer (s); J^{n} P^{re} Me Dubois (s); [two illegible signatures]. Priest: Francisco Magnes.

57. JOSEPH EDOUARD ARMAND (s)
* MARIE SUSETTE RACHAL (s)
25 July 18<u>42</u>.
Groom: Legitimate son of J. B. Armand and deceased Marie Catherine Frederique. Bride: Legitimate daughter of Bartelome Rachal and Marie Louisse Chelete. Dispensation granted from third degree consanguinity. Witnesses: Amadée Rachal (s); Jh. Lestage (s); [illegible] Rachal (s); [illegible] Rachal (s). Priest: R. Pascual.

[Ed. note. *No entry number appears. The entry is recorded on an inserted page which apparently came from another volume.]

58. JEAN BAPTISTE LATTIER (s)
#4-1821 MARIE EMELY LACOUR (x)
9 January 1821.
Groom: Legitimate son of Jean Baptiste Lattier and Pelagie Federiq, native of this parish [age illegible]. Bride: 21, native of this parish, legitimate daughter of Gaspar La Cour and Marie Felicité Brevel. Dispensation from impediment of consanguinity to third degree. Witnesses: J^{n} B^{te} Lattier, Sr. (x); Gaspar La Cour (x); J^{n} B^{te} Le Comte (s); Fçois Frederic (s); Jh. Lattier, fils (s); B^{te} Armant (s). Priest: Francisco Magnes.

59. RENÉ FRANÇOIS EPRON (s)
#5-1821 MARIE ROSALINE MASIPPE (x)
13 January 1821.
Groom: [age illegible]. Bachelor, legitimate son of René Epron and Thomasa G_____n. Bride: 18, native of this parish, legitimate daughter of Jean Massippe and Marie Lemoin, already deceased. Witnesses: Pierre Masippe (x); J. F. Hertzog (s); Pierre Gagnon (x); Fçois. Frederic (s); [two illegible signatures]. Priest: Francisco Magnes.

60. BERNARD ISURD [HISSOURA] (s)
#6-1821 EULALIE DEMESIER (x)
1 March 1821. 3 bans.
Groom: native of this jurisdiction, legitimate son of Bernardo Isurd and Margarite Grillet. Bride: native of this jurisdiction, 16, daughter of Jacque Demesier and Chatarine Beebe, already deceased. Witnesses: M^{e}

Margarite Grillet (x); Isaac Plaisance (s); Marie Josephe Demesieres (s); A. Grilliet (s); C. Grilliet (s); Ad. Lauve (s); C. Noyrit (s); Hre. Fredieu (s); Tauzin (s); Priest: Francisco Magnes.

61.
#7-1821
JOSEPH MARIA SANCHES (x)
MARIE CHARLOT ALEMAN (x)
___ April 1821 [date illegible]
Groom: 24, bachelor, native of [illegible], legitimate son of Joseph Sanches and Maria Josepha y Barbo. Bride: [age illegible], native of this parish, natural daughter of Pierre Aleman and Marie Thérèse Langlois. 3 bans. Witnesses: Joseph Sanches (x); Luis Procela (s); Jos. (?) Henry (s). [Two illegible signatures.] Priest: Francisco Magnes.

62.
#8-1821
JUAN JOSEPH ACOSTA (x)
MARIA JACINTA CASTRO (x)
23 April 1821. 3 bans.
Groom: bachelor, 23, native of Nacogdoches, legitimate son of Joseph Andres Acosta and Maria de la Concepcion Padillo. Bride: 24, native of San Antonio de Bexar, legitimate daughter of Antonio Castro, already deceased, and Maria Guadalupe Leyva. Witnesses: José Andres Acosta (x); Ma. Guadalupe Leyva (x); Cazenave (s); Jn. Mora (s); Luis Procela (s). Priest: Francisco Magnes.

63.
#9-1821
JEAN BTTE. VACOCU (x)
MARIE ASPASY RIS (x)
23 April 1821. 3 bans
Groom: 21 years, 11 months; native of this parish, legitimate son of Mr. Louis Bacocu and Marie Magdaline Peraut, already deceased. Bride: 22, native of this parish, legitimate daughter of Jean Ris and Marie Françoise Vacocu. Dispensation for impediment of consanguinity in second degree. Witnesses: Jeann Ris (x); Louis Vacocu (x); Joseph Vacocu (x); Hillaire Bourdelon (s); Lufroy Bordelon (s); Cazenave (s). Priest: Francisco Magnes.

64.
#10-1821
JEANN BAPTISTE ANTY (x)
MARIE LOUISE LATTIER (x)
28 April 1821. 3 bans.
Groom: 20, native of this jurisdiction, bachelor, legitimate son of the marriage of Jeann Btte Anty and Marie Cyprienne Dervan. Bride: 14, legitimate daughter of the marriage of François Lattier and Marie Pelagie Slettre. Witnesses: Jn. Btte. Anty, the father (x); François Lattier (x); Jn. Bte. Lattier, son (s); Mc. Sompayrac (s); Bte. Lecomte (s); Jh. Lattier (s); Jn. Egne. Michamps (s); Fçois. Frederic (s). Priest: Francisco Magnes.

65. MICHEL RAMBIN (x)
#11-1821 MARIE PHANY BOLLIU [BEAULIEU] (x)
27 May 1821. 3 bans.
Groom: 56, native of this parish, widower of Marie Thérèse Mayoux, by his first nuptials, by which marriage he had seven children. Bride: 17, native of this parish, legitimate daughter of Pierre Bolliu and Marie Thérèse Bodoin, already deceased. Witnesses: Pierre Dubois (s); Luis Procela (s); Pierre Laffitte (s); José Serafin Gonzales (s). Priest: Francisco Magnes.

66. RICHARD GUILLAUME HERTZOG (s)
#12-1821 HENRIETTE AMIRE PROUDHOMME (s)
30 July 1821. 3 bans.
Groom: 24 native of Bordeaux, legitimate son of Henri Mathieu Hertzog and Jeanne Lartigue. Bride: 16(?), native of this parish, legitimate daughter of Antoine Proudhomme and Marie Lambre. Witnesses: Prudhomme (s); Marie Lambre (s); J. F. Hertzog (s); B^{min} Metoyer (s); Janin (s); ___ Prudhomme; ___ Hertzog (s); H. Landreau, fils (s); Suzette _____ (s). Priest: Francisco Magnes.

[Ed. note: Groom signed as Richard W. Hertzog, indicating that he spelled his middle name in the English manner.]

67. MANUEL HILAIRE BORDELEAU (s)
#13-1821 MARIE MODESTE TONTON PERAUT (x)
7 August 1821. 3 bans.
Groom: 19, native of this parish, bachelor, legitimate son of Hypolite Bordeleau and Marie Thérèse Trichel. Bride: 21, native of this parish, legitimate daughter of Jean Chrisostom Peraut and Marie Louisse Salvan, already deceased. Witnesses: Chrisostom Peraut (s); Athanasse Trichel (s); T. Grilliet (s); Jean B^{te} Fonteneau (s); F^{tin} Perot (s); J. Grilliet (?) (s); Henry Triche (s); Hy^{te} Bordelon (s). Groom signed as Hillaire Bourdelon. Priest: Francisco Magnes.

68. FRANÇOIS BESSON (s)
#14-1821 MARIE SUSET DERVAN (x)
7 Aug 1821. 3 bans.
Groom: 23, native of this parish, bachelor, legitimate son of [Julien Besson], already deceased, and of Marie [de l'Incarnation Perot]. Bride: 21, native of this parish, legitimate daughter of Gaspar Dervan and Marie Suset Peraut. Dispensation granted from the impediment of consanguinity. Spouses are the children of two sisters. Witnesses: Marie Peraut (x); J^{n} B^{tte} Dervan (s); J^{n} V. Vacocu (s); Bauvard St. Amand (s);

T. Grilliet (s); F^{tin} Perot (s). Priest: Francisco Magnes.

> [Ed. note: Bracketed information above is torn away from the original entry; data is provided from the baptismal record of the groom dated 1 October 1797. See Elizabeth Shown Mills, *Natchitoches, 1729-1803: Abstracts of the Catholic Church Registers of the French and Spanish Post of St. Jean Baptiste des Natchitoches in Louisiana*, Vol. II, Cane River Creole Series (New Orleans: Polyanthos, 1977), #2846. No indication of the tear is apparent on the microfilm copy of the film, since the filmers did not place a blank sheet behind the torn page; data from the entry on the following sheet fills the torn space, resulting in a somewhat garbled entry on the microfilm.
>
> The identification of the bride's mother in the above record as Marie SUSET does appear on the original entry. However, the bride's baptismal record in Mills, *Natchitoches, 1729-1803*, #2968, and numerous other records of the family identify this mother as Marie JOSEPHE.

69. TORIVIO DUVIN (x)
#15-1821 MARIA JOSEFA DEL REFUGIA SOTO (x)
23 August 1821. 3 bans.
Groom: 23, native of San Antonio de Bexar, bachelor, son of Ma [torn] Duvin and Micaela Sosa, already deceased. Bride: [torn], native of Nacogdoches, legitimate daughter of Cristoval Soto and Josefa Barbara Chirino, already deceased. Witnesses: Juan Vimines (?) (x); Pedro Ocon (x); François Serpentini (s); Ignacio de los Santos Coy (s). Priest: Francisco Magnes.

> [Ed. note: Please read above comments regarding the condition of the original and the microfilm.]

70. IGNACIO ELDE (x)
#16-1821 MARIA JESUSA DE LOS STOS. COY (x)
11 September 1821. 3 bans.
Groom: 26, native of Nacogdoches, bachelor, legitimate son of Francisco Elde and Maria Zarigoza (?) Cruz, already deceased. Bride: 19, native of Nacogdoches, single, legitimate daughter of Joseph de los S^{tos}. Coy and Maria Concepcion Chopa. Witnesses: José de los S^{tos}. Coy (s); Pedro Procela (s); Fçois Serpentini (s); Celedonio Longoria (x); Juan Belanger (s). Priest: Francisco Magnes.

71. PIERRE MASSIPPE (x)
#17-1821 MARIE FRANÇOISE ARTHEMISSE RACHAL (x)
17 September 1821. 3 bans.
Groom: 30, native of this jurisdiction, legitimate

son of Jeann Massippe and Marie Lemoine, both already deceased. Bride: 26, native of this jurisdiction, legitimate daughter of L^{s} B^{my} Rachal and Marie Françoise Grillet, already deceased. Witnesses: L^{s} Bertelmie Rachal (s); Richd W. Hertzog (s); B^{min} Metoyer (s); P. Compère (s); A. B. Rachal (s). [One illegible signature]. Priest: Francisco Magnes.

72. LOUIS SOSIER (s)
#18-1821 MARIE ASELY DU ROSSÉ (x)
10 October 1821. No bans.
Groom: 37, native of New Orleans, legitimate son of François Sosier, already deceased, and Felicité Dubornée. Bride: 34, native of New Orleans, widow of deceased Ramon Antonio Lasada to whom she was married in her first nuptials. Family members have informed the priest that there is no blood relationship between the parties, and the bride and groom have declared before witnesses that they have six children, three boys and three girls, which they not yet have legitimized because there was no notary public in their jurisdiction. Witnesses: Joseph Tauzin (s); C. De la Rue (s). Priest: Francisco Magnes.

73. VALERIO LAVOMBE (s)
#19-1821 MARIE OSINNE DAVID (x)
26 November 1821. 3 bans.
Groom: native of Guasita [Ouachita], aged 25, legitimate son of Sr José Lavombe of the French nation and Maria Louisa Courterie, a free woman of color. Bride: native of this parish, 22, natural daughter of Sr Luis David, white, already deceased, and Magdalena Grappe, a free woman of color. Witnesses: Magdalena Grappe (x); Louis Lamata, godfather (x); Pelagie Grappe, godmother (x); L^{s} Lamat, *fils* (s); Jean B^{te} Fontenau (s); Ath. Triche (s). Groom signed as Ba La riobaume. Priest: Francisco Magnes.

[Ed. Note: The identification of Valery de la Baume as legitimate appears to be correct despite the fact that intermarriage between races was illegal at the post where Valery was born (and elsewhere in Louisiana). The count Joseph de la Baume moved from Ouachita to Texas, residing at both Nacogdoches and San Antonio. The 1804 and 1805 censuses of Nacogdoches identify de la Baume as a widower, living in the village since 1802; the 1806 census states that he is married to "Feliciana, mulatto," and has five children aged 1 to 13. The marriage apparently occurred in Nacogdoches, and would have been legal in that province. Valery and his siblings would have been legitimized at the time of the marriage, as with the Sosier [Saucier]-Du Rossé children above.

74. #20-1821

JEAN BTTE. METOYER (s)
MARIE SUSET METOYER (x)
29 November 1821. 3 bans.
Groom: 21, native of this parish, legitimate son of Louis Metoyer and Thérèse [no last name]. Bride: 17, native of this parish, legitimate daughter of Pierre Metoyer and Marie Perine [no last name], already deceased. All are free people of color. Dispensation granted from impediment of consanguinity in second degree; spouses are children of two brothers. Witnesses: Louis Metoyer (x); Pierre Metoyer (s); Thérèsse Metoyer (x); Auguste Langlois (s); E. Roques (s); C. N. Roques (s); Jerome Sarpy (s); M^{l}. Llorens (s); J^{n}. Landreau (s); J^{n}. B^{te}. Metoyer, *fils* Augustin (s); Aug^{te}. Metoyer (s); J^{n}. B^{te}. D^{om}. Metoyer (s).
Priest: Francisco Magnes.

[Ed. note: Mother of groom was Marie Thérèse Le Comte. Mother of bride was Marie Perine Le Comte. See Gary B. Mills, *The Forgotten People: Cane River's Creoles of Color* (Baton Rouge: Louisiana State University Press, 1977), 75, 85-86.]

75. #21-1821

JOSEPH FRANCISCO ROND (s)
MARIA AURORA BESSON (x)
31 December 1821. 3 bans.
Groom: 21, native of Nacogdoches, legitimate son of Michel Rond, already deceased, and Maria Juana Rossier. Bride: 14, native of this parish, legitimate daughter of J^{n}. Baptiste Besson and Marie Jeann Pierverde, Witnesses: Jean B^{te}. Besson (s); Vidal (s); Louis Closeau (s); A. Chaugnier [Chatagnier?] (s); H^{re}. Fredieu (s). Priest: Francisco Magnes.

76. #1-1822

ANDRES BERMEA (x)
MARIA FRANCESCA JUANA CALDENAS (x)
12 January 1822. 3 bans.
Groom: 26, native of the Rio Grande, bachelor, legitimate son of Mathias Bermea, already deceased, and Encarnacion Salenas. Bride: 18, single, native of San Antonio de Bexar, legitimate daughter of Francisco Caldenas and Maria Trinidad Dias. All parties are Spaniards. Witnesses: José Laflor (x); José Toro [Soso?] (s); Manuel Marunos (x); José Vineda (s); Isaac Plaisance (s). Priest: Francisco Magnes.

77. #2-1822

JEANN LALANDE (x)
MARIE SELESINE DAVION (x)
17 January 1822. 3 Bans.
Groom: 47, native and resident of this parish, widower of Marie Adelayde Vercher. Bride: 24, native of this parish, legitimate daughter of deceased Dom-

inique Davion and Pelagie Gagné. Witnesses: Pelagie Gagné (x); Michel Chamard (s); Pre Ternier (s); Ml Barberousse (s); Fçois Rouquier, *fils* (s); Jn Btte Davion (x); Fçois Scopini (s). Priest: Francisco Magnes.

78. ISUBE ISOURD (s) [EUSEBE HISSOURA]
#3-1822 MARIE EMÉ BASCOCU
2 February 1822. [Number of bans illegible]
Groom: [age illegible]. Single, legitimate son of Bernarde Isourd, already deceased, and Marie Margarite [Grillet]. Bride: _5 years, legitimate daughter of Andres Bacocu and Magdalena Ra[ymond]. Witnesses: Margaret Grillet (x); Chrisostomé Vacocu (s); Isaac Plaisance (s); A. Grillet (s); Fçois Chabus (s); Remy Totin (x); Louis Vacocu, *pere*. Priest: Francisco Magnes.

79. MANUELLE LAFFITTE (x)
#4-1822 MARIE SALOME PROCELA (x)
29 Jan 1822. [Number of bans illegible]
Groom: 22, son of Paul Bouet Laffite and Marianne Soto. Bride: 16, daughter of Todos(?) Santos Procela, alreday deceased, and Maria Jetrudis Hivarvo, all of this jurisdiction. Witnesses: Pedro Procela (s); Josef Arocha (s); Luis Procla (s); Césaire Fontenau (s); Morantin(?) (s). Priest: Francisco Magnes.

80. VALERY [LE COURT] (x)
#5-1822 MARIE SILBY METOYER (x)
2 February 1822. 3 bans.
Groom: 24, native of this parish, quadroon son of Marie Ursulle, a free mulatress [*métisse*]. Bride: 18, native of this parish, single, legitimate daughter of Dominique Metoyer and Margarita [Le Comte], all free people of color. Witnesses: Dominique Metoyer (x); Manuel Llorens (s); Jn Bte Metoyer, *fils* Atin (s); Augte Metoyer (s); Jn Bte Metoyer, *fils de* Louis (s); Maxlle Metoyer (s). Priest: Francisco Magnes.

[Ed. note: Marie Ursulle was of mixed French-Indian parentage, rather than French-Negro. See note accompanying Entry 2837 in Mills, *Natchitoches, 1729-1803*. Of the numerous documents dealing with Ursulle, all identify her as *métisse* or *métive* except three instances in which she or her children appeared before officials in company with mulattoes.]

81. MICHEL MENANSON (x)
#6-1822 MARIE JOSEPHE ADELISE BAUDOIN (x)
11 March 1822. 3 bans.
Groom: 24 (29?), native of [illegible], Isle de Sto Domingo, legitimate son of Charles Menanson and of

Magdalenne Dupuis, already deceased. Bride: single, native of this parish, legitimate daughter of Pierre Baudoin and Anne Rovin. Witnesses: Pierre Beudoin (x); Charles Mananson, *fils* (x); S.P.(?) Russell (s); B. Chenal (s); Athanase Brossé (s); Louis P^{re} Pillet (s). Priest: Francisco Magnes.

82. #7-1822

PIERRE GEODFROY LAVESPÈRE (x)
MARIE FROSINE LEMOINE (x)
13 March 1822. 3 bans.
Groom: 23, native of this parish, bachelor, legitimate son of Francisco Lavespère and Marie Louisse Dervan. Bride: 16, native of this parish, legitimate daughter of Jeann B^{tte} Lemoin and Marie Felicité La Casse. Witnesses: J^{n} B^{te} Lemoin (x); Chas F. Benoist (s); J. F. Hertzog (x); Epron (s); Fç^{ois} Fredieu (s); Baltasard Brevelle (s). Priest: Francisco Magnes.

83. #8-1822

LOUIS GASPARD DERVAN (x)
MARIE MERANTE POISSOT (x)
10 April 1822. 3 bans.
Groom: [no age, no birthplace], legitimate son of J^{n} B^{tte} Dervan, already deceased, and Marie Elenne Brevelle. Bride: 18, widow of deceased Leon Totin, by which marriage she had one daughter who died a year after the death of her father, legitimate daughter of Paul Poissot and Marie Louise Anty, all natives of this parish. Witnesses: Paul Poissot (x); L^{s} Derbanne (s); J^{n} E^{gne} Michamps (s); Auguste Langois (s). Epron *dit* Renois (s); Fç^{ois} Fredieu (s). Priest: Francisco Magnes.

84. #9-1822

CRISOSTOMÉ VASCOCU (s)
MARIE MARCELITE RIS (x)
13 April 1822. 3 bans.
Groom: 19, native of this parish, bachelor, legitimate son of Louis Vacocu and Marie Magdalenne Perau, already deceased. Bride: 18, legitimate daughter of Jeann Ris and Marie Françoise Vacocu. Dispensation from impediment of consanguinity in second degree, resulting from the brother-sister relationship of the groom's father and the bride's mother. Witnesses: J^{n} Vacocu, for my father(s); Jean Ris (x); Apolinar de Marmela (s); Remy Totin (x); Juan Lazarin (s); Isehe Issoury (x). Groom signed as Chrisostomé Vacocu. Priest: Francisco Magnes.

85. #10-1822

JOSEPH VASCOCU (x)
MARIE MIRAMIS VASCOCU (x)
13 April 1822. 3 bans.
Groom: 22, bachelor, legitimate son of Andres Vacocu and Marie Magdelenne Raimon, already deceased.

Bride: legitimate daughter of Louis Vascocu and Marie Magdalenne Peraut, already deceased. Dispensation granted from impediment of consanguinity in second degree, the bride and groom being children of two brothers. Witnesses: Jean V. Vacocu, for my father (s); Marie Eulalye Vascocu (x); Remy Totin (x); Appolinar De Marmela (s); Juan Lazarino (s); Isebe Issouray (s). Priest: Francisco Magnes.

86. SILVESTRE JULIAN RACHAL (s)
#11-1823 MARIE HELAINE LAVESPÈRE (x)
18 April 1822. 3 bans.
Groom: 22, bachelor, native of this parish, legitimate son of Julian Rachal and Marie Louisse Vrevel, already deceased. Bride: 21, native of this parish, legitimate daughter of François Lavespère and Marie Louisse Dervan. Witnesses: F. Lavespère (s); Julien Rachal (s); S. Compère (s); J^{n}. Frederic (x); F^{çois}. Frederic (s); J^{n}. E^{gne}. Mechamps (s). Priest: Francisco Magnes.

87. CLAUDE ANTOINE CHOPPIN (s)
#12-1822 MARIE DELPHINE LAMBRE (s)
6 July 1822. 3 bans.
Groom: 30, bachelor, native of the city of Lyon in France, legitimate son of Jean Baptiste Choppin and Magdalene Souvone [Louvone?], both already deceased. Bride: 18, legitimate daughter of Remy Lambre and Marie Susette Proudhomme, native of this parish. Witnesses: B^{min}. Metoyer (s); Aurore Lambre (s); A^{d}. Lauve (s); J. A. Huppé (s); Prudhomme (s); S. Compère (s); Metoyer (s); Ch^{s}. Noyrit (s); V. Lambre (s); Lambre (s); J. F. Hertzog (s); B^{te}. Lecomte (s); J^{n}. P^{re}. M^{e}. Dubois (s); Marie Prudhomme (s); [one illegible signature]. Priest: Francisco Magnes.

88. IGNACIO LOPEZ (s)
#13-1822 MARIE DEVES (x)
17 July 1822. 3 bans.
Groom: 45, native of Santa Maria de los Parros; bachelor, legitimate son of Santiago Lopez and Maria Antonia Adams, already deceased. Bride: 22, native of Guasita [Ouachita], legitimate daughter of Juan Deves and Maria Nancy Arman [Harmon], both already deceased. The groom is a Spaniard; the bride an American. Witnesses: Michel Chamard (s); Marie Therresse Andres Bascocu (x); José Davis, "her elder brother," (x); James Quinnally (s); Manuel Floer (Hoer?) (s); Man^{l}. Bustam^{te}. (s); Pantalleon (s). Priest: Francisco Magnes.

[Ed. note: Baptismal registrations of Marie and two other children born at Ouachita to Davis and Zadock Harmon's daughter, Nancy, are to be found at St. Paul de Mansura.]

89. JOSÉ ANDRES AYALA (x)
#14-1822 MARIA RAFAELA MARTINEZ (x)
29 July 1822. 3 bans.
Groom: 32, native of Monterrey, legitimate son of Nicolas Ayala, already deceased, and Petra de Aro. Bride: 16, single, native of Bexar, legitimate daughter of Dolores Martinez [father] and Maria Manuela Gomez. Sponsors: [illegible] Parela(?) and Mª de Sezar Cevallos. Witnesses: J. B^{te} Landreau (s); Joseph Marie Mondez (x); Juan de la Peña (s); Isebe Issoury (s). Priest: Francisco Magnes.

90. PEDRO OCON (x)
#15-1822 MARIA IGNACIA PROCELA (x)
31 July 1822. 3 bans.
Groom: 26, bachelor, native of S^{n} Antonio de Bexar, legitimate son of Jose Antonio Ocon and Josefa Sandoval. Bride: about 20, native of Nacogdoches, widow of José Flores, by which marriage she had one daughter Maria Josefa, aged 3. Sponsors: Juan Lazarino (s); Maria Josefa Flores. Witnesses: Juan José Cavaros? (s); Pedro Hernandez (s). Priest: Francisco Magnes.

91. JOSÉ MARIA MURQUEZ (x)
#16-1822 MARIA JUANA LEONOR AROCHA (x)
20 August 1822. 3 bans.
Groom: 26, native of Bexar, legitimate son of Joaquin Murques, already deceased, and Masalina Medina. Bride: native of Nacogdoches, legitimate daughter of José Damion Arocha and Mª Antonia Flores. Witnesses: Josef Damion Arocha (s); Juan Lazarino (s); Manuel Llorens (s); Josef Mª Bustamen^{te} (s); Juan José Cavrio? (s). Priest: Francisco Magnes.

92.* CHARLES FR^{CS} BENOIT (s)
MARIE SUSETTE RACHAL
28 October 1825
Nuptial benediction given to the marriage already performed civilly by the parish judge. Witnesses: P^{re} Sebastien Compère; J^{n} B^{te} Charleville. Priest: Anduze.

93.* JOSEPH TOUSSAINT JANNIN
MARIE ANT. PRUDHOMME
28 October [1825]
Groom: born at Vannes, department of Morbihan, major and legitimate son of deceased Julien Jeannin and Marie Louise Jobert. Bride: native of this parish, minor and legitimate daughter of Antoine Prudhomme and Marie

----
*These entries carry no year or entry number in the margin.

Lambre. Witnesses: J^{n} F^{s} Hertzog (s) and P^{re} Delouche. Priest: Anduze.

94.* EUGENE MECHAMPS (s)
ANNA CATHERINE MULER (x)
14 June 1826
Groom: native of Paris, major and legitimate son of deceased Eugene Mechamps and [at this point a parenthesis is inserted with the words "de nom___ public."] Bride: born in Mayenne, Wurtemberg, major and legitimate daughter of Frederic Muller and Barbara Muler. Witnesses: Joseph Derbanne (s); L^{s} Derbanne (s); P.N. Rost (s); F^{çois} Dupuis? (s). Priest: Anduze.

95.* MARCELINO DE LA GARZA
DOLORES RODRIGUEZ
16 June 1826
Groom: major son of José L__ de la Garza and Maria F^{çoise} Sou, residents of S. Antonio de Veyal [Bexar]. Bride: major daughter of Joachin Rodriguez and Jacoba Segoure, living at Veyal. Witnesses: Theodore Grillet and [illegible]. Priest: Anduze.

96.* JOHN CAVERT
DIANA WALKER
2 August 1826
Groom: 22, born in Adams County, Mississippi, of Benj.? Cavert and Thebeta Morgan. Bride: a widow, about 17, born in state of Tennessee of Joal Walker? and Mary Jually?. Witnesses: Jos. H. Hartley (s); John Davis (x); Samuel D. Clark (s). Priest: Anduze.

97.* JN BTE VACOCU
MARIE SEVERINE OCANA [O'CONNOR]
28 August 1826
Groom: son of deceased L^{s} Vacocu and deceased Marie Magdeline Pero. Bride: legitimate and major daughter of deceased J^{n} Ocana and Felicité Torres of the parish of Natchitoches. Witnesses: Antonio Ariano (s); L^{s} D[illegible]. Priest: Anduze.

98.* ANARTHASIO BAREL [ATHANASIO BARELA]
MARIA CONCEPTION FEREL
24 November 1826
Groom: major and legitimate son of Feliciano Barel and Maria Josefa Caro of Nacogdoches. Bride: daughter of Joseph Guadeloupe Ferel and Maria Josefa Villegar of the parish of St Antoine de Vejars [San Antonio de Bexar]. Witnesses: Antonio Menchaca (s); Manuel Gallion (x); Feliz Barel (x). Priest: Anduze.

----

*These entries carry no year or entry number in the margin.

99.* JN BTE FAUSTIN PLAISANCE
GENEVIÈVE ALINEIDE LE VASSEUR
16 December 1826
Groom: major and legitimate son of Bertrand Plaisance and Marie Barbe Grillet, both residents of this place. Bride: minor and legitimate daughter of deceased Emanuel Levasseur and Geneviève Gonin. Witnesses: Theodore Grillet (s); Donatien Vascocu (x); Ludger Le Vasseur (s). Priest: Anduze.

100.* EDOUARD LESTANG ROUBELOT
MARIE ROSE SOLIGNY
6 February 1827
Groom: major son of Pierre Roublot, resident of Bayou Pierre. Bride: major daughter of Joseph Soligny. Witnesses: Pierre Lafitte (s); Benoit Bertrand (s); Joseph Valentine (s). Priest: L. Dusassoy.

101.* MARTILIEN ANDRÉ VAAST COQU
MARIE BARBE JEANRIS
5 December 1826
Dispensation given from impediment of blood relationship. Witnesses: Spire Bordelon (s); C^{h}. Vacocu (s); Jn. V. Vascocu (s). Priest: L. Dusaussoy.

102.* SPIRE BORDELONE
ZELINE GRILLET
5 December 1826
Spouses are residents of Camté. Married at residence of Ch^{me}. Vaast cocu. Witnesses: Mme. Vacocu (s); H^{te}. Bordelone, *fils* (s); F^{tn}. Perot (s). Priest: L. Dusaussoy.

103.* CEZAIRE FONTENEAU
MARIE LOUISE BOURDELON
3 December 1826
Married at Campté home of Mlle. Fanchonette Triché. Witnesses: Pierre Trichel (s); Louis Closeau (s); Louis Perot. Priest: L. Dussassoy.

104.* LUDGER LEVASSEUR
MARIANNE TRICHÉ
3 December 1826
Married at home of Mlle. Fanchonette Trichel at Camté. All parties are residents of this post. Witnesses: Pierre Trichel (s); Louis Closeau (s); Louis Perot (s). Priest: L. Dussasoy.

----
*These entries carry no year or entry number in margin.

105.* PAUL FIRMIN RACHAL
MARIE CEPHALIDE TERNIER
27 February 182?
Groom: minor son of Dominique Rachal and Marie Rosalie Vercher. Bride: minor daughter of Pierre Ternier *dit* Grenoble and Marie Rosalie Gagnier. Married at the home of Dominique Davion. Witnesses: L^{s} G^{me} Rachal (s); Neuville Prudhomme (s); Clement Rachal (s). Priest: L. Dussasoy.

106.* FRANÇOIS MASSIPPE
LOLETTE BOISSIER
26 December 1826
Groom: major son of Jean Massippe. Bride: minor daughter of Alexandre Boissier, living on Côte Joyuse. Witnesses: Ch^{les} F. Benoist (s); P^{re} Chaler; Fç^{ois} Frederic. Priest: L. Dussasoy.

107.* DAVID DORTOLAN
MARGUERITE ELIE
27? April 1827
Groom: major son of Jean Ortolan, living at Rivière aux Cannes. Bride: minor daughter of Celestin Elie, resident of Camté. Married at home of David Brown at Campté. Witnesses: Landry Ely (s); M^{l} Barberousse (s); Louis Geoffrois (s); F^{s} Perot. Priest: L. Dussasoy.

108.* VICTOR DAMAS RACHAL
MARIE HENRIETTE ARMAND
23? April 1827
Groom: major son of Dominique Rachal and Marie Rosalie Vercher. Bride: minor daughter of Jean Baptiste Armand and Catherine Frederic. Married at home of Mr. Armand. Witnesses: C^{me} Perot (s); C? Plaisance (s); Lestan Langlois (s). Priest: L. Dussasoy.

109.* NEUVILLE PRUDHOMME
MARIE MERANTE LAMBRE
28 April 1827
Groom: major son of Antoine Prudhomme and Marie Lambre. Bride: minor daughter of deceased Remi Lambre and Marie Susanne Prudhomme. Married at home of Antoine Prudhomme "after necessary dispensation." Witness: Janin, D.M. (s). Priest: L. Dussasoy.

110.* ETIENNE DAVION
CELINE LAFITTE
21 April 1827
Groom: major son of Dominique Davion and Pelagie Gagné. Bride: minor daughter of Mr. *Cadet* [the younger]

---

* These entries carry no year or entry number in margin.

Lafitte and Marianne Donmanuel [De Soto], at home of Mr. Dominique Davion. Witnesses: Landry Ely (s); Louis Geoffrois (s); F^{s}. Perot (s). Priest: L. Dussasoy.

111.* HYPPOLITE BORDELON
CELEMINE FONTENOT
25 January 1827.

[Ed. note: Entry is almost entirely faded.]

112.* BARTHELEMI LUDGER RACHAL
MARIE MELISA RACHAL
18 Nov 1826
Dispensation given for impediment of blood relationship in fourth degree. Witnesses: Epron *dit* Renois (s); J^{n}. F. Hertzog (s); P. S. Compère (s). Priest: L. Dussasoy.

113.* LOUIS SILVIE
MARIE CLAIRE GRAPPE
12 February 1827
Groom: major son of William Case. Bride: daughter of Felicité Grap. Residents of Camté. Witnesses: Louis Perot (s); Cesaire Fontenau (s); S^{re}. Bordelon (s); H^{te}. Bordelon, *fils* (s). Priest: L. Dussasoy.

114.* DENIS CASENAVE
MARIE DESIRÉE RAMBIN
4 February 1827
Groom: major son of Michel Casenave and Marie Riss. Bride: minor daughter of Michel Rambin and Marie Thérèse Mayou. Married at home of François Rambin at Bayou Pierre. Witnesses: Rosemond Chamard? (s); Fç^{ois}. Rambin (s). Priest: L. Dussasoy.

115.* JOSEPH LAFITTE
M[AR]IE CELINE ROUBELOT
3 February 1827
Groom: minor son of Cesaire Lafitte and Isabelle Leyton. Bride: minor daughter of Pierre Roubelot and Marie Magdeleine Bastien [Prudhomme], at home of Cesaire Lafitte. Witnesses: Vital Flores (s); Clement Laffitte (s). Priest: L. Dussasoy.

116.* JOSEPH ALPHONSE DOMINGO
CATHERINE SOLIGNY
3 February 1827
Bride is daughter of Marie Marguerite Mallough?. Witnesses: Vital Flores (s): Cesair Laffitte (s); Priest: L. Dussasoy.

----

*These entries carry no year or entry number in margin.

117* EDOUARD LESTANG RAMBIN
MARIE MARIANNE LAFITTE
3 February 1827
Groom: major son of Michel Rambin and Marie Thérèse Mayou. Bride: minor daughter of Cesaire Lafitte and Isabelle Leyton. Married at home of Cesaire Lafitte. Witnesses: Pedro Flores (s); Vital Flores (s). Priest: L. Dussasoy.

118.* FRANÇOIS METOYER
MARIE COTTON-MAÏS
26 April 1827
Groom: major son of François Metoyer, mulatto inhabitant of Isle Brevelle. Bride: minor daughter of Antoine Cotton-Maïs, inhabitant of Isle Brevelle. At house of Augustin Metoyer on Isle Brevelle. Witnesses: Augustin Metoyer, Nerestan Roque, Louis Metoyer. Priest: L. Dussasoy.

119.* JUAN CRUZ
MARIE JESUS AROCHE
16 June 1827
Groom: major son of Lumin Cruz and Maria Antonia Sosa?. Bride: minor daughter of Damien Aroche and Antonia Flores. Witneses: Mr. Bertrand? (x); Gagnon? (s). Priest: L. Dussasoy.

120.* AMBROISE LE COMTE
JULIA BUARD
2 June 1827
Groom: minor son of Jean Baptiste Le Comte, deceased, and Cephalide Lambre. Bride: minor daughter of deceased Jean Louis Buard and Eulalie Bossier. At home of Placide Boissier at Natchitoches. Witnesses: Prudhomme, *fils* (s); P. E^{te}. Bossier (s); C. Choppin (s). Priest: L. Dussasoy.

121.* FIRMIN POISSOT
CELESTE LAFFITE
19 March 1827
Groom: major and legitimate son of Athanase Poissot and Hélène Pavie. Bride: minor and legitimate daughter of Paul Boëte Lafitte and Marianne Sotto, his wife. Witnesses: Mr. George Devis?; Honoré Fredieu?; and Charles Bussi. Priest: E. Anduze. Recorded in register at a later date [unspecified] by Rev. J. B. Blanc.

122.* JN. BTE. ARMAND
MARIE LOUISE ADELAIDE NOFFRE
19 May 1827
Groom: major son of Jean B^{te}. Armand and Marie Catherine

---

*These entries carry no year or entry number in margin.

Frederic, his wife. Bride: major daughter of deceased Adrien Hughe Noffré and deceased Marie Adeline Denuertre, his wife. Witnesses: Epron *dit* Renois; Fçois Frederic. Priest: Louis Dussasoy. Copy recorded in register at a later, unspecified, date by Rev. J. B. Blanc. [cf. Reg. 8.]

123.* PIERRE METOYER
MARIE DENEIGE METOYER
19 May 1827.
Ratification of civil marriage. Groom: major son of Pierre Metoyer, free mulatto, and inhabitant of Isle Brevelle, and of deceased Marie Perrine [Le Comte], his wife. Bride: minor daughter of Joseph Metoyer of Isle Brevelle and of Marie Pelagie Lecour his wife. Dispensation from impediment of blood relationship. Witnesses: Fçois Frederic (s); Epron *dit* Renois. Priest: L. Dussasoy.

124.* JEAN BTE. LEMOYNE
FELICITÉ LACASSE
20 May 1827
Groom: major son of Jean Bte. Lemoine and Felicité LaCasse, his wife. Bride: major daughter of Étienne LaCasse and deceased Dorothée Massipe, his wife. Dispensation from impediment of consanguinity resulting from bride and groom being cousins. Witnesses: Nicolas Furlong, Epron *dit* Renois, Pierre N. Gagnon. Priest: L. Dussasoy. Copy entered into register at a later, unspecified date by Rev. J. B. Blanc.

125* FÇOIS. BAUDOIN
HORTENSE ORTOLON
12 June 1827
Groom: major son of Nicolas Baudouin and Marie des Neiges [Malbert], both deceased. Bride: major daughter of Jean Ortolan and Ecolastie Brown. Married at home of Baptiste Chenal (s); Rivière aux Cannes. Witnesses: Bte. Chenal, Athanase Brosset. Priest: L. Dussasoy. Copy entered into register at a later, unspecified date by Rev. J. B. Blanc.

[Ed. note: The surname of Mme. Baudouin is to be found within numerous entries in Mills, *Natchitoches, 1729-1803* and *Natchitoches, 1800-1826*.]

126. SIMON *dit* TRICHEL (x)
#1-1827 JEANNE SIMEON (x)
11 July 1827. 1 ban.
Groom: major and natural son of Marie Jeanne, a free woman of color living at Campté, in the parish of

---

*These entries carry no year or entry number in margin.

Natchitoches. Bride: major and legitimate daughter of Charles Simeon and Marie Bisante Perez, free people of color also living at Campti. Witnesses: V. Cherbonier; Alexandre L. De Blieux; Louis Lamatte. Priest: Blanc.

127. #2-1827 JEAN BTE. CLOUTIER
SUZETTE LAMBRE
24 July 1827. 2 bans.
Groom: major and legitimate son of Jean Pierre Cloutier and Marie Salvan, inhabitants during their lives of this parish of Natchitoches. Bride: minor and legitimate daughter of deceased Remy Lambre and Susanne Prudhomme, also living in the parish of Natchitoches. Witnesses: Victorin Metoyer, Felix Cherbourne, Ch. Noyrit, A. Choppin. Priest: Blanc.

128. #3-1827 THOMAS BASK [BASQUES]
TRANQUILLINE LECOURT
5 November 1827. No bans.
Groom: major and legitimate son of Mariano Bask and Conception Morin, residents of Rivière aux Cannes. Bride: minor daughter of Bmy. LeCourt and of Luison [Ursulle]. Witnesses: Ariede Garguon?; William Penn; Lestan Langlois. Priest: Blanc.

[Ed. note: For identity of the bride's mother, see Tranquilline's baptismal entry in Mills, *Natchitoches, 1800-1826*, #440, and its accompanying note.]

129. #4-1827 LESTAN PRUDHOMME
LAÏZA LAMBRE
12 November 1827. 3 bans.
Groom: major and legitimate son of A. Prudhomme and Marie Lambre, residents of Isle de Brevelle, parish of Natchitoches. Bride: minor and legitimate daughter of deceased Remy Lambre and deceased Suzette Prudhomme, former residents of the parish of Natchitoches. Witnesses: Jn G. Hertzog; Victorin Metoyer; A. Choppin; B. Metoyer; "and others." At home of B. Metoyer, after dispensation from impediment of consanguinity in second degree. Priest: Blanc.

130. #5-1827 ZENON *dit* MÉZIÈRES (x)
EULALIE SIMEON (x)
5 December 1827. 2 bans.
Groom: free man of color, major and natural son of Marie Bernar, free woman of color living at Campti, parish of Natchitoches. Bride: major and legitimate daughter of Charles Simeon and Marie Bisente Perez, all free people of color living at Campti.

Witnesses: Charles Simeon (s); François Xavier de Glaudon (s); Charles Simeon, *fils* (s); Joseph Lazarin (x). Priest: J. B. Blanc.

131.
#6-1827
VALSIN LAMBRE (s)
CLARISSE HERTZOG (s)
27 December 1827.
Dispensation granted for the double impediment of consanguinity in second and third degrees; additional dispensation for marriage during the prohibited octave of Christmas. Groom: major and legitimate son of deceased Remy Lambre and Suzanne Prudhomme, residents of this parish during their lifetime. Bride: minor and legitimate daughter of Sr. J^{n}. F. Hertzog and Desirée Prudhomme, also residents of this parish of Natchitoches. Witnesses: A. Prudhomme (s); Richard W. Hertzog (s); Benjamin Metoyer (s); Jean Jacques Lambre (s). At home of J^{n}. F. Hertzog (s). Priest: J. B. Blanc. [cf. Reg. 8.]

132.
#1-1828
NICHOLAS FURLONG (s)
MARIE AZELINE DAVION (x)
9 March 1828. 1 ban.
Dispensation granted for other 2 bans and for prohibition against marriage during period of Lent. Groom: major and legitimate son of James Furlong and Anasazia Doyle, widower in first nuptials of Catherine Kenbe, native of Ayrlande [Ireland], actually a resident, at this time, of the parish of Natchitoches. Bride: minor and legitimate daughter of deceased Dominique Davion and Pelagie Gagnier. Witnesses: J. Victor Boissier (s); D. Bunel (s); Robert H. Russel (s); Saml. P. Russell (s); P^{re}. Pomié (s). Priest: J. B. Blanc. [cf. Reg. 8.]

133.
#2-1828
JEAN BTE. DERBANNE (x)
MARIE EMILIE TRICHEL (s)
7 April 1828. 3 bans.
Groom: major and legitimate son of deceased Jean B^{te}. Derbanne and Marie Perot, widower from first nuptials of Marie Lucie Plaisance, inhabitants of the parish of Natchitoches. Bride: minor and legitimate daughter of Jean B^{te}. Trichel and Marie Modeste Fonteneau, widow from first nuptials with deceased Raymond Durand, also a resident of this parish. Witnesses: Cezaire Fontenau (s); J^{n}. B^{te}. Fontenau (s); Theodore Chabot (s); C^{me}. Perot (s). Priest: J. B. Blanc [cf. Reg. 8.]

134.
#3-1828
JEAN BTE. TRICHEL (s)
MARIE CEPHALIDE PEROT (s)
14 April 1828. 2 bans.

Groom: major and legitimate son of deceased Jean Bte. Trichel and Marie Modeste Fonteneau, resident of the parish of Natchitoches. Bride: minor and legitimate daughter of deceased Cezaire Perot and Marie Delphine Poissot, also residents of the parish of Natchitoches. Witnesses: Louis Trezzini (s); Cesaire Fonteneau (s); Victor Boissier (s); Evariste Boissier (s); Louis Trezzini (s); Charles ?. Lewis (s); W. R. Johnson (s). Priest: Blanc. [cf. Reg. 8.]

135. AIMÉ CARON (s)
#4-1828 CATHERINE PRUDENCE MONDE
15 April 1828. 2 bans.
Groom: major and legitimate son of deceased Hypolite Rodolphe Carron and Belgire de Beance (Berriere?), native of Lyon, France, now a resident of this parish of Natchitoches. Bride: minor and legitimate daughter of deceased Fçois. Monde and Marianne Guarrand, native of St. ? of Cuba, now a resident of this parish. Bride has consent of her mother. Witnesses: C.E. Greneaux (s); Dassise Bossier (s); Victor Sompayrac (s); Narcisse Prudhomme (s); A. Sompayrac (s). Priest: Blanc.

136. GEORGE LABERSHE
#5-1828 PELAGIE LEMOINE
17 April 1828. 3 bans.
Groom: major and legitimate son of deceased George Labershe and Helene Laberche?, native of Rayene? in Dalmatie, now a resident of this parish of Natchitoches. Bride: major and legitimate daughter of Charles Lemoine and Jeanne Lebrun, widow from first nuptials with Jean Baptiste Ferrier, also a resident of this parish. Witnesses: Nicola Gracia; Jean Pierre Marie Dubois; Claude Chèze. Married in chapel at Cloutierville. Priest: Blanc.

137. DERZELIN GALIEN (x)
#6-1828 PHELONIZE LATTIER (x)
14 July 1828. 3 bans.
Groom: natural and minor son of Marie Jeanne Crete, resident of parish of Natchitoches. Bride: minor and legitimate daughter of Fçois Lattier and Marie Sheletre. Dispensation given from impediment of consanguinity in third degree. Groom marries with consent of his tutor, Alexis Cloutier. Ceremony performed at home of Fçois. Lattier (x). Witnesses: J. Bte. Lattier (s); Ls. Bmy. Rachal (x); Jean Pierre Cloutier (s); Fçois. Frederic (s). Priest: Blanc. Dispensation from impediment of consanguinity in third degree. [cf. Reg. 8.]

138. FRANÇOIS VALERY (s)
#7-1828 MARIE MAURINE
23 August 1828
Ratification of civil marriage performed 30th of last October. Groom: major and legitimate son of Jean B[te] Valery and Julienne Toures. Bride: minor daughter of [E]stevan Maurin and Marie Ceraflor [Telesfora] de la Serda, all residents of the parish of Natchitoches. Marriage in chapel at Rivière aux Cannes in presence of F[çois] Derbanne (s); Joseph Crevier Deschervaux (s); Narcisse? Rachal (s). Priest: Blanc. [cf. Reg. 8.]

[Ed. Note: Marginal notarion in Book 11 identifies groom as JEAN BAPTISTE Valery, while text identifies him as François. The original entry in Book 8 identies him only as François.]

139. LUGER LANGLOIS (s)
#8-1828 MARIE LOUISE ADLET (x)
24 August 1828
Ratification of civil marriage performed in September 1825. Groom: legitimate son of Augustin Langlois and Marie Celeste Verger, all residents of the parish of Natchitoches. Bride: minor and legitimate daughter of Jean B[te] Adlet and Marie Denise Dolet, all residents of the parish of Natchitoches. Married at chapel at Rivière aux Cannes, in presence of J[h] Crevier Deschervaux (s); F[çois] Derbanne (s). Dispensation given for impediment of consanguinity in third degree. Priest: Blanc. [cf. Reg. 8.]

140. FRANÇOIS CHABUS (s)
#9-1828 MARIE JOSEPH[E] ADELAŸDE HESSER (x)
28 August 1828. 3 bans.
Groom: major and legitimate son of deceased F[çois] Chabus and Marie Anne Malige, inhabitants of the parish of Natchitoches during their lives. Bride: minor and legitimate daughter of Christien Hesser and Marie Françoise Adelaÿde Rambin, also residents of the parish of Natchitoches. Witnesses: A. Sompayrac (s); Christian Hesser (s); A[d] Lauve (s); L[s] Tauzin (s); J. D. Bossier (s); P. Baulos (s). Priest: Blanc.

141. NOEL *dit* COINDET (x)
#10-1828 NATTALIE *dite* MÉZIÈRES
29 December 1828. 3 bans.
Groom: natural son of Marie Jeanne, a free woman of color and resident of parish of Natchitoches. Bride: natural and major daughter of Marie Jeanne,

a free woman of color, also residing in the parish of Natchitoches. Married in "the church of this parish" in presence of Manuel Llorens (s); J^{n} B^{te} Metoyer *fils* Aug^{tin}(s); J^{h} Metoyer *fils* A^{tin} (s). Priest: Blanc.

142. JN BTE HUPPÉ (s)
#1-1829 SUZETTE PRUDHOMME (s)
19 January 1829. 3 bans.
Groom: native of Bayonne, department of Basse Pyrénées, major and legitimate son of Pierre Huppé and Marie Henyazau?, residents of the town of Bayonne. Bride: widow of deceased J^{n} B^{te} Le Comte, major and legitimate daughter of A^{ne} Prudhomme and Marie Lambre, residents of this parish of Natchitoches. Witnesses: C. Noyrit (s); C. Davis (s); Marie Prudhomme (s); Prudhomme (s); F. B. Sherburne (s); Richd W. Hertzog (s); J. F. Hertzog (s); Neuville Prudhomme (s); V. Lambre (s); Lestan Prudhomme (s); Amire R. Hertzog (s); V. Rouquier (s). Priest: Blanc.

143. LS. SOLASTIE RACHAL
#2-1829 MARIE CEPHIZE BROSSET
15 February 1829
Rehabilitation of civil marriage celebrated 30 April 1827, after dispensation given for impediment of consanquinity in third degree. Groom: legitimate and major son of deceased A^{ne} Rachal and Marie Louise Lemoin, widower from first nuptials with Heloïse St. André. Bride: minor and legitimate daughter of Philippe Brosset and Marie Thérèse Brevel. At chapel of Rivière aux Cannes. Witnesses: Silvestre Hernan (x) [Hernandez]; Jacques Valcour *dit* Le Comte (s); Brosset (s); Louis J^{n} Rachal (s). Priest: Blanc. [cf. Reg. 8.]

144. RAIMOND VACOCU
#3-1829 MARCELITE DERBANNE
19 March 1829. No bans.
Groom: major and legitimate son of deceased André Vascocu and Magdeleine Raimond, residents of the parish of Natchitoches during their lifetimes. Bride: major and legitimate daughter of deceased Gaspar Derbanne and deceased Marie Josephe Peraut, residents of the parish of Natchitoches during their lifetimes. Witnesses: Cezaire Fontenau; Athanase Trichel; Spire Bordelon. Priest: Blanc.

145. JEAN BTE. DERBANNE
#4-1829 MARIE LOUISE ST. ANDRÉ
23 April 1829. 1 ban.
Groom: widower from first nuptials with Marcelite Dupré, major and legitimate son of deceased Jean

Bte. Derbanne and Hélène Brevel, residents of the parish of Natchitoches during their lifetimes. Bride: minor and legitimate daughter of deceased André St. André and Marie Rachal, residents of this parish of Natchitoches. Witnesses: Fçois Marie Normand; Charles Fçois Benoist, Jean Louis Deslouche. Married at the church in Cloutierville. Priest: Blanc. Dispensation to marry during Easter octave.

146. FELIX ST. ANDRÉ
#5-1829 MARGUERITE PLUNKET
23 April 1829.
Rehabilitation of civil marriage [no date given]. Dispensation from 3 bans and from prohibition against marrying during the octave of Easter. Groom: major and legitimate son of deceased André St. André and Marie Rachal, residents of this parish of Natchitoches. Bride: minor and legitimate daughter of William Plunket and Marie Littleton, residents of this parish of Natchitoches. Married in the chapel at Rivière aux Cannes in presence of Sylvestre Rachal, François Derbanne, Charles Fçois Benoist. Priest: Blanc.

147. [Recording of the bishop's visit and blessing of the new church at Natchitoches.]

148. GUILLAUME GILLE DUPART (s)
#6-1829 MARCELITE CORTEZ (s)
18 May 1829. 1 ban.
Groom: major and legitimate son of Guillaume Dupart and Ann Prudhomme of the parish of St. James, state of Louisiana. Bride: minor and legitimate daughter of deceased Jean Cortez and Marcelite Josephine Rouquier of the parish of Natchitoches. Witnesses: A. Prudhomme (s); C. Davis (s); Narcisse Prudhomme (s); V[*euve*] Cortes (s); Jn. Laplace (s); John C. Carr (s); Chas. A. Bullard (s). Priest: Blanc.

149. NOËL [MÉZIÈRES] (x)
#7-1829 MARIE DELOÏZE *dite* PERAUT (x)
18 May 1829. 2 bans.
Groom: major and natural son of Marie Jeanne *dite* Mézières, a free woman of color living in this parish of Natchitoches. Bride: major and natural daughter of Pelagie *dite* Grappe, a free woman of color living at Campti, parish of Natchitoches. Witnesses: André Chamard (s); Ls. Balthazar (s); Charles Simon, *fils* (s). Priest: Blanc.

150. LS DUNOYE BOSSIER (s)
#8-1829 MARIE CELINA HESSER (x)
3 June 1829. Rehabilitation of civil marriage performed 21 May 1825. Groom: major and legitimate

son of deceased F^{çois} Bossier and Marie Pelagie Lambre, residents of this parish of Natchitoches during their lifetimes. Bride: minor daughter of Christian Hesser and Marie Adelaïde Rambin, residents of the parish of Natchitoches. Witnesses: Widow Jean Louis Buard (s); Ve Jean B^{te} Buard (s). Priest: Blanc.

151. #9-1829
FRANÇOIS DERBANNE (s)
TRANQUILLINE LE COUR [LA COUR] (x)
11 June 1829. 3 bans.
Groom: widower from first nuptials with deceased Carmelite Langlois, major and legitimate son of deceased J. B^{te} Derbanne and deceased Hélène Brevel, residents of this parish during their lifetimes. Bride: minor and legitimate daughter of Gasparite LaCour and Felicité Brevel, also residents of this parish of Natchitoches. Dispensation from impediment of consanguinity in second degree. Witnesses: J. B. C. Rachal (s); L^{s} Derbanne; Dr. Normand (s); Clement Rachal (s); Gasparite La Cour (x). At the chapel in Cloutierville. Priest: Blanc. [cf. Reg. 8.]

152. #10-1829
LOUIS MONET
MARIE LOUISE COTTON-MAŸS
23 July 1829.
Rehabilitation of civil marriage performed 17 May 1825. Groom: major and natural son of Marie Louise LeComte, a free man of color and resident of the parish of Natchitoches. Bride: natural daughter of Antoine Cotton-Maÿs and Marie Louise [Bellepeche], her father and mother, residents of the parish of Natchitoches. At the chapel of St. Augustine on Isle à Brevel. Witnesses: Étienne Lacaze and Cezaire Le Cour. Priest: Blanc.

[Ed. Note: For identity of the wife of Antoine Cotton-maïs see Entry 409.]

153. #11-1829
ÉTIENNE LACAZE
CAROLINE LEMOINE
23 July 1829.
Rehabilitation of civil marriage performed 6 April 1823. Groom: major and legitimate son of Étienne Lacaze and Dorothée Massipe, residents of this parish of Natchitoches. Bride. Major and legitimate daughter of Jean B^{te} Lemoine and Felicité LaCase, also residents of this parish of Natchitoches. Dispensation from impediment of consanguinity in second degree. Married at chapel of St. Augustine, Isle à Brevel. Witnesses: Louis Monet; Cezaire Le Cour. Priest: Blanc.

154.
#12-1829

CEZAIRE LE COUR
GERTRUDE MAURINE
23 July 1829.
Ratification of civil marriage performed about five years earlier. Groom: natural son of Barthelemy Le Cour and Marie Ursulle, residents of the parish of Natchitoches. Bride: daughter of Stave [Esteban] Maurine and Marie Celaphore [Maria Telesfora de la Cerda] also residents of this parish of Natchitoches. Performed at the chapel of St. Augustine on Isle à Brevel in presence of Etienne LaCaze and Louis Monet. Priest: Blanc.

155.
#13-1829

NAZARIO ORTIS
DES NEIGE ARAGON
23 July 1829.
Groom: major and legitimate son of Jean B^{te} Ortis and Jeanne Ross, residents of this parish of Natchitoches. Bride: daughter of Jean Baptiste Aragon and Marie Valbois, also residents of this parish of Natchitoches. Married at chapel of St. Augustine on Isle à Brevel in presence of Etienne LaCaze and Louis Monet. Priest: Blanc.

156.
#14-1829

EMILE DUPARTE
MARIE ROSE BALTAZAR
25 July 1829.
Ratification of civil marriage performed 10 May 1825. Groom: major and natural son of Victoire Mulon, native of New Orleans and now a resident of the parish of Natchitoches. Bride: legitimate daughter of Jean B^{te} Baltazar and Marie Rose [Metoyer], all free people of color. Married at chapel of St. Augustine on Isle à Brevel, in presence of Jean B^{te} Metoyer and Manuel Llorens. Priest: Blanc.

157.
#15-1829

NARCISSE METOYER
MARIE CEPHALIDE [DAVID]
19 November 1829.
Ratification of civil marriage performed four or five years earlier. Groom: legitimate and major son of Dominique Metoyer and Marguerite [Le Comte], free people of color and residents of the parish of Natchitoches. Bride: natural daughter of Magdeleinne [Grappe] a free woman of color and resident of the parish of Natchitoches. Married in the chapel at Cloutierville in presence of Jean B^{te} D^{que} Metoyer, *cadet*; F^{çois} Bertile [Trichel]. Priest: Blanc.

[Ed. note: For maternity of the groom see Mills, *Forgotten People*, 75, 84. For baptism of the bride, see Mills, *Natch. 1800-1826*, #179 [Marie Stephalie]. The surname of the bride appears in Succession of Narcisse Dominique Metoyer, partly transcribed in Succ. Bk.

12, pp.175-79 and Conv. Bk. 22 (Mortgages), pp. 280-81, Office of the Clerk of Court, Natchitoches. Cephalide's mother, Magdeleine Grappe, was the mother of several quadroon children who used the surname David. The marriage of one of these identified the father as "Sr. Luis David, white, already deceased." See No. 73, this volume. François Berthilde Trichel, prior to 1830, was often called simply François Berthilde.]

158. FRANÇOIS ADLET
#16-1829 EUPHROSINE SHELETRE
19 November 1829. 3 bans.
Groom: major and legitimate son of Jean B^{te} Adlet and Victoire Brevel, residents of the parish of Natchitoches. Bride: minor and legitimate daughter of deceased Jean B^{te} Sheletre and deceased Euphrosine Rachal, residents of this parish of Natchitoches during their lifetimes. Married at chapel at Cloutierville in presence of Clement Rachal, Pierre Sheletre, and Sanguinette Hubert Benoist. Priest: Blanc.

159. PRUDENT RACHAL
#17-1829 ADELE ARMAND
30 November 1829. 3 bans.
Groom: minor and legitimate son of Dominique Rachal and Rosalie Verchere, residents of this parish of Natchitoches. Bride: minor and legitimate daughter of Jean Baptiste Armand and Catherine Fréderic, residents of this parish of Natchitoches. Married at the home of Jean B^{te} Armand in presence of L^{s} Derbanne, Firmin Rachal, Jean B^{te} Armand, Jr. Priest: Blanc.

160. JOSEPH T. ROBINSON
#18-1829 ARSENE TRICHEL
3 December 1829. 3 bans.
Groom: major and legitimate son of Joseph T. Robinson, native of Dublin, Ireland, now a resident of this parish of Natchitoches. Bride: minor and legitimate daughter of deceased Emanuel Trichel and Euphrosine Prudhomme, also residents of this parish of Natchitoches. Dispensation from prohibition against marriage during Advent. Married at home of Sr. Fleming in presence of Michael Boyce, Wm. Long, Pierre Gagnon. Priest: Blanc.

161. EMANUEL HERNAND
#19-1829 MARIE AGATHE NOLASCO
8 December 1829. 3 bans.
Groom: major and legitimate son of deceased Jerome Hernand and Marie Nanon Rachal, residents of the parish of Natchitoches. Bride: minor and legitimate daughter of deceased Pierre Nolasco and Magda-

leine La Bery, also residents of this parish of Natchitoches. Dispensation granted from impediment of consanguinity in 2nd and 3rd degrees and from prohibition against marriage during Advent. Ceremony at chapel at Cloutierville in presence of Charles Fçois Benoist (s); J. P. Cloutier (s); and J. Bte Derbanne (x). Priest: Blanc. [cf. Reg. 8.]

162. SILVESTRE HERNAND
#20-1829 LAIZA VERCHER
9 December 1829. 3 bans.
Groom: major and legitimate son of deceased Jerome Hernand and Marie Nanon Rachal, residents of the parish of Natchitoches. Bride: minor and legitimate daughter of Jacques Verchere and Euphrosine Gallien, residents of this parish of Natchitoches. Dispensation from impediment of consanguinity in 4th degree and from prohibition against marriage during Advent. Ceremony at chapel in Cloutierville in presence of Marc Sompayrac (s); Antoine Bmy Rachal (s); Pierre Baulos (s). Priest: Blanc. [cf. Reg. 8.]

163. FRANÇOIS LATTIER (s)
#21-1829 MARIE FRANÇOISE PHANNIE PLAISANCE (s)
31 December 1829. 3 bans.
Groom: minor and legitimate son of Fçois Lattier and Marie Pelagie Sheletre, residents of this parish of Natchitoches. Bride: minor and legitimate daughter of Bertrand Plaisance and Marie Barbe Grillet, also residents of this parish of Natchitoches. Dispensation from prohibition against marriage during Octave of Christmas. Witnesses: François Lattier, Sr (x); Bertrand Plaisance (x); Ad Lauve (s); Clement Rachal (s); Ludger Rachal (s); Cme Perot(s); Isaac Plaisance (s). Priest: Blanc. [cf. Reg. 8.]

164. LOUIS FLORENTIN METOYER (x)
#1-1830 MARIE THEODOZE CHAGNAU (x)
19 January 1830. 3 bans.
Groom: minor and legitimate son of Dominique Metoyer and Marguerite [Le Comte], free people of color and residents of this parish of Natchitoches. Bride: minor and natural daughter of Felicité [Grappe], a free woman of color also living in this parish of Natchitoches. Married in the parish church in presence of Dominique Metoyer (x); Felicité (x); Manuel Llorens (s); Jn Bte Metoyer *fils* Augtin(s); Fçois Gacion [Metoyer] *fils* Gtin [Gustin --i.e.: Augustin]. Priest: Blanc. [cf. Reg. 8.]

[Ed. note: For baptism of Marie Louise Theodoze/Theodore Chagneau, daughter of Felicite Grappe, see Mills, *Natch. 1800-1826,* No. 190.

165.
#2-1830 JOSEPH METOYER
MARIE ANTOINETTE COINDET
26 January 1830. 3 bans.
Groom: minor and legitimate son of Augustin Metoyer and Marie Agnes [Poissot], free people of color and residents of the parish of Natchitoches. Bride: minor and natural daughter of Marie Rose Metoyer, also a free person of color. Married in chapel on Isle Brevel, after dispensation from impediment of consanguinity in second and third degrees, in presence of Emanuel Laurens [Llorens], J. B.te Metoyer and Pierre Metoyer, *fils*. Priest: Blanc.

[Ed. note: For surname of groom's mother see Mills, *Forgotten People*, 74, 81-83. *Ibid.*, 100-101, identifies the bride's father as Sieur Jacques Antoine Coindet.]

166.
#3-1830 MARCEL LAPLANTE
DAMASCENE GALLIEN
4 February 1830. 3 bans.
Groom: major and legitimate son of Louis La Plante and Marie [blank], residents of the parish of Natchitoches. Bride: minor and legitimate daughter of deceased Louis Gallien and Céleste Anty, her father and mother, also residents of this parish of Natchitoches. Married at chapel in Cloutierville, in presence of Jean B.te Lattier, Jean Pierre Cloutier, and J. B.te Clement Rachal. Priest: Blanc.

167.
#4-1830 NEUVILLE LECOUR
MARIE OSITTE METOYER
15 February 1830. 3 bans.
Groom: a man of color, major and natural son of Bmy. Le Court and Marie Louise, residents of the parish of Natchitoches. Bride: minor and legitimate daughter of Pierre Metoyer and Marie Henriette [Cloutier], residents of this parish of Natchitoches. Married in chapel of St. Augustine, Isle a Brevel, in presence of Charles Nerestan Roque, Joseph Metoyer, Fç.ois Gacion Metoyer. Priest: Blanc.

[Ed. note: Neuville's baptismal record identifies him as Jean Baptiste Neuville, son of Marie URSULLE, a free *metive*. The full name of his half-Indian mother was Marie Louise Ursulle, called "Louison." See Mills, *Natch. 1800-1826*, No. 16 for his baptismal entry and Mills, *Forgotten People*, 94-95 for a discussion of his parentage. *Ibid.*, 86-87 identifies the mother of Marie Ositte.

168. GABRIEL ST. ANNE PRUDHOMME (s)
#5-1830 MARIE AGLAE PRUDHOMME (s)
17 February 1830. 2 bans.
Groom: major and legitimate son of Jean Baptiste Prudhomme and Marie Thérèse Victoire Aillaud Ste. Anne, residents of this parish of Natchitoches. Bride: minor and legitimate daughter of Narcisse Prudhomme and Marie Thérèse Elisabeth Metoyer, residents of this parish of Natchitoches. Dispensation from double impediment of consanguinity in 2nd and 3rd degree and from the announcement of the 3rd ban. Married at home of J. B^{te} Prudhomme, in presence of P^{re} Phanor Prudhomme (s); Prudhomme, *fils* (s); Narcisse Prudhomme (s); M^{ie} Thérèse Prudhomme (s); Lambre Prudhomme (s); Prudhomme (s); V. Metoyer (s); Narcisse Prudhomme, *fils* (s); Jean Prudhomme (s); Janin, D.M. (s); A. Sompayrac (s). Priest: Blanc.

169. ABEL NAPOLEON SERS
#6-1830 MARIANNE PAMELA JOHNSON
28 February 1830.
Groom: major and legitimate son of Pierre Jean Abel Sers and Sophie Ducrois, native of La Bessonier, department of Tarn, France, now a resident of the parish of Natchitoches. Bride: minor and legitimate daughter of deceased John Johnston and deceased F^{çoise} Greneaux, also a resident of this parish of Natchitoches. Dispensation given from prohibition against marrying during Lent. Married in chapel at Cloutierville in presence of Marc Sompayrac, Ch. Greneaux, A. Dolichamp. Priest: Blanc.

170. MELICE ANTY
#7-1820 HENRIETTE ARMAND
17 April 1830. 3 bans.
Groom: major and legitimate son of Jean B^{te} Anty and Marie Cyprienne Derbanne, residents of this parish of Natchitoches. Bride: widowed from first nuptials with deceased Victor Rachal, major and legitimate daughter of Jean B^{te} Armand and Catherine Frederic, also a resident of this parish of Natchitoches. Dispensation from prohibition of marriage during Octave of Easter. Witnesses: Ludger Rachal; Florian Derbanne, Sévère Lattier, and Batoche Brevel. Priest: Blanc.

171. LOUIS BALTHASARD
#8-1830 ANTOINETTE COTTON-MAYS
1 May 1830. 3 bans.
Groom: natural son of Marie Rose Metoyer, a free person of color and resident of this parish of Natchitoches. Bride: minor and legitimate daughter of

Antoine Cotton Maÿs and Marie Louise [Bellepeche], free people of color and residents of this parish of Natchitoches. Marriage in chapel of St. Augustine on Isle à Brevel, in presence of Emanuel Laurens [Llorens], Joseph Metoyer *fils* Augustin, and Pierre Metoyer, *fils*. Priest: Blanc.

[Ed. note: For identity of wife of Cotton-maïs, see entry 409.]

172. AUGUSTE METOYER
#9-1830 MARIE THÉRÉSE CARMELITE ANTY
1 May 1830.
Rehabilitation of civil marriage performed 6 April 1824. Groom: major and legitimate son of Augustin Metoyer and Marie Agnes [Poissot]. Bride: daughter of Suzanne Metoyer and resident of this parish of Natchitoches. Performed in Chapel of St. Augustine on Isle á Brevel, in presence of Jean B$^{t.e}$ Metoyer, Charles Nerestan Roques. Priest: Blanc.

[Ed. note: For identity of groom's mother, see Mills, *Forgotten People*, 74, 81-83.]

173. PIERRE GAGNON
#10-1830 HENRIETTE DUBOIS
24 June 1830. 3 bans.
Groom: major and legitimate son of deceased P$^{r.e}$ Gagnon and deceased Thérèse Valentin, residents of the parish of Natchitoches during their lifetimes. Bride: minor and legitimate daughter of Fç$^{o.is}$ Dubois and Eleonore Risse, also residents of this parish of Natchitoches. Witnesses: Jean B$^{t.e}$ Perot, Derzelin Perot, Samuel Russel, Bénigne Davenport. Priest: Blanc.

174. EMANUEL DUPRÉ
#11-1830 MARIE MARGUERITE METOYER
19 August 1830. 3 bans.
Groom: minor and "legitimate-natural" son of Adelaÿde [Mariotte], a free woman of color and resident of this parish of Natchitoches. Bride: major and legitimate daughter of D$^{q.ue}$ Metoyer and Marguerite [Le Comte], free people of color and residents of this parish of Natchitoches. Married at chapel of St. Augustine on Isle à Brevel in presence of Ch. N. Roque, Joseph Metoyer, and Octave Henry [Henry Octave Deronce]. Priest: Blanc.

[Ed. note: for parentage of the groom see Mills, *Forgotten People*, 91-94. *Ibid*, 75, 84, identifies mother of the bride.] Deronce, also a free man of color of Cane River, appears with his name written in full in the following entry.]

175. JACQUES PORTER
#12-1830 ADELAŸDE ARSENE COTTON-MAŸS
24 August 1830. 3 bans.
Groom: major and natural son of Perine Metoyer, a free man of color and resident of this parish. Bride: minor and legitimate daughter of Antoine Cotton-Maÿs and Marie Louise [Bellepeche].* Married at chapel of St. Augustine on Isle à brevel in presence of Joseph Metoyer, *fils* Augustin, Pierre Metoyer, *fils*, and Henry Octave Deronce. Priest: Blanc. *[See entry 409]

176. AVIT DAVION
#13-1830 MELANIE PERAULT
14 September 1830. 3 bans.
Groom: major and legitimate son of deceased D^{que} Davion and Pelagie Gagné, residents of this parish of Natchitoches. Bride: minor and legitimate daughter of L^{s} Derzilin Perault and Melanie Trichel, also a resident of this parish of Natchitoches. Dispensation from impediment of consanguinity in 3rd and 4th degrees. Witnesses: J. J^{que} Lambre; P. Gagnon; L^{s} Geofroi. Priest: Blanc.

177. JOSEPH LA BAUME (s)
#14-1830 MARIE JEANNE GRAPPE
4 October 1830. 3 bans.
Groom: son of Joseph La Baume and Hortance Couturier, a native of Nacogdoches and resident of the town of San Ferdinand de Bejar, province of Texas. Groom has presented the certificate of Reverend Refugio de la Garca, pastor of that said town, dated 12 July 1830, stating that La Baume is free to marry. Bride: major and natural daughter of Magdeleine Grappe, a free woman of color and a native of this parish of Natchitoches. Witnesses: François Frederic, St. Cyr de la Baume, Louis David (x). Groom signed as José de Labaume (s). Witness St. Cyr signed as St. Cyr Pedero de la Baume (s). Priest: Blanc.

178. GEORGE WILLIAM GANIE [GUNNY] (s)
#15-1830 MARIE REINE ROŸER (s)
12 October 1830. 2 bans.
Groom: major and legitimate son of deceased Wilson Ganie and Susanne Ganie, native of the Isle of Gonzi [Guernsey?], now in this parish. Bride: minor and legitimate daughter of François Roÿer and Marie Pelagie Adlet, also a resident of this parish. Witnesses: John A. Dunn (s); W. L. Cockerille (s); David? Russell (s); Fenilon W. Ragland. Groom signed as G. W. Gunny (s). Priest: Blanc.

179. EMANUEL TRICHEL (x)
#16-1830 MARGUERITE ADELAÏDE SUDERLINE (x)
4 November 1830. 1 ban.
Groom: major and natural son of Marie Cilezie Trichel, a free woman of color. Bride: natural and minor daughter of Melite Suderline, also a free woman of color. Witnesses: Henry Octave [Deronce] (s); Cyrille Duprat (s); Charles Simon (s). Priest: Blanc.

[Ed. note: Bride's name is also spelled Sudderline.]

180. LEZIN [ONESIME] EUGÈNE TAUZIN (s)
#1-1831 MARIE HELMINA GINGER (s)
17 January 1831. 3 bans.
Groom: major and legitimate son of Joseph Tauzin and Marie Chamard, a resident of this parish of Natchitoches. Bride: minor and legitimate daughter of Jean Agues Ginger and deceased Helmina Miller, natives of Platten in "Allemagne" [Germany]. Witnesses: Lille Sarpy (s); A^e^ Chamard (s); ?. H. Rueg (s); L^s^ Tauzin (s); B. Ba__ [Bart? Bant?] (s). Priest: Blanc.

181. PAUL VICTOR SOMPAYRAC (s)
#2-1831 MARIE SEPHALIDE ELISA PRUDHOMME
19 January 1831. 1 ban.
Groom: major and legitimate son of Ambroise Sompayrac and Josephine Briant, resident of this parish of Natchitoches. Bride: minor and legitimate daughter of Narcisse Prudhomme and Marie Thérèse Elisabeth Metoyer. Witnesses: Messieurs Marc Sompayrac (s); Louis Sompayrac (s); Charles Emanuel Greneaux (s); A. Sompayrac (s); Narcisse Prudhomme (s); Briant Sompayrac (s); Marie Thérèse Prudhomme (s); Narcisse Prudhomme, *fils*; St. Anne Prudhomme (s); J. V. Bossier (s); Prudhomme (s). Groom signed as V. Sompayrac. Priest: Blanc.

182. FIRMIN SOTO (x)
#3-1831 SOPHIE GONIN (x)
12 February 1831. 3 bans.
Groom: major and legitimate son of Jean Soto and "Dame [blank] whose name is unknown," native of the environs of St. Antoine, province of Texas, and now a resident of this parish of Natchitoches. Bride: major and legitimate daughter of F^çois^ Gonin and Marie Barbe Frederick, native of this parish of Natchitoches. Witness: Laurent Soto (x); Chrisostomé Perot (s); Prudent Rachal (s); Derzilin Rachal (s). Priest: Blanc.

183. FELIX FRANÇOIS GRACIEN PAUL (s)
#4-1831 FRANÇOISE ADELAŸDE ROUBIEU (s)
14 March 1831. 1 ban.
Groom: major and legitimate son of deceased F^çois^

Paul and deceased Jeanne Françoise Mayeu, native of the town of Nantes, department of Loire-Inferieure, France, and now a resident of New Orleans. Bride: minor and legitimate daughter of F[ç][ois] Roubieu and Marie Ozitte Rachal, native of the parish of Natchitoches. Dispensation from prohibition against marrying during Lent. Witnesses: Ausite Rachal (s); F[s] Roubieu (s); Ocsar Roubieu (s); Alexander L. Deblieux (s); P. S. Compère (s); Charles F. Benoist (s); L[s] Chevalier (s); G. F? Hertzog (s). Priest: Blanc.

184. DAUNOYE VERCHER
#5-1831 MELISSAIRE MARIE GALLIEN
19 March 1831. 2 bans.
Groom: major and legitimate son of Jacque Vercher and Euphrosine Gallien, native of this parish of Natchitoches. Bride: minor and legitimate daughter of deceased Louis Gallien and Marie Celeste Anty. Dispensation from impediment of consanguinity in second degree. Witnesses: Sévère Lattier; Ludger Langlois; Felix Langlois. Priest: Blanc.

185. JEAN RENAUDE AGUESSE (x)
#6-1831 MARIE MARCELITE POISSOT (x)
11 April 1831. 1 ban.
Groom: major and legitimate son of deceased Jean Renaud Aguesse and Marie Louise Massip, residents of this parish of Natchitoches. Bride: minor and legitimate daughter of Paul Poissot and Marie Louise Anty, residents of this parish of Natchitoches. Witnesses: Charles G. Lewis (s); Silvestre Bossier (s); G. A. Ragan (s); Jacques __uilly? (s). Priest: Blanc.

186. JOSEPH DERBANNE (s)
#7-1831 MARIE LOUISE HANZELMAN (x)
11 April 1831. 1 ban.
Groom: widower of first nuptials with deceased Catherine Brosset. Legitimate and major son of Pierre Derbanne and Marie Leclerc, residents of this parish of Natchitoches during their lives. Bride: native of Germany, now a resident of this parish of Natchitoches, with permission of Bertrand Plaisance (x), her tutor. Witnesses: A[d] Lauve (s); L[s] Derbanne (s); C. L. Greneaux (s); I. Deterville (s). Priest: Blanc.

#187. ETIENNE ROI (x)
#8-1831 MARIE CLEMANTINE SHELETTRE (x)
19 April 1831. 3 bans.
Groom: native of the parish of St. Landry des Opeloussas, major son of deceased Noël Roi and Celeste

Wayble, and now a resident of this parish of Natchitoches. Bride: minor and legitimate daughter of Pierre Shelettre and Eulalie Bossier, resident of this parish of Natchitoches. Witnesses: J^{n}. B^{te}. Lille Sarpy (s); A^{m}. Le Comte (s); Eulalie Bossier (x); Pierre Shelettre, *fils* (s); L. Alexandre Buard (s). Priest: Blanc.

188. EMANUEL DERBANNE
#9-1831 AIMÉE PEROT
21 April 1831.
Groom: major son of Gaspar Derbanne and Marie Joseph Perot. Bride: major and legitimate daughter of François Perot and Marie Louisse Agatte Labery. Ratification of civil marriage performed 22 April 1829, with dispensation from impediment of consanguinity in second degree. Witnesses: Placide Derbanne; Louis Dersilin Perot. Priest: Blanc.

189. FRANÇOIS JEAN BAPTISTE FONTENEAU
#10-1831 MARIE CELINA PEROT
23 April 1831. 1 ban.
Groom: major and legitimate son of deceased Jean B^{te}. Fonteneau and Marie Pompose Lafitte, native of this parish of Natchitoches. Bride: minor and legitimate daughter of Jean Chrisostomé Faustin Perot and Marie Celeste Bordelon, native of this parish of Natchitoches. Married at the house of Dlle. Françoise Trichel, district of Campti, after dispendation from impediment of consanguinity in 3rd and 4th degrees. Witnesses: Cezaire Fonteneau, Hypolite Bordelon, Athanaze Pierre Trichel. Priest: Blanc.

190. PIERRE BAULOS
#11-1831 VICTOIRE EMANDÉE JHONSTON
2 May 1831. 3 bans.
Groom: major and legitimate son of F^{çois}. Baulos and Marie Guibert, native of the town of Bureau?, department of La Gironde in France. Bride: minor and legitimate daughter of deceased Jhon Jhonston and deceased Victoire Greneau, native of this parish of Natchitoches. Married in the church at Cloutierville. Witnesses: P. Bossier; Marc Sompayrac; Charles E. Greneaux. Priest: Blanc.

191. ANTOINE FREDIEU
#12-1831 MARIE LOUISE VACOCU
17 May 1831. 1 ban.
Groom: major and legitimate son of deceased Auguste Fredieu and deceased Marie Jeanne Sorel, residents of this parish during their lifetimes. Bride: minor and legitimate daughter of deceased Louis Vacocu and Celeste Jean Risse, also a resident of this parish.

Bride's mother gives consent, after dispensation from impediment of affinity in second and third degrees. Married in the district of Campti in presence of Messieurs P. Trichel, Faustin Perot, and Chrisostomė Vacocu, "and others" [unnamed]. Priest: Blanc.

192. ANTOINE LENOIR (x)
#13-1831 ADELAŸDE DUBOIS (x)
7 May 1831. 1 ban.
Groom: natural son of Lally [Eulalie] Carle, widower in first nuptials of Marie des Neiges Derbanne, resident of this parish. Bride: major and legitimate daughter of Fçois Dubois and Eleonore Jean Risse, also a resident of this parish of Natchitoches. Witnesses: Messieurs P. Gagnon (s); Celestin Ely (x); Louis Acoit (x); "and others." Priest: Blanc.

193. MARCELIN TAUZIN (s)
#14-1831 MARIE CONSTANCE LEVASSEUR (s)
20 June 1831. 3 bans.
Groom: major and legitimate son of Jph. Tauzin and Marie Chammard, resident of this parish of Natchitoches. Bride: minor and legitimate daughter of deceased Jean Fçois Trichel. Witneses: Jh Tauzin (s); Me Françoise Trichel (s); E. C. Tauzin (s); J. B. Trichel (s); Aphe Sompayrac (s); L. E. Tauzin (s); Louis Closeau (s); B. Dranguet (s); Chamard Tauzin (s). Priest: Blanc.

194. CHARLES LEMOINE
#15-1831 FELICITÉ LEMOINE
23 June 1831.
Rehabilitation of civil marriage celebrated 4 February 1828, after dispensation from impediment of consanguinity in 2nd degree. Groom: major and legitimate son of Ane Lemoine and Geneviève Belle Garde resident of this parish of Natchitoches. Bride: minor and legitimate daughter of J. Bte Lemoine and Felicité LaCase. Nuptial benediction given at residence of Mr. Marc Sompayrac. Witnesses: Valentine Dubois, Abel Sers. Priest: Blanc.

195. VALENTINE DUBOIS
#16-1831 HELOISE LEMOINE
23 June 1831
Ratification of civil marriage performed 1 October 1829. Groom: major and legitimate son of J. Bte Dubois and Rosette Shelettre, resident of this parish of Natchitoches. Bride: minor and legitimate daughter of Antoine Le Moine and Geneviève Belle Garde, resident of this parish of Natchitoches. Nuptial benediction given at residence of Mr. Marc

Sompayrac. Witnesses: Charles Lemoine, Abel Sers "and others." Priest: Blanc.

196. JPH. METOYER
#17-1831 MARIE DOROLYSE COINDET
25 June 1831. 3 bans.
Groom: major and legitimate son of Joseph Metoyer and Pelagie [Le Court], free people of color and residents of Natchitoches Parish. Bride: minor and natural daughter of Marie Rose Metoyer [and Jacques Coindet], native of this parish. Marriage in chapel of St. Augustine on Isle Brevelle, after dispensation from impediment of consanguinity in 2nd and 3rd degrees. Witnesses: Henry Octave [Deronce]; Emile Dupart; J. B[te] Metoyer "and others." Priest: Blanc.

[Ed. note: For documentation of parentage given above in brackets, see Mills, *Forgotten People*, pp. 76, 84, 100-01.]

197. PIERRE VICTOR BOUIS (s)
#18-1831 MARIE EMELIE CHAMARD (s)
29 June 1831. 2 bans.
Groom: major and legitimate son of Jacques Antoine Bouis and Marie Magdeleine Aryand, a native of the town of Marseille, department of Bouches-des-Rhône in France, now a resident of the parish of Natchitoches. Bride, minor and legitimate daughter of André Chammard and Felicité Saucier, resident of this parish of Natchitoches. Witnesses: A[e] Chamard (s); Felicité Chamard (s); E. C. Tauzin (s); L. E. Tauzin (s); B. Dranguet (s); Lille Sarpy (s); T. Deterville (s); N. Chamard (s). Priest: Blanc.

198. LOUIS MAURIN (s)
#19-1831 SUZETTE METOYER (x)
2 July 1831. 1 ban.
Groom: major son of Marie Susette [no last name], a free man of color of New Orleans, who now is in this parish. Bride: major and legitimate daughter of Augustin Metoyer and Dame Agnes [Poissot]; widow of deceased Elisée Roque in first nuptials and a resident of this parish of Natchitoches. Married at church of St. Augustine of Isle à Brevel, in presence of Manuel Llorens (s); Jerome Sarpy (s); Charles Nerestan Rocques (s); Seraphine Llorens (s). Priest: Blanc.

[Ed. note: In a procuration given to A. Chateigner of New Orleans by the widow of the above Louis Amadée Morin, soon after his 1844 death, Morin's mother is identified as "Mme. Sanitte Morin" of New Orleans. See Doc. 342, Robert B. DeBlieux Collection, Historic New Orleans Collection, New Orleans. For identification of Dame Agnes, see Mills, *Forgotten People*, 82-83.]

199. NOËL PLAUDE (x)
#20-1831 DENISE POISOT (x)
4 July 1831. 2 bans.
Groom: major and legitimate son of Vincent Plaude and Victoire Crois, a native of the parish of St. Fç^{ois} in Canada and now a resident of this parish. Bride: minor and legitimate daughter of Paul Poissot and Marie Anty, native of this parish of Natchitoches. Witnesses: J. V. Bossier (s); P. Evariste Bossier (s); L. D. Bossier (s); Chrisostomé Perot (s); Wesley Cure? (s). Priest: Blanc.

200. ISAAC BIRTT
#21-1831 MARIE HÉLÈNE LEMOINE
11 August 1831.
Rehabilitation of civil marriage dated 14 April 1830. Groom: native of Greenwige [Greenwich], Connecticut, now in the parish of Natchitoches. Bride: legitimate daughter of deceased Charles Lemoine and Jeanne Le Brun, widow of [So]Lastie Derbanne in first nuptials, and a resident of the parish of Natchitoches. Marrie at the church in Cloutierville in presence of Jean Morantine, Fç^{ois} Bethl [François Berthilde Trichel?] "and others." Priest: Blanc.

201. JEAN MARIE BRET LACOUR
#22-1831 FRANÇOISE LA COUR
31 August 1831. 3 bans.
Groom: minor and legitimate son of Jean Marie Bret Lacour and Josephine Gillard, residents of the parish of Rapides. Bride: minor and legitimate daughter of Gilbert LaCour and Hélène Geoffrion, also residents of the parish of Rapides. Married at the home of Mr. Bret La Cour in the parish of Rapides, after dispensation from impediment of consanguinity in 2nd degree. Witnesses: Joseph Gillard, J. B^{te} Gillard, Leandre La Cour "and others." Priest: Blanc.

[Ed. note: The bride's name was first written in the marginal notation as La Court; then the "t" was crossed through. The name appears in text as La Cour.]

202. JUAN DE LUNA (x)
#23-1831 GUADALUPE FUENTES (x)
[illegible] September 1831. 1 ban.
Groom: major and legitimate son of Pedro de Luna and Serafina Trego, native of San Antonio, now in the parish of Natchitoches. Bride: legitimate daughter of Ramond Fuentes and Juanna Goutieres, native of San Antonio and now in the parish of Natchitoches. Witnesses: Ignacio de los Santos Coy (s): Manuel Sanctes (x); Paulo Ocon (x). Priest: Blanc.

203. MICHEL [LA CAZE (x)
#24-1831 MARIE DELPHINE LAISA (x)
24 October 1831. 3 bans.
Groom: free man of color, natural son of Rosalie and native of this parish of Natchitoches. Bride: minor and natural daughter of Marguerite Denize, a free woman of color and a native of this parish. Married in the church of St. François des Natchitoches in presence of Marguerite Denize (x); P^{re}. Metoyer, Jr. (s); J^{h}. A^{tin}. Metoyer (s); Tanasite [Athanase] Metoyer (s). Priest: Blanc.

[Ed. note: For baptismal entries on the above bride and groom see Mills, *Natch. 1800-1826*, Nos. 1102 and 1843.]

204. LS. ALEXANDRE BUARD (s)
#25-1831 MARIE VIRGINIA PRUDHOMME (s)
25 October 1831. 2 bans.
Groom: minor and legitimate son of deceased Jean Louis Buard and Eulalie Bossier, native of this parish of Natchitoches. Bride: minor and legitimate daughter of Louis Narcisse Prudhomme and Marie Thérèse Elisabeth Métoyer, resident of this parish of Natchitoches. Married at home of Sr. Narcisse Prudhomme after dispensation from impediment of consanguinity in second, third, and fourth degrees. Witnesses: Narcisse Prudhomme (s); Vve. J. L. Buard (s); M. T. Elisabeth Metoyer (s); J. B. Prudhomme *fils* (s); Metoyer (s); A^{e}. Le Comte (s); Phanor Prudhomme. Priest: Blanc.

205. J. BTE. BESSON
#26-1831 CLARISSE SOREL
27 October 1831
Groom: minor and legitimate son of B^{te}. Besson and deceased Marie Jeanne Pievert, resident of this parish of Natchitoches. Bride: major and legitimate daughter of Dominique Sorel and Marie David, inhabitants of this parish of Natchitoches. Married in the Church of the Nativity at Campti, in presence of Michel Boice, Louis Closeau, Honore Fredieu, "and others." Priest: Blanc.

206. JULIUS C. SAUNDERS (s)
#27-1831 MARIE PHELOE ADLET (x)
[English] 1 December 1831. 1 ban.
Groom: son of John Saunders and Elisabeth Compton, born in Davidson County, Tennessee and now residing in Natchitoches. Bride: minor and legitimate daughter of Valentin Adlet and Selesie Brosset. Married at home of Joseph Derbanne after dispensation from prohibition against marrying during Advent. Witnes-

ses: William McConault (s); A. Le Comte (s); Bertrand Plaisance (x); Isaac Plaisance (s); A. C. Kimball (s). Priest: Blanc.

207. ISAAC PLAISANCE (s)
#1-1832 MARIE ZELINE LATTIER (x)
4 January 1832. 2 bans.
Groom: major and legitimate son of Bertrand Plaisance and Marie Barbe Grillet, resident of this parish of Natchitoches. Bride: minor and legitimate daughter of François Lattier and Marie Pelagie Shelettre, resident of this parish of Natchitoches. Married at home of François Lattier after dispensation from prohibition against marriage during the Epiphany. Witnesses: J. Bte. Prudhomme, Jr. (s); J. P. Bossier (s); Honoré Fredieu (s); Marie Barbe Grillet (x); Fçois. Lattier (x); Bertrand Plaisance (x); Marie Pelagie Sheletre. Priest: Blanc.

208. JEROME THOMASSIE (x)
#2-1832 MARIE ADELINE GALLIEN (x)
5 January 1832. 2 bans.
Groom: major and legitimate son of Louis Thomassie and Marie Catherine Lattier, residents of this parish of Natchitoches. Bride: widow of deceased Joseph Lattier in first nuptials, legitimate daughter of deceased Nicolas Gallien and Marie Le Court, resident of this parish of Natchitoches. Married at the church in Cloutierville, after dispensation from prohibition against marriage during the Epiphany and dispensation from impediment of affinity in second degree. Witnesses: J. Bte. Lattier (s); Dr. F. M. Normand (s); Sévère Lattier (s). Priest: Blanc.

209. J. BTE. McTAER (s)
#3-1832 CELIMEN VERCHERE (x)
2 February 1832. 2 ans.
Groom: major and legitimate son of George McTaier and deceased Marie Louise Mayou, resident of this parish of Natchitoches. Bride: minor and legitimate daughter of deceased Berony [Beloni] Verchere and Marie Orizille Gallien, resident of this parish of Natchitoches. Witnesses: George Mactaer (s); François Terence Chaler (s); Noël Gallien (x); Ch. F. Benoist (s). Priest: Blanc.

210. FRANÇOIS CHALER
#4-1832 MARIE LOUISE LATTIER
14 February 1832. 1 ban.
Groom: major son of Marie Lite [Marcellite] Dupré, widower of deceased Azelie? [ink blot covers most of name] Langlois in first nuptials, resident of this parish of Natchitoches. Bride: widow of deceased

Ignace Anty, in first nuptials; major and legitimate daughter of F$^{ç\underset{.}{o}is}$ Lattier and Marie Pelagie Shelettre, resident of this parish of Natchitoches. Married at the home of Sr. François Lattier in presence of Ch. Benoist, F$^{ç\underset{.}{o}is}$ Lattier, *fils*; J. B$^{\underset{.}{te}}$ Charleville "and others." Priest: Blanc.

211. #5-1832 HENRY OCTAVE DERONCE
MARIE ASPAZIE ANTY METOYER
15 February 1832. 2 bans.
Groom: major and natural son of Henriette Messy, a free woman of color and resident of this parish of Natchitoches. Bride: daughter of Suzanne Metoyer, widowed from first nuptials with Maxil Metoyer, also a woman of color of this parish of Natchitoches. Married at church of St. Augustine of Isle à Brevel, in presence of Nerestan Rocque, Joseph Metoyer, Emanuel Laurens [Llorens]; "and others." Priest: Blanc.

212. #6-1832 SÉVÈRE LATTIER
MARIE TRANQUILLINE LACOURT [LA COUR]
16 February 1832. 3 bans.
Groom: major and legitimate son of F$^{ç\underset{.}{o}is}$ Lattier and Marie Pelagie Shelette, resident of this parish. Bride: Widowed from first nuptials with F$^{ç\underset{.}{o}is}$ Derbanne, minor and legitimate daughter of Gasparite Derbanne [La Cour] and Felicité Brevel, also a resident of this parish. Married in the church at Cloutierville in presence of F$^{ç\underset{.}{o}is}$ Lattier; Ch. F. Benoist; F$^{ç\underset{.}{o}is}$ Challer, "and others." Priest: Blanc.

[Ed. note: The identification of the bride's father as Gasparite DERBANNE is incorrect. An attempt has been made by someone to erase the word Derbanne; but the correct name, La Cour, has not been inserted.]

213. #7-1832 JEAN BTE. CECILE (x)
MARIE ADELAYDE [MARIOTTE] (x)
19 March 1832. 2 bans.
Groom: major and natural son of Cecile, a free woman of color and resident of the parish of Natchitoches. Bride: Major and natural daughter of Adelaÿde Mariotte, also a woman of color of this parish. Married in the church of St. François des Natchitoches, in presence of Joseph A$^{\underset{.}{tin}}$ Metoyer (s); Athanase "Tanasite" Metoyer (s); St. Cyr "Sincir" Metoyer (s); "and others." Priest: Blanc.

214. #8-1832 JOSEPH DEROQUE (s)
MARIA GUADELUPE [CORDERO]
31 March 1832. 3 bans.
Groom: major and legitimate son of Nicolas Duroque

and Manuela Sanctes of this parish of Natchitoches. Bride: widow in first nuptials with deceased Precilliano Fuentos, daughter of Antoine Cordero and Theodora Renderne?, also a resident of the parish of Natchitoches. Witnesses: George Monroe (s); Fr. Bertille [Trichel] (s); Marie Magdeliene La Renaudière (x). Priest: Blanc.

215.
#9-1832

FÇOIS GACION METOYER
MARIE FLAVIE [MÉZIÈRES]
25 April 1832. 3 bans.
Groom: major and legitimate son of Augustin Metoyer and Agnes Metoyer, resident of this parish. Bride: natural daughter of Phannie [Marie Euphrosine "Fanny" Mézieres], a free person of color and resident of this parish. Marriage at Chapel of St. Augustin de l'Isle à Brevel, after dispensation from prohibition against marrying during Octave of Easter. Witnesses: Jean Bte Atin Metoyer, Emanuel Laurens [Llorens]; Joseph Metoyer. Priest: Blanc.

[Ed. note: Surname of bride is found in tutor's bond posted by the widowered F. G. Metoyer in August 1833. See *Old Natchitoches Records*, Vol. 2, No. 119, Cammie G. Henry Collection, Northwestern State University, Natchitoches. For documentation of Flavie's maternity, see Elizabeth Shown Mills, "(De) Mézières-Trichel-Grappe: A Tri-Caste Lineage of the Old South," to be published in 1985 in *The Genealogist*: Journal of the Association for the Promotion of Scholarship in Genealogy.]

216.
#10-1832

LS. LA MATHE (x)
MARIE JOSEPHE SIMON (x)
28 April 1832. 3 bans.
Groom: natural and minor son of Louis Lamathe and Celeste Perot, a person of color. Bride: legitimate daughter of Charles Simon and Marie Vicente Perres, free people of color of this parish of Natchitoches. Witnesses: Charles Simon, Jr. (s); Simeon Trichel (s); Fçois Bertille [Trichel] (s); Charles Simon (s). Priest: Blanc.

217.
#11-1832

CEZAIRE FONTENEAU, JR. (s)
MARIE EUGENIE McTAER (s)
[illegible]1 May 1832. 3 bans.
Groom: minor and legitimate son of Cezaire Fonteneau and Felicité Laffite. Bride: widow in first nuptials with William Russel, minor and legitimate daughter of deceased George McTaer and deceased Marie Louise Mayou, all residents of the parish of Natchitoches. Married in the chapel at Campti in presence W. H. Russell (s); F. Robinson (s); Louis Genty (s); Charles Geo. Lewis (s); G. McTaer; Samuel Russel (s). Priest: Blanc. [cf. Reg. 8.]

218. JULES VICTOR BOSSIER (s)
#12-1832 LOUISE VICTOIRE DESIRÉE SOMPAYRAC (s)
21 June 1832. 3 bans.
Groom: major and legitimate son of deceased F$^{ç\underline{ois}}$ Paul Bossier and deceased Catherine Pelagie Lambre, residents of this parish of Natchitoches during their lifetimes. Bride: minor and legitimate daughter of A$^{\underline{se}}$ Sompayrac and Josephine Briant, also residents of this parish of Natchitoches. Witnesses: A. Sompayrac (s); V$^{\underline{e}}$ Sompayrac (s); P. E. Bossier (s); C. E. Greneaux (s); A. Sompayrac (s); J$^{\underline{n}}$ Laplace (s); Briant Sompayrac (s); Evariste A. Bossier (s); J$^{\underline{h}}$ Tauzin (s); M$^{\underline{c}}$ Sompayrac (s); Wm. Paillette (s); P? Prudhomme (s); D. Bossier (s); A. Le Comte (s); E.A.? Buard (s). Priest: Blanc.

219. JUAN BTA. FRANCISCO GONZALES (x)
#13-1832 MARIE CLARISSE SHELETTRE (x)
10 July 1832. 3 bans.
Groom: major and legitimate son of Juan B$^{\underline{tta}}$ Gonzales and Maria Manuela? Sepulveda, native of the province of Texas, now a resident of the parish of Natchitoches. Bride: minor and legitimate daughter of deceased Jean Pierre Shelettre and Eulalie Bossier, native of this parish of Natchitoches. Witnesses: Eulalie Bossier (x); D. Bossier; A. Le Comte (s); P. Bertin (s). Priest: Blanc.

[Ed. note: Groom's name is given in text and in margin as Francisco Gonzales. However, the mark of "Juan B$^{\underline{ta}}$ Gonzales" appears at the end of the document in the position where groom's signature normally appears.]

220. GREGORIO JARNAC (x)
#14-1832 LOUISE BREVEL (x)
25 July 1832.
Ratification of civil marriage. Groom: major son of L$^{\underline{s}}$ Jarnac and Anna Maria de la Cerda. Bride: major daughter of Guillaume Brevel and Paula Whiteman. All reside in this parish. Witnesses: P. Bertin; Oscar Roubieu. Priest: Blanc.

221. ONESIME RACHAL (x)
#15-1832 MARIE AIMÉ LESTAGE (x)
1 August 1832. 3 bans.
Groom: minor and legitimate son of Jean B$^{\underline{te}}$ Rachal and Roseline Derbanne, all residents of this parish. Bride: widowed from first nuptials with A$^{\underline{tin}}$ Gutieres, major and legitimate daughter of deceased Barthelemy Lestage and Pelagie Frederic. Witnesses: Ludger Rachal; [illegible] Bossier. Priest: Blanc.

222. ISAAC RACHAL (x)
#16-1832 MARIE AZELIE RACHAL (x)
9 August 1832. 3 bans.
Groom: major and legitimate son of deceased J. B[te] Barthelemy Rachal and Marie Pelagie Brevel, residents of this parish in their lifetimes. Bride: minor and legitimate daughter of Sr. L[s] Barthelemey Rachal, Jr. and of M. Louise Chelette, residents of this parish. Dispensation from impediment of consanguinity in 3rd degree. Witnesses: Bmy. Rachal (x); Marie Louise Shelette (x); C[me] Perot (s); L[s] Derbanne (s); Clement Rachal (s). Priest: Blanc.

223. FRANCISCO DIAZ (x)
#17-1832 JOANNA GUTIERES (x)
20 August 1832
Groom: major and legitimate son of Julian Diaz and Manuela Huertes, natives of Islandi?, parish of Caens?, now living in this parish of Natchitoches. Bride: widowed from first nuptials with Raimond Fuentes, daughter of Adout Gutiere and Gertrude del Garde, residents of the parish of Natchitoches. Witnesses: Juan de Luna (x); Guadelupe Fuentes (x); P. Bertin (s). Priest: Blanc.

224. MARTIN GONZALES (x)
#18-1832 MARIA LORETA DE GUADALOUPE (x)
27 August 1832
Groom: legitimate and minor son of Ignacio Gonzales and Maria Guadeloupe Ramez, residents of this parish of Natchitoches. Bride: minor and natural daughter of Marie Gertrude Ruis, also a resident of this parish. Witnesses: Juan de diaz Castro (x); Maria Onesia? de Monteziore? (x); P. Bertin (s). Priest: Blanc.

225. JN. BTE. NARCISSE KERY (s)
#19-1832 MARIE LISE LACOURT [LA COUR] (x)
5 October 1832. 2 bans.
Groom: widower from first nuptials with deceased Marie Uranie Derbanne, major and legitimate son of Pierre Kery and Marie Rosalie Frederic, all residents of this parish of Natchitoches. Bride: widow from first nuptials with Emanuel Rachal, major and legitimate daughter of Gasparite LaCourt and Felicité Brevel, all residents of this parish. Witnesses: Mc Sompayrac (s); Derzelin Rachal (s); Thomas A. Morgan (s). Priest: Blanc.

226. FRANCISCO CARDENES (x)
#20-1832 ANDREA FLORES (x)
1 November 1832
Ratification of civil marriage. Groom: legitimate

son of Bicente Cardenes and A___tel? Arauno, residents of the parish of Natchitoches. Bride: major daughter of Fr. Flores and Trinidad Commacho, a native of S. Antonio, now living in this parish. Witnesses: Tomas Garcia (s); P. Bertin (s). Priest: Blanc.

227. ISIDORE ROCK PLAISANCE (s)
#21-1832 MARGUERITE LISE PLAISANCE (x)
8 November 1832.
Groom: minor and legitimate son of Bertrand Plaisance and Marie Barbe Grillet, inhabitants of this post. Bride: minor and legitimate daughter of Jn. B^{te} Plaisance and Marie Joseph Palvado, inhabitants of this parish. Married at home of Dame Widow J. B^{te} Plaisance, after dispensation from impediment of consanguinity in second degree. Witnesses: Isaac Plaisance (s); Faustin Plaisance (s); Tranquillin LeComte (s). Priest: Blanc.

228. JEAN USTACHE GRAVIER (s)
#1-1833 CATHERINE PRUDENCE MONDE (s)
21 January 1833. 3 bans.
Groom: major and legitimate son of Jean Gravier and deceased Dame Jeanne de Guillaume?, native of [illegible] de [illegible] in Lot-et-Garonne, France. Bride: widow from first nuptials with Aimé Carron, major and legitimate daughter of François Monde and Marie Anne Garrau, native of Vargues? in Cuba, now living in this post. Witnesses: J. B^{te} Lille Sarpy (s); J. V. Bossier (s); T. Deterville (s); L. Sompayrac (s). Priest: Blanc.

229. ANTOINE DOLYCHAMP (s)
#2-1833 MARIE AGATH RACHAL (x)
31 January 1833. 3 bans.
Groom: major and legitimate son of A______[ink blot] Dolychamp and Anne Claunbe?, native of the town of Lyon, department of Rhône, France, now residing in this parish. Bride: widow from first nuptials with deceased Hilaire Lavespère, major and legitimate daughter of Louis Rachal and Marie Grillet, native of this parish of Natchitoches. Married in the home of the bride. Witnesses: Mc Sompayrac (s); Clement Rachal (s); A^{ne} B^{my} Rachal (s); F. M. Normand, Dr. (s); C. Noyrit (s). Priest: Blanc.

230. JEAN BTE. AUGER GILLARD (s)
#3-1833 ROSELLA MARGUERITE DEBLANC (s)
6 February 1833.
Groom: minor and legitimate son of Jean Baptiste Gillard and Cecile Lacour, resident of the parish of Rapides. Bride: minor and legitimate daughter

Fçois Jules? DeBlanc and Marguerite LaCour, residents of the parish of Rapides. License issued by Judge of the parish of Rapides and dispensation given from the impediment of consanguinity in second degree. Marriage performed at Rapides in presence of relatives. Witnesses: Bte Gillard (s); Bret LaCour (s); Jn Gillard (s); Gilbert LaCour (s); E. Jn Gillard (s). Priest: Blanc.

231.
#4-1833

SAMUEL RHEA REID (s)
MANETE RACHAL (s)
7 February 1833. 2 bans.
Groom: resident of the parish of Natchitoches. Bride: widow from first nuptials with deceased Narcisse Rachal, also residing in the parish of Natchitoches. Witnesses: P. S. Compère (s); Mc Sompayrac (s); Silvestre Rachal (s). Priest: Blanc.

232.
#5-1833

CHARLES LEMOINE (x)
MARIE ADELAIDE FAVROT (x)
10 February 1833.
Ratification of civil marriage performed 11 March 1831. Groom: major and legitimate son of J. Bte Lemoine and Felicité Lacaze, resident of the parish of Natchitoches. Bride: minor and legitimate daughter of Augustin Favrot and Celeste Lacase, resident of this parish of Natchitoches. Witnesses: Charles le Roy (s); Isaac Birtt (s). Married at church of St. Augustin de l'Isle Brevelle after dispensation from impediment of consanguinity in second degree. Priest: Blanc.

233.
#6-1833

PIERRE DELAUNAY (x)
DELIZE POISSOT (x)
7 February 1833. 3 bans.
Groom: minor and legitimate son of Pierre Delaunay and Marie Dupont, native of the parish of Opeloussas, now residing in this parish. Bride: minor and legitimate daughter of Paul Poissot and Marie Louise Anty, native of this parish of Natchitoches. Permission given by the respective parents. Witnesses: Damas Poissot (x); J. Bte Lille Sarpy (s); François Dubois (s); Joseph Dubois (s). Priest: E. D'haund.

234.
#7-1833

PEDRO DEL RIO
MARIA EULALIA SANCHEZ
10 February 1833. 1 ban.
Groom: minor and legitimate son of Manuel Delrio, a native of Nacogdoches, and Maria Line Paria of this parish of Natchitoches. Bride: minor and legitimate daughter of deceased Jossé Leander Sanchez and deceased Maria Tomasa Martinez, both natives of the parish of San Antonio de Vega. Witnesses: Jossé Ramirez; André Chamard. Priest: E. D'haund.

235. PEDRO BELA (x)
#8-1833 MARIA ANTONIA CANTONNA (x)
15 February 1833. 1 ban.
Groom: widower in first nuptials with Gertrudes de los dolores Garza?, legitimate son of Nicolas Bela and Maria Incarnacion Ramires?, originally of Lamargie?, now residing in this post. Bride: widow in first nuptials with Ossé Caro, legitimate daughter of Warline? (Warlupe? -- i.e.: Guadalupe?] Cantoana and Maria Santa Cruz, also a resident of this parish of Natchitoches. Witnesses: Ignacio Racio (x); Antonia Rodriguez (x); P. Bertin (s); [Rev.] E. D'hound (s). Priest: Blanc.

236. WILLIAM PRESTON HICKMAN (s)
*#9-1833 MARYANNE BAILLOT (x)
19 March 1833.
Groom: lawful son of William Hickman and Mary Webster, native of North Carolina and now residing in the parish of Natchitoches. Bride: lawful daughter of Auguste Baillio and of Felonize Lessart [Layssard], residents of the parish of Rapides. Married at the Rapides plantation of Mr. Auguste Baillio. Witnesses: Peter T. Hickman (s); B. Jarreau (s); Joseph Lattier (s); Fs. Baillio (s). Priest: Blanc. [cf. Reg. 8.]

237. FRANCOIS FLEMING (s)
*#11-1833 CELESTE LAFITTE (s)
6 April 1833. 2 bans.
Groom: minor and legitimate son of Bartholomew Fleming and Marie Thérèze Constance Fonteneau, resident of this parish. Bride: widowed from first nuptials with Firmin Poissot, major and legitimate daughter of Paul Boëte Lafitte and Marie Anne de Soto, natives of this parish. Married at the Church of the Nativity of the Holy Virgin in Campté. Witnesses: Cezaire Fonteneau (s); J. Bte. Trichel (s); Spire Bordelon (s); Constance Fleming (s). Priest: Blanc. Groom signed as Francis Fleming. [cf. Reg. 8.]

238. CHARLES SIMON (s)
#12-1833 TONTON PEROT (x)
29 April 1833. 3 bans.
Groom: a free man of color, legitimate and major son of Charles Simon and Bissente Perez, native of the parish of Opeloussas. Bride: a free woman of color, natural and major daughter of Pelagie Grappe, and a resident of this parish of Natchitoches. Married at the Church of the Nativity of the Holy Virgin, Campté. Witnesses: Francis Fleming (x); Pierre Laviolette (s); Pierre Trichel (s); Louis Lamatte (s) "and others." Priest: C. D'haund.

---

*There is no Entry #10

239. JOSEPH VICTOR BARBEROUSSE (s)
#13-1833 MARIE JOSEPHE CELINE HESSER (x)
7 May 1833. 3 bans.
Groom: major and legitimate son of Michel Barberousse and Manete Gagnier, natives of this parish of Natchitoches. Bride: Minor and legitimate daughter of Christian Hesser and of Marie Françoise Adelaïde Rambin, also a native of this parish of Natchitoches. Witnesses: Michel Barberousse (s): Christian Hesser (s); Honoré Fredieu (s); Jean Louis Perot (s); C.me Perot (s); Adoph Sompayrac (s); Charles G. Lewis (s). Priest: E. D'haund.

240. TRANQUILLINE LECOMTE (s)
#14-1833 [ILLEGIBLE] PLAISANCE? (x)
[illegible] May 1833. [Number of bans illegible].
Groom: major and legitimate son of Jacques LeComte and of Marie [illegible] Brosset, native of this parish of Natchitoches. Bride: minor and legitimate daughter of Jean Baptiste Plaisance and of Marie Josephe Palvado, native of this parish of Natchitoches. Witnesses: J.n B.te Lille Sarpy (s); F.tin Plaisance (s); C. E. Greneaux (s); Edouard? Plaisance (s).

[Ed. note: According to the LeComte-Plaisance marriage contract now filed in *Old Natchitoches Records, Vol. 2* (pp. 149-51), Cammie Henry Collection, the given name of the bride is CELESTE. According to the Natchez, Mississippi, marriage record of the groom's parents, a copy of which is to be found in Folder 804, Melrose Collection, Northwestern State University, the middle name of Demoiselle Brosset was SILVIE.]

241. JEAN LAPLACE (s)
#15-1833 MARIE JOSEPHINE CLARA CORTEZ (s)
11 May 1833. 1 ban.
Groom: major and legitimate son of Pierre Laplace and Marie Cortez, native of Navarre in Basses-Pyrénées, France, actually residing in this parish. Bride: minor and legitimate daughter of deceased Jean Cortez and Marcellite Josephine Rouquier, native of this parish of Natchitoches. Married at the home of Widow Cortez in this parish, after dispensation from impediment of consanguinity in 2nd degree. Witnesses: James Bloodworth (s); Louis G. DeRussy (s); Odille Cortes (s); V.e Cortes (s); Marcelitte Dupare néé Cortes (s); Lieutenant Francis Lee (s); B. V. Cortes (s); Widow Rouquiere (s); Emelie De Russy (s); Chas. A. Bullard (s); Julia Ann Bullard (s); Eliza Pavie (s). Priest: Blanc.

242. LOUIS PORTER (x)
#16-1833 MARIE AGLAE METOYER (x)
14 May 1833. 3 bans.
Groom: major and natural son of Perine Cecile, a free man of color and resident of this parish. Bride: minor and legitimate daughter of Dominique Metoyer, Jr. and Adelaÿde [Rachal], all free people of color and residents of this parish of Natchitoches. Witnesses: J. Bte. Ls. Metoyer (s); Serafin Llorens (s); Jn. Bte. Dque. Metoyer (x); Pre. Metoyer, Jr. (s). Priest: Blanc.

243. JEAN MARIE GILLARD (s)
#17-1833 MARGUERITE EMILIE GILLARD (s)
22 May 1833. 3 bans.
Groom: major and legitimate son of Joseph Gillard and Petronille La Cour, residents of the parish of Rapides. Bride: minor and legitimate daughter of Jean Baptiste Gillard and Cecile La Cour, also residents of Rapides. Married at Rapides after dispensation from double impediment of consanguinity in second degree. Witnesses: Joseph Gillard (s); Jean Baptiste Gillard (s); Jean Marie Bret La Cour (s/ Janmari Bret Lacour); Apollinaire Baillio (s); "and others." Groom signed as John M. Gillard. Priest: E. D'haund. [cf. Reg. 8.]

244. ATHANAZE VIENNE METOYER (s)
#18-1833 MARIE EMELIA METOYER (x)
27 May 1833. 3 bans.
Groom: major and legitimate son of Pierre Metoyer and deceased Marie Perine [Le Comte], all free people of color and residents of this parish of Natchitoches. Bride: minor and legitimate daughter of Jean Baptiste Dominique Metoyer and Adelaïde Rachal, also free people of color and residents of this parish. Married at St. Augustine de l'Ile Brevelle after dispensation from impediment on consanguinity in second degree. Witnesses: Pierre Metoyer (s); Jean Baptiste Dominique Metoyer (s); Florentin Conant (s); Pre. Metoyer, Jr. (s); "and others." Priest: D'haund.

245. FRANÇOIS HENRY TRICHEL (s)
#19-1833 MARIE AMIRE PEROT (s)
8 June 1833. 3 bans.
Groom: major and legitimate son of deceased Emanuel Trichel and Euphrosine Prudhomme, native of this parish of Natchitoches. Bride: minor and legitimate daughter of Jean Chrisostomé Perot and Marie Suzanne Rachal, native of this parish of Natchitoches. Witnesses: Jn. Bte. Perot (s); Louis Closeau (s); Spire Bordelon (s); J. Cme. Perot. Priest: Blanc.

246. PHILIPE CYRIAQUE BROSSET (s)
#20-1833 MARIE CAROLINE SHELETRE (x)
11 June 1833. 3 bans. Married at Rivière aux Cannes. Groom: minor and legitimate son of Philipe Brosset and Marie Thérèse Brevel, native of this parish of Natchitoches. Bride: minor and legitimate daughter of Jean Baptiste Sheletre, deceased, and of deceased Euproisine Rachal, native of this parish of Natchitoches. Witnesses: M^{c}. Sompayrac (s); Philipe Brosset (x); Tranquillin Leconte (s); Sévère Lattier (s). Priest: Blanc.

247. JEAN JOSEPH RACHAL (x)
#21-1833 NANETTE DENYS (x)
9 July 1833. 0 bans.
Groom: major and legitimate son of deceased Louis Rachal and of Marie Labery, native of this parish of Natchitoches. Bride: major and legitimate daughter of deceased J. B^{te}. Denys and of Marie Elisabeth Baudoin, also a native of this parish of Natchitoches. Married at the Cloutierville church. Witnesses: Jean Fabre (s); Abel Sers (s); Hilaire Rachal (s). Priest: Blanc. [cf. Reg. 8, sheet 21.]

248. JUAN BIAREAL
#22-1833 MARIA ANTONIA IBARBE
5 July 1833. 0 bans.
Bride and groom are both natives of the parish of Natchitoches. Witnesses: Miguel Ibarbo and Felipo Gevarra. Priest: D'haund.

249. JOSEPH OZEME METOYER (s)
#23-1833 CATHERINE DAVID (x)
30 July 1833. 3 bans.
Groom: minor and legitimate son of Dominique Metoyer and Marguerite [Le Comte], all free people of color and natives of this parish. Bride: major and natural daughter of Magdeleine [Grappe], a free woman of color, also residing in this parish. Married at St. Augustin de l'Isle Brevelle. Witnesses: Emanuel Laurens (s/ Manuel Llorens); J. B^{te}. Metoyer (s/ J. B. D. Metoyer); Selaphin Laurens (s/ Serafin Llorens); D^{que}. Metoyer (x). Priest: Blanc. [cf. Reg. 8.]

250. ADAM GUINGER (s)
#24-1833 MARIE AZELIE PEROT (x)
5 August 1833. 3 bans.
Groom: major and legitimate son of Jean Agues Guinger and deceased Helmine Miller, native of Platten Hart in Germany, actually residing in this parish of Natchitoches. Bride: minor and legitimate daughter of deceased F^{çois}. Perot and of Marie Manote Fonteneau, all

residents of this parish of Natchitoches. Married at the chapel of the Nativity at Campté. Witnesses: Jph. T. Robinson (s); Francis Fleming (s); Christeno Guinger (s); L^{s} G^{me} Rachal (s). Priest: Blanc. [cf. Reg. 8.]

251. #25-1833 JEAN BAPTISTE SAINTVILLE MARIOTTE (x)
MARIE CEPHALIDE METOYER (x)
19 August 1833.
Groom: natural and minor son of Adelaide Marie. Bride: minor and legitimate daughter of Dominique Metoyer and Marguerite Le Compte, all free people of color and residents of this parish of Natchitoches. Married at the chapel of St. Augustine on Isle Brevelle. Witnesses: Joseph Augustin Metoyer (s); Nerestan Roque (s); Ozeme Dominique Metoyer (s); Athanaset Metoyer (s/ Tanasite Metoyer). Priest: D'haund. [cf. Reg. 8.]

252. #26-1833 LUFROY DUPREZ (x)
ELIZABETH POIRIER (x)
2 September 1833. 0 bans.
Groom: legitimate son of Pierre Duprez and Françoise Le Cour. Bride: legitimate daughter of Jean Baptiste Poirier and Elisabeth Diser. Witnesses: Marc Sompayrac (s); Sylvestre Rachal (s); Clement Laroche (s). Married at Cloutierville where "said parties have declared their wish to legitimize Joseph Leon, Sylvestre Numa, Athanase Dufroy, Marie Françoise, Elisa, and Antoine Valmont who were born to them before their marriage. . . ." Priest: D'Haund. [cf. Reg. 8.]

253. #27-1833 FRANÇOIS PLACIDE DACISE BOSSIER (s)
MARIE JEANNE PHANNIE HERTZOG (s)
19 September 1833. 1 ban.
Groom: major and legitimate son of deceased Paul François Bossier and Catherine Pelagie Lambre, native of this parish. Bride: major and legitimate daughter of J. Fçois Hertzog and Desirée Prudhomme. Married at home of J. Fçois Hertzog. Witnesses: J. Fçois Hertzog (s); Desirée Hertzog (s); P. E. Bossier (s); A. Le Comte (s); Lestan Prudhomme (s); V. Lambre (s); Janin, D.M. (s); Neuville Prudhomme (s); B^{te} Cloutier (s); Compère (s); J. V. Bossier (s). Priest: D'haund.

254. #28-1833 ETIENNE DERZILIN RACHAL (s)
FRANÇOISE IRENE BROSSET (s)
15 October 1833. 1 ban.
Groom: major and legitimate son of J. B^{te} Bmy. Rachal and Pelagie Brevel, native of this parish of Natchitoches. Bride: minor and legitimate daughter of Philipe Brosset and Marie Thérèze Brevel, native of this parish of Natchitoches. Marriage at home of Sr.

Philipe Brosset, after dispensation from impediment of consanguinity in second degree. Witnesses: J. B^te^ Clement Rachal (s); Terence Challer (s/T. Challer); J. B^te^ Charleville (s/ John B. Charleville); Philippe Brosset (x). Bride signed as hi. Raine f. Brosset. [cf. Reg. 8.]

[Ed. note: Original entry in Reg. 8 is accompanied by the following note: "Reverend Père, you will please consider this as a special license to celebrate a marriage between Mr. Etienne Derzelin Rachal and Miss Irene Brosset, both of this parish. Respectfully, C. E. Greneaux, Parish Judge, Natchitoches, Oct. 13th 1833." Special license is in English.]

255. BALTAZARD BREVEL (s)
#29-1833 MARIE LOUISE MASSIPE (x)
19 October 1833. 0 bans.
Rehabilitation of civil marriage previously contracted. Groom: legitimate and major son of J. B^te^ Brevel and Françoise Poissot, native of this parish of Natchitoches. Bride: major and legitimate daughter of Jean Massipe and Marie Lemoine, also a native of this parish. Legitimation of children: Baltazar, aged 10 1/2; Lise, aged 7 years on 26 September. Witnesses: J. B^te^ Armand (s); Ls. Chevalier (s); Isaac Rachal (s). Priest: Blanc. [cf. Reg. 8.]

256. MARCEL DE SOTO (s)
#30-1833 DELIZE WALACE (x)
10 November 1833. 0 bans.
Rehabilitation of civil marriage contracted 28 August 1826. Groom: son of Marcel de Soto and Marie Baillio. Bride: major daughter of James Walese and Hyacinthe Ganier, residents of this parish of Natchitoches. Witnesses: Fçois Rambin (s); Pierre Boëte Lafitte (s/ Pierre Laffitte); André Michel Rambin (s/ André Michelle Rambin). Priest: Blanc. [cf. Reg. 8.]

257. FRANÇOIS (JOSEPH) LAFITTE (s)
#31-1833 MARIE CATHERINE RAMBIN (s)
10 November 1833. 0 bans.
Rehabilitation of civil marriage contracted 3 March 1829. Groom: legitimate son of Pierre Lafitte and Ursule Conion. Bride: major and legitimate daughter of François Rambin and Marie Damas[cen]e de Soto, residents of this parish of Natchitoches. Ceremony performed at home of Pierre Boëte Lafitte. Witnesses: Pierre Lafite (s/ Pierre Laffitte); André Michel Rambin (s/ André Michelle Rambin); François Rambin (s). Priest: Blanc. [cf. Reg. 8.]

[Ed. note: Groom is identified in margin as François Lafitte and in text as Joseph Laffite. The original in Reg. 8 is signed by the groom as Joseph Laffite.]

258. #32-1833
PIERRE ROBLEAU (x)
MARIA BACILLA GRANDE (x)
10 November 1833. 0 bans.
Groom: son of Pierre Robleau and Magdeleine Prudhomme, residents of this parish of Natchitoches. Bride: daughter of Julian Grande and Trinidad Flores. Married at home of Pierre Boëte Laffitte at Bayou Pierre. Witnesses: Pierre Boëte Laffite (s/ Pierre Laffitte); André Michel Rambin (s/ André Michelle Rambin); Marcel de Soto (s); Fçois Rambin (s). Priest: Blanc. [cf. Reg. 8.]

259. #33-1833
CHARLES RAMBIN (x)
MARIE CELIMINE LAFFITE (x)
10 November 1833.
Rehabilitation of the civil marriage celebrated 29 September 1831. Groom: son of Michel Rambin and Marie Thérèze Mayou, residents of this parish of Natchitoches. Bride: legitimate daughter of Cezaire Lafite and Isabel Lathon, also residents of this parish. Celebrated at home of Cezaire Laffitte at Bayou Pierre. Witnesses: Auguste Fauvelle (s); Louis N[ville] Rambin (x); Joseph Lafitte (x). Priest: Blanc. [cf. Reg. 8.]

260. #34-1833
REMY LAFITTE (x)
FELICITÉ RAMBIN (x)
11 November 1833.
Rehabilitation of civil marriage contracted 25 August 1830. Groom: legitimate son of Cezaire Laffite and Isabel Lathon, residents of this parish of Natchitoches. Bride: legitimate daughter of Michel Rambin and Marie Thérèze Mayou, also residents of this parish. Witnesses: August Fauvelle (s); Ls. N[ville] Rambin (x); Joseph Laffitte (x). Priest: Blanc. [cf. Reg. 8.]

261. #35-1833
EDMOND (ROZEMOND) CHAMARD (s)
MARIE CELEZIE CORDOVA (x)
17 November 1833.
Rehabilitation of civil marriage celebrated 18 January 1831. Groom: major and legitimate son of Ls. Chamard and Catherine Bardon. Bride: minor daughter of Marie Cordova, residents of this parish of Natchitoches. Witnesses: Marcel de Soto (s); Fçois Rambin (s); Paul Cazenave (s). At home of Fçois Rambin. Priest: Blanc. [cf. Reg. 8.]

[Ed. note: Groom's name is given in text as Edmond Chamard. He signed as Rosemond Chamard.]

262. JOSSÉ LOPEZ (s)
#36-1833 MARIE MILAGIE McDONATO (s)
17 November 1833.
Rehabilitation of civil marriage contracted in September 1832. Groom: major and legitimate son of Ossé Lopez and Maria Marcelina, native of the Rio Grande. Bride: legitimate daughter of Luca McDonald and Maria Rosalis Simon Golser?, residents of this parish of Natchitoches. Witnesses: Fçois Rambin (s); Paul Cazenave (s); Marcel de Soto (s). Groom signed as Ossé vio Lopez. Priest: Blanc. [cf. Reg. 8.]

263. NARCISSE CORDOVA (x)
#37-1833 MARIE GENEVIÈVE ADLET (x)
18 November 1833.
Rehabilitation of civil marriage contracted in April 1831. Groom: son of Pedro Cordova and Maria [illegible] Ruis, residents of this parish of Natchitoches. Bride: minor and legitimate daughter of J. $B^{t.e}$ Timothé Adlet and Marie Desneiges Prudhomme, natives of this parish of Natchitoches. Witnesses: Fçois Rambin (s); Thimothé Adlé (x); Ignacio Gongre (s/ Ignacio Gongora). Priest: Blanc. [cf. Reg. 8.]

264. CHARLES EMANUEL GRENEAUX (s)
#1-1834 MARIE ELISA TAUZIN (s)
6 January 1834. 1 ban.
Groom: native of this parish of Natchitoches, major and legitimate son of deceased Emanuel Greneau and Victoire Emeranthe Bossier, residents of this parish of Natchitoches. Bride: minor and legitimate daughter of Louis Jph. Tauzin and Marie Eugenie Murphy, a native of this parish of Natchitoches. Witnesses: Joseph Tauzin; J. $B^{t.e}$ Trezzini (s); Victor Bossié; Joseph Louis Tauzin (x); Eugenie Tauzin (s); M^{c}. Sompayrac (s); J. V. Bossier (s); T. E. Tauzin (s); A. Le Comte (s); Benj. V. Cortes (s); A. L. Deblieux (s); Charles G. Lewis (s). Priest: Blanc.

265. JN BTE GRANDCHAMPT (s)
#2-1834 MARIE AZELIE ADLÉ (s)
28 January 1834. 3 bans.
Groom: major and legitimate son of deceased Raymond Villadary Grandchampt and Anne Guidon, native of Perigueux, department of Dordogne in France. Bride: minor and legitimate daughter of Jean Baptiste Adlé and Marie Victorine Brevelle, natives of this parish of Natchitoches. Witnesses: Antoine Barthélemy Rachal (s); Marc Sompayrac (s); Jn. Fabre (s); P. Baulos (s); J. Reynaud (s). Priest: D'haund.

266. JEAN PIERRE SHELETTRE
#3-1834 MARIE HYACYNTHE PASSANEAU
11 February 1834. 2 bans.
Groom: legitimate and major son of deceased Jean Pierre Shelette and Eulalie Bossier. Bride: minor and legitimate daughter of Toussain Passaneau and Marie Jossé Henriette Ganier, all residents of this parish of Natchitoches. Married at home of Mr. Peter McDannel. Witnesses: Jean Geuffant (s); Pierre Trichel (s); Peter McDannel (x). Priest: D'haund. [cf. Reg. 8.]

267. DOMINIQUE LANGE (x)
*#4-1834 MARIE PHILOMENE (x)
9 February 1834.
Ratification of civil marriage celebrated the past year. Groom: major son of Dque. Lange and Adelaÿde, residents of this parish of Natchitoches. Bride: minor and natural daughter of Marie Mariotte, also a resident of this parish of Natchitoches. Ceremony at Church of St. Augustin on Isle à Brevel. Witnesses: Ch. N. Rocque (s); Ema^{l}. Laurens (s/ Manuel Llorens). Priest: Blanc. [cf. Reg. 8.]

268. PIERRE RABALAIS (x)
*#6-1834 MARIE AZELIE DE ROUSSEAU (x)
8 April 1834.
Groom: legitimate and major son of Joseph Rabalais and Marie Baudouin. Bride: minor and legitimate daughter of Pierre De Rousseau and of Caroline La Case, all residents of this parish of Natchitoches. Married at Cloutierville. Witnesses: Jacques Vercher (s); Pierre De Rousseau (x); Octave Rachal (x). Priest: Blanc. [cf. Reg. 8.]

269. JEAN FRANÇOIS CORTES (s)
#7-1834 MARIE EMELIE DE RUSSY (s)
17 April 1834
Groom: major and legitimate son of deceased Jean Cortez and Marcelite Josephine Rouquier, native of this parish. Bride: minor and legitimate daughter of Louis Gustave de Russy and Elizabeth Claire, native of New York, actually residing in this parish. Witnesses: Lewis G. De Russy (s); V. Cortes (s); Elisa De Russy (s); J. B^{te}. Cloutier (s); W. L. Cockerille (s); Benj. Walker (s); Francis Lee (s); D. R. Hopkins (s). Priest: Blanc. [cf. Reg. 8.]

----

*There is no # 5

270. MATHIEU LEON BOUDRIGE (s)
*#8-1834 MARIE LOLLETE VASCOCU (x)
24 April 1834
Groom: major and legitimate son of Antoine Boudrige and Gabriele Couteret, native of Thiers, department of Puy-de-Dôme in France, now a resident of this parish. Bride: major and legitimate daughter of deceased Louis Vascocu and Marie Magdeleine Perot, a native of this parish. Witnesses: C. E. Greneaux (s); F^{s}. Lepeintre (s); Ch^{me}. Vascocu. Priest: Blanc.

271. JOSEPH PEROT
*#9-1834 MARIE ROSALIE FORT
29? April 1834
Groom: major and natural son of Pelagie Grappe, a free man of color and a native of this parish. Bride: minor and natural daughter of Marie Angelique [Metoyer], a free woman of color. Witnesses: Pierre Trichel, Cezaire Fonteneau, Hilaire Bordelon "and others." Married at Campti church. Priest: Blanc.

272. JOSSÉ CHABANNE
*#10-1834 MARIE TRICHEL
5 May 1834
Groom: major and legitimate son of Lino Chabanne and Barbara Chavis, native of Nacogdoches. Bride: natural daughter of Simeon Trichel and Marie Jeanne, free people of color and residents of this parish. Witnesses: Jean Jacques Lambre, Jean Prat, Pierre Trichell, Martin Chabanne. Priest: D'Haund.

273. JULIEN BESSON
*#11-1834 MARIE CEPHALIDE LENOIR
6 May 1834. 3 bans.
Groom: major and legitimate son of deceased Jean Baptiste Besson and Marie Jeanne Piedvert. Bride: minor and legitimate daughter of Antoine Lenoir and Marie Desneiges Derbanne, all residents of this parish. Witnesses: Faustin Perot, Cesaire Fonteneau, Jerome Rachal, Pierre Trichel, "and others." Priest: D'Haund.

274. LOUIS RACHAL
*#12-1834 MARIE CATHERINE RACHAL
8 May 1834.
Groom: major and legitimate son of Julien Rachal and Melanie Lavespère. Bride: legitimate daughter of Louis Julien Rachal and Marie Reine Tomassi, all residents of this parish. Witnesses: Ch^{s}. F^{s}. Benoist;

----

*These entries do not appear on the NSU microfilm of Register 11.

François Marie Normand, S. H. Sanginette "and others." Priest: D'haund.

275.
#13-1834
MICHAEL COLEGAN (s)
MISSOURY BURNETT (x)
15 May 1834. 1 ban.
Groom: legitimate son of John Colegan and Nolla Derenny, native of Muligan, Londonderry county, in Ireland. Bride: legitimate daughter of Peter Burnett and Ignace [Agnes?] Reynolds; both actually residing in the parish of Natchitoches. Witnesses: John Sibley (s): John H. Mahle (s); Joseph Criswell (s); Wm. Ferguson (s); William M. Payne (s). Priest: D'haund.

Ed. note: The phrase "both actually residing in the parish of Natchitoches" follows the names of the bride's parents. However, the sense of the text suggests that it could refer to the two parties being married.]

276.
#14-1834
REMI CASIMIR PEROT (s)
JULIA FLEMING (s)
27 May 1834.
Groom: major and legitimate son of Casimir Perot and Delphin Poissot, a native of the parish of Natchitoches. Bride: major and legitimate daughter of deceased Barthelemi Fleming and Marie Thérese Fontenau, also a resident of this parish of Natchitoches. Married at Campti in the Church of the Nativity of the Blessed Virgin. Witnesses: Thomas Gardiner, M.D. (s); Firmin Perot (s); Michael Boyce (s). Priest: D'haund. [cf. Reg. 8.]

277.
*#15-1834
SEVERIN ROUGEOT (x)
FLORENTINE DE PERCUNA (x)
2 June 1834
Groom: legitimate and major son of J^{n}. B^{te}. Rougeot and Isabelle Ledé, residents of the parish of Opelousas. Bride: major and legitimate daughter of deceased Pierre Nolasque Depercuna and Magdeleine La berrie, resident of this parish of Natchitoches. Witnesses: Silvestre Rachal (s); B^{tte}. Adlé (s); H. Eudos? (s).

278.
*#16-1834
LOUIS NARCISSE VANIER (s)
MARIE LAISA RACHAL (x)
2 June 1834
Groom: major and legitimate son of J^{n}. B^{te}. Vanier and Marie Joseph D'agenêt, native of Canada. Bride: minor and legitimate daughter of Antoine Rachal and Françoise Rachal, residents of this parish of Natchitoches. Witnesses: Silvestre Rachal (s); Leander

----

*These entries do not appear on the NSU microfilm of Register 11.

Lacour, Jr. (s); Antoine Rachal (x). Priest: D'haunds.

279. BENJAMIN FRANKLIN CHAPMAN (s)
*#17-1834 HENRIETTE SIBLEY (s)
5 June 1834.
Groom: lawful son of Simeon B. Chapman and Ann Bohannon, a native of Virginia now residing in this parish. Bride: lawful daughter of John Sibley and Eulalie Malige, residing in this parish. Canonical dispensation given for unspecified reason. Witnesses: John Sibley (s); Francis Lee (s); B. V. Cortes (s); Thos. Anderson (s); Henry Jones (s); W. L. Cockerille (s); B. Leonard (s). Priest: D'haunds.

280. DAVID LACASA (x)
*#18-1834 MARIE EGLANTIN ANTY (x)
22 June 1834.
Groom: major and legitimate son of Etienne Lacasa and Marie Felicité [Dorothée] Massip. Bride: minor and legitimate daughter of Valerie Anty and Marie Aspasie Derbanne. Witnesses: Pierre Massip (x); Jos. Crevier Descherveaux (s). Priest: D'haunds.

281. EDMOND DUTHIL (s)
#19-1834 MARIE HENRIETTE LACASE (s)
23 June 1834
Groom: minor and legitimate son of Jacques Duthil and of Françoise Marzelle, native of Sibourne, department of Gironde in France. Bride: minor and legitimate daughter of deceased Jacques Lacase and Fanny Massip, resident of this parish of Natchitoches. Witnesses: J^{n}. J^{h}. Dumarest (s); Ludger Rachal (s); Felix Langlois (s); F^{s}. Roubieu (s). Married at Isle Brevelle residence of Jacques Lacase. Priest: D'haunds.

282. FELIX LANGLOIS (s)
#20-1834 MARIE CLARA ARMAND (x)
24 June 1834. 2 bans.
Groom: major and legitimate son of August Langlois and Marie Celeste Verger, residents of this parish of Natchitoches. Bride: minor and legitimate daughter of Jean B^{te}. Armand and of Catherine Féderic, residents of this parish of Natchitoches. Married at residence of J. Bte. Armand on Ile Brevelle. Witnesses: J^{n}. B^{te}. Armand (s); J^{n}. J^{h}. Dumarest (s); Terence Chaler (s). Priest: D'haunds.

283. ALFRED K. EDENS (s)
#21-1834 MARIE LOUISE PEROT (s)
21 August 1834. 3 bans.

----

*These entries do not appear on the NSU microfilm of Register 11.

Groom: major and legitimate son of John Edens and Luivina Lankford, native of Illinois. Bride: minor and legitimate daughter of Derzilin Perot and Melanie Trichell, native of this parish of Natchitoches. Married at chapel of the Nativity, Campti. Witnesses: Louis Derzilin Perot (s); Henry F. Trichel (s); Pierre Trichell (s). Priest: D'haund. [cf. Reg. 8.]

284. PATRICK BERRY (s)
#22-1834 M. EMMA HERMINIA CARR (s)
8 September 1834.
Groom: major and lawful son of Sylvester Barry and Mary Donnaghan of Wexford, a county in Ireland. Bride: lawful and major daughter of the late John Charles Carr and Henriette Rouquier. Married at the home of Mr. Wm. Carr. Witnesses: John Carr (s); Henry Jones (s); Michael Boyce (s); Henriette Carr (s); Oscar W. Carr (s); C. E. Carr (s); Ve Rouquier (s). Priest: D'haund.

285. FIRMIN PEROT (s)
#23-1834 MARIE CEPHALIDE DOLET (s)
22 September 1834. 1 ban.
Groom: legitimate and minor son of Casimir Perot and Delphin Poissot, residents of this parish of Natchitoches. Bride: minor and legitimate daughter of deceased Pierre Dollet and of Marie Pompos Prudhomme, also residents of this parish of Natchitoches. Married at home of Athanas Poissot. Witnesses: J^{n} B^{te} Trichel (s); Gabriel Perot (s); Bernard St. Amand (s); Ambrose Sompayrac (s); B^{tte} Adlé (s); C. E. Greneaux (s); [one illegible signature, possibly Steph. H. B_____]. Priest: D'haund.

286. JUAN JOSSE IBARBO (x)
#24-1834 MARIE AURORE AZELIE DUBOIS (x)
27 November 1834.
Groom: legitimate and major son of Juan Ibarbo and Maria Mora, residents of this parish of Natchitoches. Bride: major and legitimate daughter of Antoine Du bois and Josette Malige, all residents of this parish of Natchitoches. Witnesses: Lille Sarpy; P. Bertin. Priest: D'haund.

287. MICHEL ANTY (x)
#25-1834 MARIE BASILICE MORANTINE (s)
29 December 1834. 1 ban.
Groom: major and legitimate son of Silvestre Anty and Marie Zemire Baudouin, a resident of this parish of Natchitoches. Bride: major and legitimate daughter of Jean Morantine and deceased Marie Magdelene

Federic, also a resident of this parish of Natchitoches. Witnesses: Thomas A. Morgan (s); Jean Moratin (x); Simon (s); Ch^{les} F. Benoist (s); Mc Somperact (s); Victor Rachal (s). Priest: Français. [cf. Reg. 8.]

[Ed. note: Bride's signature spelled her name as Basilice; document spells it Basilis. Original entry in Reg. 8 contains added note "done at Rivière aux Cannes . . . at the home of Jean Moranty."]

288.
#1-1835

PIERRE PHANOR PRUDHOMME (s)
SUSANNE LISE METOYER (s)
12 January 1835.
Groom: major and legitimate son of Emmanuel Prudhomme and Catherine Lambre. Bride: minor and legitimate daughter of François Benjamin Metoyer and Marie Aurore Lambre. Dispensation from impediment of consanquinity in second and third degrees. Witnesses: B^{n} Metoyer (s); Metoyer (s); Aurore Metoyer (s); Lambre Prudhomme (s); Prudhomme, *fils* (s); J. Bte. Cloutier (s); A. Lecomte (s); Lise Ruelle (s); Français, priest (s). Officiating priest: D'haund.

289.
#2-1835

BALTAZAR BREVELLE, JR. (x)
MARIE EULALIE BOSSIER (x)
13 January 1835. 3 bans.
Groom: legitimate and major son of Baltazar Brevel and Marie Louise Thérèse, resident of this parish of Natchitoches. Bride: widow in first nuptials of deceased Jean Pierre Schelettre, major and legitimate daughter of Soulange Bossier of Opelousas and Eleonore [illegible] of Avoyelles. Witnesses: J. B^{te}. Armant, Jr. (s); Lestan Langlois (s). Priest: Français.

[Ed. note: Although Baltazar, Jr. was a native of Natchitoches, his baptism was performed by an Opelousas pastor in 1812 and was registered at St. Paul the Apostle Church, Mansura. See Alberta Rousseau Ducote, *Early Baptism Records, St. Paul the Apostle Catholic Church, 1796-1824, Avoyelles Parish* (Mansura: St. Paul's Church, 1980), p. 82. Numerous other Natchitoches baptisms were likewise performed by Opelousas and Avoyelles pastors and recorded in [illegible] priest was in residence at Natchitoches -- including Baltazar's sister Marie Amire Brevelle.

The mother of Marie Eulalie Bossier was Eleonore Himel (var. Imel, Ymelle, etc.) The name as it appears in the text seems to be Ione or Jone, although Imé was probably meant. Eulalie Bossier was born and baptized at Natchitoches. See Mills, *Natchitoches, 1729-1803*, No. 2179.]

290. MICHEL LATTIER (x)
#3-1835 MARIE EMELIA VERCHER (x)
13 January 1835. 3 bans.
Groom: major and legitimate son of Joseph Latier and deceased Marie Françoise Schelettre, residing in the parish of Claiborne. Bride: major and legitimate daughter of Jean Pierre Vercher and of Marie Emelie Schelettre, resident of this parish of Natchitoches. Dispensation from impediment of consanguinity in second and third degrees. Witnesses: B. Jarreau (s); T. Chaler (s); Narcisse Querry (s). Priest: Français.

291. OBADIAH D. OAKS (s)
#4-1835 MARIE AN CYNTHIANA SCHAMP
12 February 1835.
Groom: major and legitimate son of Josiah Oaks and Catherine Delinsworth of the state of New York. Bride: minor daughter of George Schamp and Marie Pelagie Desneige Adlet. Witnesses: Antoine Adlet (x); John R. Dunn (s); Daniel M. Heard (s); Henry Burgher (s); Fournier (s); [one illegible signature, possibly Francois Box or Cox, Jr.]. Priest: D'haund.

292. EDOUARD MURPHY (s)
#5-1835 ADELAIDE HESSER (s)
February 1835. 2 bans.
Groom: minor and legitimate son of deceased Edouard Cesaire Murphy and deceased Adelaïde Buard. Bride: major and legitimate daughter of Christian Hesser and Adelaïde Rambin, widow in first nuptials of deceased François Chabus, all residents of this parish of Natchitoches. Witnesses: Christian Hesser (s); J. Victor Barberousse (s); Alexandre L^{s} Deblieux (s); C. E. Greneaux (s); J. V. Bossier (s); A. Lecomte (s); L. A. Buard (s); F. C. (T.E.?) Tauzin (s); F? Feble? (s); Adolph Sompayrac (s); Jules Luvini (s). Priest: D'haund.

[Paraph:] "Marriage No. 5, having been contracted with two impediments of consanguinity of the third degree, either through ignorance or by this not having been declared, has been revalidated by me, the undersigned, on 2 June 1877. Natchitoches, 9 June 1877, P. F. Dicharry, Adm."

293. ATHANASE DENIS (x)
#6-1835 MARIE SUZETTE VERCHER (x)
17 February 1835. 3 bans.
Groom: major and legitimate son of Jean Baptiste Denis and Elisabeht Baudoin, residents of this parish of Natchitoches. Bride: major and legitimate

daughter of Jacques Vercher and Frozine Gallien, also natives of this parish of Natchitoches. Witnesses: Louis Derbanne (s); Ane (One?) Denis (s); Isaac Plaisance (s); I. R. Plaisance (s); Jacques Vercher (s); A.ne B.my Rachal (s). Priest: Français. [cf. Reg. 8.]

294. CELESTIN LACASE (x)
#7-1835 ELISA ROUQUIER (x)
2 March 1835
Groom: major son of Rosalie Lacase. Bride: minor daughter of Suzette Rouquier. All are residents of the parish of Natchitoches [and free people of color]. Witnesses: François Jacques Rouquier (x); J.n B.te Rouquier (x): Français, priest. Officiating priest: D'haund.

295. MANUEL GUTIERES (s)
#8-1835 ISABELLE MEDILLEN
31 March 1835
Groom: major son of Antonio Gutieres and Stephania Molane. Bride: major and legitimate daughter of Michel Medillen and of Geonneva Gommez of the parish of Mataguade, presently residing with her spouse at the place of the Adayes in the present parish. Dispensations given from the announcement of 3 bans and from prohibition against marriage during an inappropriate period of the Church calendar. Legitimation of five children: Bernarda, Petra, Manuela, Manuel, Sever. Witnesses: André Chamard (s), sacristan of the church; Manuel Bustamente (s); Joseph San Miguel (x); André Rossales (x). Priest: Alonzo?.

296. EDWARD ORLANDO BLANCHARD (s)
#9-1835 MARIE ELISA BLUDWORTH (s)
18 May 1835
Groom: major son of Thomas Blanchard and of Aney Newton, natives of Norfolk, Virginia. Bride: legitimate and major daughter of James Bludworth and Marie Aimé Rouquier, residents of this parish of Natchitoches. Dispensation given from publication of bans and from the impediment of disparity of faiths. Witnesses: Marie Aimé Rouquier, resident of this parish of Natchitoches; James Bludworth (s); C. Pavie (s); A. Sompayrac (s); Jos. B. Many (s); Chas. A. Bullard (s); Narcisse Prudhomme (s); Louis G. De Russy (s). Priest: D'haund.

297. SEVER LAFFITTE (s)
#10-1835 ELISABETH LEE (x)
15 May 1835
Ratification of civil marriage contracted before a justice of the peace. Groom: major and legitimate son of Pierre Boëte Laffitte and [Ursulle] Felicité

Gagné. Bride: legitimate and major daughter of Isaac Lee and Mary Ann Parker, residents of Rapides Parish. Witnesses: Pierre Boëte Laffitte (s); Chrysostomé Vascocu (s); Clement Laffitte (s). Priest: D'haund. At home of Pedro Flores near Bayou Banchez. [cf. Reg. 8.]

298. #11-1835
JAMES WALLACE (x)
MARY GLASS (x)
16 May 1835
Ratification of civil marriage contracted before a justice of the peace. Groom: major and legitimate son of James Wallace and Marie Hyacinthe Gagné. Bride: legitimate and major daughter of William Glass and Mary Russell, all residents of the parish of Natchitoches. Celebrated at home of Pedro Flores near Bayou Banchez. Witnesses: Pierre Lafitte (s); Joseph Jean B.te Prudhomme (s). Priest: D'haund. [cf. Reg. 8.]

299. #12-1835
MAXIMILIEN WALLACE (x)
NANCY LEE (x)
16 May 1835
Ratification of civil marriage contracted before a justice of the peace. Groom: major and legitimate son of James Wallace and Marie Hyacinthe Gagnié. Bride: major and legitimate daughter of Isaac Lee and Mary Ann Parker, actually residing in this parish of Natchitoches. Witnesses: Pierre Laffitte (s); Joseph J.n B.te Prudhomme (s); Clement Laffitte (s). At home of Pedro Flores. Priest: D'haund. [cf. Reg. 8.]

300. #13-1835
ANTOINE LENOIR (x)
LISE DEROUANNE (x)
1 June 1835
Groom: Widower in second nuptials of Adelaïde Dubois, major and legitimate [natural] son of Antoine LeNoir and of Eulalie Carles. Bride: minor and legitimate daughter of Michel Derouanne and Euphrosine Rachal, all residents of this parish of Natchitoches. Witnesses: P. Trichell; Jean Guiffan? (s); Cesaire Fonteneau, Jr. (s). Priest: D'haund.

301. #14-1835
ETIENNE BREVILLE CHELETRE (x)
MARIE AZELIE FREDERIC (x)
2 June 1835. 3 bans.
Groom: major and legitimate son of Jean Baptiste Cheletre and Euphrozine Rachal. Bride: minor and legitimate daughter of François Frederic and Marie Felicité Lavespère; all residents of this parish of Natchitoches. Dispensation from impediment of consanguinity in third degree. Witnesses: Joseph Crevier Descheraux (s); Lestan Langlois (s); Melisse

Anty (s); Jean Pommier Miller (s); François Latier, Jr. (s). Priest: Français. [cf. Reg. 8.]

302. FRANÇOIS XAVIER ARCHINARD (s)
#15-1835 MARIE ANNE CEPHALIDE METOYER (s)
2 June 1835
Groom: major and legitimate son of François Archinard and Louise Rapicault, residents of the parish of Rapides. Bride: minor and legitimate daughter of François Benjamin Metoyer and Marie Aurore Lambre, residents of this parish. Witnesses: François Benjamin Metoyer (s); Pierre Victorin Metoyer (s); Valsin Lambre (s); Aurore Metoyer (s); L. Archinard (s); J. F. Hertzog (s); Metoyer (s); Phanor Prudhomme (s); V. Lambre (s); P. S. Compère (s); Prudhomme (s); C. Noyrit (s); Narcisse Prudhomme (s); A. Lecomte (s). Priest: D'haund.

303. ATHANASE OLIVER BROSSET (s)
#16-1835 MARIE ZELINE ADLET (x)
16 June 1835
Groom: minor and legitimate son of Philippe Brosset and Marie Thérèse Brevelle. Bride: minor and legitimate daughter of Jean Baptiste Adlet and Marie Victoire Brevelle, all residents of this parish of Natchitoches. Marriage at home of Mr. J^{n} B^{te} Adlet at Rivière aux Cannes after dispensation from impediment of consanguinity in second degree. Witnesses: J^{n} B^{te} Adlé (s); J. B^{te} Clement Rachal (s); Etienne Derzelin Rachal (s). Priest: D'haund. [cf. Reg. 8.]

304. JN. BTE. LEMOIN (x)
#17-1835 MARIE CEPHALIDE LEMOINE (x)
6 July 1835
Groom: major and legitimate son of Antoine Lemoine and Marie Genèvieve Bellegarde. Bride: minor and legitimate daughter of Jean Baptiste Lemoine and Felicité Lacase; all residents of this parish of Natchitoches. Dispensation from impediment of consanguinity in second degree. Witnesses: J^{n} B^{te} Lemoine (s); Ambroise Lemoine (s); Valentin Dubois (s). Priest: D'haund.

305. LUCIEN JARAU (s)
#18-1835 ATHANAISE BROSSET (s)
14 July 1835. 3 bans.
Groom: major and legitimate son of Jean Jarau and Lucile Tounoir, resident of the parish of New Orleans. Bride: minor and legitimate daughter of Philippe Brosset and Marie Thérèse Brevelle, a resident of this parish of Natchitoches. Witnesses: Louis Derbanne (s); Breuville Perot (s); Bernard

Jarau (s); Auguste Bayou (s); Thomas A. Morgan (s); Philippe Brosset (x); Mc Sompayract (s). Priest: Français.

306.
#19-1835

CHARLES GEORGE LEWIS (s)
JANE E. H. COWAN (s)
20 July 1835. 0 bans.
Groom: major and lawful son of Charles Lewis and Mary Barron of Baltimore, Maryland, now residing in this parish of Natchitoches. Bride: lawful and minor daughter of William Cowan and Sarah Henderson of Richmond, Virginia, also residing now in this parish. Witnesses: Will. L. Cockerille (s); G. W. Airey (s); Lewis G. De Russy (s); Fred. Williams (s); John P. Russell (s); John Sibley (s); Helene Sibley (s); T? H. Cowan (s); Thom. Hoding? (s); J. Cable (s). Priest: D'haund.

307.
#20-1835

BREVILLE PEROT (s)
MARIE CATHERINE VERCHER (s)
3 August 1835. 0 bans.
Groom: major and legitimate son of deceased Chrysostomé Perot and Marie Louise Salvan. Bride: minor and legitimate daughter of Jean Pierre Vercher and Marie Emelie Shelettre; all inhabitants of this parish of Natchitoches. Witnesses: Oliver Brosset (s); Lucien Jarreau (s); Zephore Brosset (s). Priest: D'haund. [cf. Reg. 8.]

308.
#21-1835

JEAN JOSEPH ALEXANDRE PLAUCHÉ (s)
MARIE OPHELIA PRUDHOMME (s)
8 September 1835. 1 ban.
Groom: major and legitimate son of Jean Baptiste Plauché and Dame Mathilde Ste. Amand, residents of New Orleans. Bride: minor and legitimate daughter of Louis Narcisse Prudhomme and Dame Marie Thérèse Elisabeth Metoyer, residents of this parish of Natchitoches. Witnesses: Narcisse Prudhomme (s); Phanor P. Prudhomme (s); Edouard Forstall (s). Priest: D'haund.

309.
#22-1835

JN BTE NARCISSE QUIERRY (s)
MARIE CEPHALIDE GALLIEN (x)
6 October 1835
Groom: widower in second nuptials with Marie Lise LaCour, legitimate and major son of Pierry Quierry and Marie Rosalie Frederic, residents of this parish of Natchitoches. Bride: major and legitimate daughter of Louis Gallien and of Marie Celeste Anty, also residents of this parish. Married at Bayou Derbanne. Witnesses: François Marie Normand (s); Pierre Baulos (s); Jacques Vercher (s); Derzilin Rachal (s); Priest: D'haund. [cf. Reg. 8.]

310. YOUWELL WISBY(x)
#23-1835 [MARIE ZELINE ESTEVE]
13 October 1835. 3 bans.
Groom: major and legitimate son of Patrik Wisby and Roda Dial, resident of the parish of Opelousas. Bride: minor daughter of Berlandine Esteve, resident of this parish of Natchitoches. Witnesses: Lucien Jarau (s); Pierre Oneziphor Brosset (s/ P. Ziphor Brosset); Isaac Birtt (s); François Lattier, *fils* (s). Priest: Français.

[Ed. note: Bride's name is erroneously given in marginal notation as Roda Dial; the entry identifies Dial as the groom's mother and Esteve as the bride.]

311. JOSE DOLORES CORTINES (x)
#24-1835 MARIA ANTONIA EZECHIEL DE LOS SANTOS COY (x)
3 November 1835. 0 bans.
Groom: major and legitimate son of Ignatio Cortines and Gertrude Procella. Bride: minor and legitimate daughter of Manuel de los Santos Coy and Maria Guadaloup Chirino; all natives of this parish of Natchitoches. Witnesses: Manuel de los Santos Coy (s); Aę Chamard (s); Nicolas Français, priest; [one illegible signature]. Officiating priest: D'haund.

312. JOHN HARDY (s)
#25-1835 JOSEPHINE TARBY (x)
15 December 1835
Ratification of civil marriage, after obtaining dispensation from impediment of disparity of faiths. Witnesses: Eugenie Lemee (s); Stephanie Fournier (s); Eugenie Bussy (s). Priest: Français.

[Paraph:] "Eugenie Tarby being *empechee* [hindered] in faith of which I have affixed my signature [for her]. Français."

[Ed. note: Both the marginal notation and the text give the name of the bride as Josephine. The priest seems to have erred in signing her name as Eugenie.]

313. STANISLAS ETIENNE D'ANGLAS (s)
#26-1835 MARIE HENRIETTE CARR (s)
28 December 1835. 1 ban.
Groom: major and legitimate son of Etienne D'Anglas and Adelaīde de Langlade, born at Nîmes, department of Gard in France, now residing in this parish. Bride: major and legitimate daughter of Charles John Carr and Henriette Rouquier, resident of this parish of Natchitoches. Witnesses: Benjamin Metoyer (s); Ambroise Sompayrac (s); François Rouquier (s); Felix Paul (s); James Bludworth (s); Henriette Carr (s). Priest: Français.

314. FRANCISCO SOTO (x)
#27-1835 MARIA BENETA MANCHA (x)
31 December 1835. 0 bans.
Groom: major and legitimate son of Gregorio Soto and Gertrude Ximenes, native of Nacogdoches. Bride: minor and legitimate daughter of Antonio Mancha and Maria Candida Gomez, a native of San Antonio in Texas. Dispensation from publication of bans and from marriage within prohibited period of church calendar. Witnesses: José de Jesus Ramirez (x); José Maria Soto (x); Aé Chamard (s). Priest: D'Haund.

315. JACQUES AGAISSE (s)
#1-1836 MARIE LISE POISSOT (x)
11 January 1836.
Groom: major and legitimate son of Jean Renaud and Marie Louise Massip. Bride: major and legitimate daughter of deceased Paul Poissot and Marie Louise Anty; all residents of the parish of Natchitoches. Witnesses: C. L. Picque (s); Hyte Bordelon (s); Aé Chamard (s); J. P. Vercher (s). Priest: D'Haund.

316. ELOY LECOURT (x)
#2-1836 MARIE CELINE METOYER (x)
16 January 1836
Groom: son of Marie Ursul [*metive*; and Barthelemy Le Court]. Bride: legitimate daughter of Dominique Metoyer [and Marguerite Le Comte, free people of color]. All are residents of this parish. Legitimation of two children: Jacques Zepherin and Antoine Le Court. Witneses: Chas. N. Leroy (s); Trouvat (s); Emmanuel Nª Napoleon [Dupre?]. Priest: Français.
[cf. vol. 8.]

317. SYLVESTRE POSSOT (x)
#3-1836 MARIE ELISE BERNARD HELY
16 February 1836. 3 bans.
Groom: major and legitimate son of Paul Poissot and Marie Louise Anty. Bride: minor and legitimate daughter of Pierre Hely and Marie Derbanne. All are residents of this parish of Natchitoches. Witnesses: Pierre Bertin (s); Agapy Eli (s); Athanase Ely (s); David Ortolan (s); Martilien Vascocu (x). Priest: Français.

318. ELISÉE RACHAL (x)
#4-1836 MARIE CLEMENTIA RACHAL (x)
9 February 1836.
Groom: major and legitimate son of Louis Julien Rachal and Marie Reine Thomassi. Bride: minor and legitimate daughter of Manuel Rachal and Marie Lise La Cour. All are residents of this parish of Natchitoches. Dispensation from impediment of consanguinity

in third degree. Witnesses: Sylvestre Rachal (s); Louis Rachal (s); Gasparite La Cour, Jr. (s). Priest: D'haund.

319. LOUIS RAIMOND RACHAL (x)
#5-1836 MARIE CLARA LATTIER (x)
10 February 1836
Groom: minor and legitimate son of Louis Julien Rachal and Marie Reine Thomassi. Bride: minor and legitimate daughter of Joseph Lattier and Marie Adeline Gallien. Witnesses: Louis Rachal (s); Gasparite La Cour, Jr. (s); Sévère Lattier (s). Priest: D'haund.

320. VALERIE PEROT (x)
#6-1836 MARIE FELONISE CONDÉ (x)
15 February 1836
Groom: major son of Pelagie Grappe. Bride: minor daughter of Noël Condé. All are residents of this parish of Natchitoches [and free people of color]. Witnesses: Faustin del Rio (s); Nëlo [Noël] Meziere (s); P. Trichell (s). Priest: D'haund.

321. URSIN SORREL (x)
#7-1836 MARIE CÉLIMÈNE LENOIR (x)
16 February 1836
Groom: major and legitimate son of Dominique Sorrel and Marie David. Bride: minor and legitimate daughter of Antoine Lenoir and Marie Desneiges Derbanne. All are residents of this parish of Natchitoches. Witnesses: Antoine Lenoir (x); Jos. T. Robinson (s); Fçois Besson (s); Jn. Bte. Perot (s). Priest: D'haund.

322. PANTALEON MORIN (x)
#8-1836 MARIE QUIERRY (x)
18 February 1836.
Groom: major and legitimate son of Estevan Morin and Marie Telesphor Lacerda, native of Nacogdoches, State of Texas, in Mexico. Bride: major and legitimate daughter of Pierre Quierry and Marie Rosalie Frederic, residents of this parish of Natchitoches. Dispensation from announcement of bans and from prohibition against marriage within inappropriate period of Church calendar. Witnesses: Nicolas Français, priest (s); Jn. Bte. Perot (s); Pierre Bertin (s). Officiating priest: D'haund.

323. JOSEPH ZARNAC (x)
#9-1836 MARIA JOSEPHA FLORES (x)
14 March 1836
Ratification of civil marriage. Groom: major and legitimate son of François G. Zarnac and Madelena? Arnaudière [La Renaudière]. Bride: minor and legitimate

daughter of Joseph Flores and Antonia Equis. Both parties are residents of this parish of Natchitoches. Witnesses: J. B^te Lille Sarpy (s); George Monroe (s). Priest: Français.

324. HENRY THÉODORE CHABOT (s)
#10-1836 MARIE MODESTE LEVASSEUR (s)
9 April 1836.
Ratification of civil marriage. Groom: major and legitimate son of Henry Chabot and Marie Magdeleine Pigot of La Rochelle, department of Charente-Inferieure in France. Bride: major and legitimate daughter of Emmanuel Levasseur and Geneviève Gonin, residents of this parish of Natchitoches. Witnesses: Louis Frederick Martine (s); Étienne Sanglier (s).

[Ed. note: The Chabot-Levasseur marriage contract was drawn at Natchitoches 2 September 1823; see Conv. Bk. 14, p. 32. Shortly after the above ratification Chabot took his family to La Rochelle, where Marie Modeste died in 1859, according to family files of the late Docteur Roger Chabot, 18, Rue Leónce-Vieljeux, 17000 La Rochelle; see correspondence of Dr. Chabot to the editor, various dates, 1980.]

325. PIERRE LA RENAUDIÈRE (x)
#11-1836 MARIE SELIMA DERBANNE (x)
12 April 1836.
Groom: major and legitimate son of Jean Baptiste La Renaudière and Marie Françoise Boudouin. Bride: minor and legitimate daughter of Louis Solastie Derbanne and Marie Hélène Le Moine. Dispensation from impediment of affinity in fourth degree. Witnesses: N^las Chas. Leroy (s); Sylvestre Anty (x); Jordan Scroggins (s); Firmin Lattier (s). Priest: D'haund.

326. ALEXANDRE PINSON (s)
#12-1836 MARIE CAROLINE DERBANNE (x)
13 April 1836
Groom: major and legitimate son of Jean Pierre Pinson and Anastasie Beatrice Legrand, natives of Dunkerque, Department of Nord in France. Bride: major and legitimate daughter of Manuel Derbanne and Marguerite Denis, all residents of this parish of Natchitoches. Witnesses: Emile Rost (s/ Em^le Rost); Nicola Gracia (s); J^h Martineau (s). Priest: D'haund.

327. WILLIAM GAUGH (s)
#13-1836 CHARLOTTE H. COWAN (s)
12 April 1836. 0 bans.
Groom: major and legitimate son of Thomas Gaugh and Catherine Nelson. Bride: minor and legitimate

daughter of William Cowan and Sarah Hinderson, all natives of Virginie, but actually residing in this parish. Witnesses: Lille Sarpy (s); F. Williams (s); C. E. Greneaux (s); Charles G. Lewis (s); Sarah P? Cowan (s). Priest: Français. [cf. Reg. 8.]

328. LOUIS ALEXANDER BUARD (s)
#14-1836 MARIE JEANNE SUZETTE HARTZOG (s)
14 April 1836. 1 ban.
Groom: widower in first nuptials of deceased Marie Virginie Prudhomme, major and legitimate son of Jean Louis Buard and Dame Eulalie Bossier. Bride: minor and legitimate daughter of Jean François Hertzog and Marianne Desirée Prudhomme, all residents of this parish. Dispensation from impediment of affinity in third degree. Witnesses: Jean François Hertzog (s/ J. F. Hertzog); Ambroise Le Comte (s/ A. Lecomte); François Dacisse Bossier (s/ D. Bossier); Jean Baptistes valsin Lambre (s/ V. Lambre); P. E. Bossier (s); Desirée Hertzog (s); Vve Jn L. Buard (s); P. S. Compère (s); B. V. Cortes (s). Priest: D'haund.

329. JOSÉ MARIE ROBLES (x)
#15-1836 MARIE OREZILLE DENIS BABET (x)
29 April 1836
Groom: major and legitimate son of François Robleo and Marie Gertrude de Viaréal. Bride: major and legitimate daughter of Jacques Babet Denis and Maria Denis, residents of this parish of Natchitoches. Witnesses: Seth E. Belknap (s); James H. Mears (s); [one undecipherable signature, appears to be Combadagan or Combadazo] (s). Priest: D'haund.

[Ed. note: The bride appears more frequently in Natchitoches records as Orezille Jacques.]

330. JOSÉ FELICIANO CARO (s)
#16-1836 MARIE EULALIA DE LA CRUZ [ACOSTA?],
1 May 1836
Groom: Major and legitimate son of Pierre Joseph Caro and Marie Michel Equis. Bride: major and legitimate daughter of Joseph Acosta and Marie Victoriana Cruz. All are residents of this parish of Natchitoches. Witnesses: Nicolas Français, priest (s); William Fleury (s/ W. Y. Fleury); Philogene Adlé (s/ F/ P. Adlé). Priest: D'haund.

331. NEUVILLE PRUDHOMME (s)
#17-1836 MARIE CLARA PRUDHOMME (s)
21 June 1836
Groom: Widower in first nuptials of Emerante Lambre, major and legitimate son of Antoine Prudhomme and

Marie Lambre. Bride: minor and legitimate daughter of Narcisse Prudhomme and Marie Thérèse Elisabeth Metoyer. All are residents of this parish of Natchitoches. Dispensation from bans and from impediment of consanguinity in third and second degrees. Witnesses: Narcisse Prudhomme, *fils* (s); Victorin Metoyer (s/ Metoyer); Victor Sompayrac (s/ V. Sompayrac); C. E. Greneaux (s); Lestan Prudhomme (s); J. J. A. Plauché (s); Prudhomme (s); J. B. Plauché (s); A. Sompayrac (s). Priest: D'haund.

332. PAUL FIRMIN RACHAL (s)
#18-1836 MARIE MELISA GRAPPE (s)
27 June 1836. 1 ban.
Groom: major and legitimate son of Dominique Rachal and Marie Rosalie Vercher, widower in first nuptials of Marie Cephalide Ternier. Bride: minor and legitimate daughter of Jean Pierre Grappe and Marie Felicité Perot. All are residents of this parish of Natchitoches. Witnesses: Louis Perrot (s); Cesaire Fontenaut (s); Spire Bordelon (s). Priest: Français. [cf. Reg. 8.]

333. JOSEPH EVARISTE RACHAL (x)
#19-1836 MARGUERITE DERBANNE (x)
30 June 1836. 1 ban.
Groom: major and legitimate son of Joseph Rachal and Marie Manete Denis. Bride: legitimate and minor daughter of Pierre Derbanne and Marie Anastasie Davion. All are residents of this parish of Natchitoches. Dispensation from impediment of consanguinity in third degree. Legitimation of infant of three years named Victor. Witnesses: Chs. Sers (s); Pierre Syphorien Derbanne (s/ P^{ir} S^{en} Derbanne (s); Antoine Barthelemy Rachal (s/A^{ne} B^{my} Rachal). Priest: D'haund.

334. FRANÇOIS GASSION METOYER (s)
#20-1836 ROSINE CARLES (s)
4 July 1836
Groom: widower in first nuptials of Flavie De Mézières, legitimate and major son of Augustin and Marie Agnes Metoyer, all free people of color. Bride: minor daughter of Marie Rose Metoyer [and Dr. Jean Zepherin Carles], a free woman of color. All are residents of this parish of Natchitoches. Dispensation from impediment of consanguinity in third degree. Witnesses: C. N. Roques (s); J. B. L^{s} Metoyer (s); Jerome Sarpy (s). Priest: D'haund.

[Ed. note: For background details regarding parentage of the bride, see Mills, *Forgotten People*, 101.]

335. FRANÇOIS AGAISSE (x)
#21-1836 MARIE AZOLINE POISSOT (x)
15 August 1836
Groom: major and legitimate son of Jean Renaud and Marie Louise Massip. Bride: minor and legitimate daughter of Paul Poissot and Marie Louise Anty. All are residents of this parish of Natchitoches. Witnesses: Français, priest (s); Pierre Bertin (s/ P. Bertin); Renaud Agaisse (x). Priest: D'haund.

336. JULES CEZAR NAPOLEON LUVINI (s)
#22-1836 MARIE EMELIE TRICHEL (s)
1 September 1836. 1 ban.
Groom: major and legitimate son of Antoine Marie Luvini and Antoinette Hosia?, native of Lagano [Locarno], canton of Tessin [Ticino], in Switzerland. Bride: major and legitimate daughter of Jean Baptiste Trichell and Marie Modeste Fontenau, widower in second nuptials of Jean Baptiste Derbanne, and a resident of this parish of Natchitoches. Witnesses: J. B. Trezzini (s); Marcelin Tauzin (s/ M^{lin} Tauzin); C. E. Greneaux (s); J. B. Trichel (s); B. Dranguet (s); C. Delarue (s); H^{re} Fredieu (s). Priest: Français.

337. JEAN BAPTISTE GRAPPE (s)
#23-1836 MARIE ARGINE DERBANNE (x)
26 September 1836. 1 ban.
Groom: minor and legitimate son of Jean Pierre Grappe and Felicité Perot. Bride: minor and legitimate daughter of Jean Baptiste Gasparite Derbanne and Marie Lucille Plaisance. All are residents of this parish of Natchitoches. Witnesses: Honoré Fredieu (s/ H^{re} Fredieu); Paul Firmin Rachal (s/ Firmin Rachal); François Lattier, *fils* (s); Isaac Plaisance (s). Priest: D'haund.

338. EMIL COLSON (s)
#24-1836 MARIE AGLAE METOYER (x)
25 October 1836
Groom: major son of Euphrosine Gallaix, a resident of New Orleans. Bride: minor and legitimate daughter of Jean Baptiste Dominique Metoyer and Laïde Rachal, widow in first nuptials of Louis Porteur, and a resident of this parish of Natchitoches. Witnesses: Florentin Conant (s); Bernard Dauphin (s/ Brd Dauphin); Joseph Augustin Metoyer (s/ J^{h} A^{tin} Metoyer); Joseph Metoyer, *fils* (s). Priest: Français.

339. JEAN BAPTISTE LEANDRE METOYER (s)
#25-1836 SERAPHINE ELINA CRISTOPHE (s)
3 November 1836

Groom: minor and legitimate son of Jean Baptiste Metoyer and Suzette Anty. Bride: minor and legitimate daughter of Firmin Christophe and Françoise Mayeux. All are free people of color and residents of this parish of Natchitoches. Witnesses: C. N. Roques (s); J. B. L^{s} Metoyer (s); Louis Morin (s); F. Conant (s); Firmin Christoph (s); J. B^{te} Metoyer *fils* Aug^{tin} (s). Priest: Français.

340. AUGUSTIN HARTMAN (s)
#26-1836 IRENA BOSSIER (s)
3 November 1836
Groom: major and lawful son of John Hartman and Mary Kons. Bride: minor and legitimate daughter of Sylvester Cesaire Bossier and Euphrosin Arnaud. All are residents of this parish of Natchitoches. Witnesses: Sylvester Cesair Bossier (s); Paul Casenave (s); John L. Ellis (s); S. S? Bossier (s); Augustus Le Fevre (s); Debrun (s); Bossier (s); Wm. Ferguson (s). Priest: D'haund. [cf. Reg. 8.]

341. JOHN L. ELLIS (s)
#27-1836 SOPHIA BOSSIER (s)
3 November 1836
Ratification of civil marriage. Groom: major and lawful son of John Ellis and Margaret Lodge? of the state of Virginia. Bride: major and lawful daughter of Sylvestre Cesaire Bossier and Euphrosine Arnaud. Witnesses: Sylvestre Cesaire Bossier (s); Paul Casenave (s); Wm. Fergusson (s). Priest: D'haund. [cf. Reg. 8.]

342. RAPHAËL DE LA GARCE (x)
#28-1836 MARIE LOUISE LAFFITTE (x)
6 November 1836
Ratification of civil marriage. Groom: legitimate son of Alexandre de la Garce and Marie Incarnacion De Soto. Bride: major and legitimate daughter of Cesaire Laffitte and Elisabeth Latham. All are residents of this parish of Natchitoches. Witnesses: Pierre Laffitte (s); Pedro Flores (s). Priest: D'haund. [cf. Reg. 8.]

343. JOSEPH FLORE (x)
#29-1836 MARIE JOSEPHINE COLLET (x)
7 November 1836
Ratification of civil marriage. Groom: major and legitimate son of José Flores and Maria Stephania Equis. Bride: major and legitimate daughter of Jean Baptiste Collet and Marie Hyacinthe Gagnier. All are residents of this parish of Natchitoches. Witnesses: Pedro Flores (s); Manuel Laffitte (s). Priest: D'haund. [cf. Reg. 8.]

344. JEAN FLORES LAFFITTE (x)
#30-1836 MARIE BIBIANE GRANDE (s)
8 November 1836
Ratification of civil marriage. Groom: major and legitimate son of Cesaire Laffitte and Elisabeth Latham. Bride: minor and legitimate daughter of Julien Grande and Marie Trinidad Flores, all residents of this parish of Natchitoches. Witnesses: Pedro Flores (s); Manuel Laffitte (s). Priest: D'haund. [cf. Reg. 8.]

[Ed. note: Bride's name is given in text and in marginal notation as Bibiane. She signed as Vivianne.]

345. PETER FRENCH KIMBALL (s)
#31-1836 ELINIA SIBLEY (s)
1 December 1836
Groom: major and lawful son of Asa Kimball and Elizabeth Smith. Bride: minor and lawful daughter of John Sibley and Marie Lolette [Eulalie] Malige of this parish. Witnesses: John Sibley (s); B. V. Cortes (s); Thomas P. Jones (s); J. Wm. A. De Russy (s); F. Williams (s); Saml. P. Russell (s); W. L. Cockerille (s); Hry. (Iby? Tby?) J. Williams (s); Henriette Chapman (s); E. Blanchard (s); John Laplace (s). Priest: D'haund.

345*(bis) SAMUEL MYERS HYAMS (s)
#32-1836 MARIE EMELIE PRUDHOMME (s)
1 December 1836
Groom: major and lawful son of Samuel Hyams and of Miriam Levy. Bride: major and lawful daughter of Jean Baptiste Prudhomme and Marie Roseline Malig. Witnesses: John Sibley (s); Emile Sompayrac (s); George Airey (s/ G. W. Airey); George F. Williams (s); F. Williams (s); Saml' P. Russell (s); J. Cable (s); W. L. Cockerille (s); Hy? J. Williams (s); Jn. Laplace (s); P. O. Lee (s); M. Haurut (s); J. S.? Kaufman (s). Priest: D'haund.

346. PETER McDONALD (x)
#33-1836 MARIE AZELIE BOSSIER (x)
7 December 1836. 0 bans.
Groom: major and legitimate son of T____ (Jean?) McDonald and Marie Cecile Saydeck. Bride: major and legitimate daughter of Alexandre Dominique Bossier and Marie Eleonore Imel, widow in first nuptials of Eloy Rachal. Dispensation from impediment of consanguinity in third degree. Witnesses: François Gonin (x); Nicolas Français, priest (s); François Massip (x). Officiating priest: D'haund.

----

* See note on following page.

346 *(bis) PLACIDE BREVELLE (x)
#34-1833 MARIE CEPHALIDE CHELETTRE (x)
21 December 1836
Groom: major and legitimate son of Balthasar Brevelle and Marie Louise Thérèse. Bride: minor and legitimate daughter of Jn. Pierre Shelettre and of Aimée [Emelie] Eulalie Bossier. All are residents of this parish of Natchitoces. Dispensation from prohibition against marriage during forbidden period of Church calendar. Witnesses: Louis Trouvat (s); Charles Leroy (s); Etienne Roy (x). Priest: D'haund.

347. LOUIS EMANUEL GALLIEN (x)
#35-1836 MARIE AIMÉE BAUDOUIN (x)
22 December 1836
Groom: widower in first nuptials with Marie Françoise Tomassi, major and legitimate son of Nicolas Gallien and Marie Le Cour. Bride: minor and legitimate daughter of Pierre Baudouin and Ane Robin. All are residents of this parish of Natchitoches. Witnesses: F. M. Normand (s); Thomas A. Morgan (s); Ls. Derbanne (s). Priest: D'haund.

347 *(bis) JOSÉ GUADALUPE CARDENAS (s)
#1-1837 PETRA CORDOBA (x)
14 January 1837
Groom: major and legitimate son of Francisco Cardenas and Maria Josepha de la Garsa. Bride: minor and legitimate daughter of José Cordovoa and Manuela Sanchez. Witnesses: José Gregoria Ybarbo (s); José Maria Chabanne (x); Antonio Ramones (x). Priest: D'haund.

---

* In order to make entry numbers from Register 11 (whose entries are not consecutively numbered in the original) fall into numerical sequence with Register 12 (which is numbered but begins erroneously with entry 348 instead of 351), three entries in Register 11 must be assigned a bis. The clerk who applied numbers to entries in the latter register apparently miscounted the number of entries actually appearing in the former.]

REGISTER 12

[Ed. Note: Register 12 actually begins with Entry 2 for the year 1837. Entry 1 is to be found at the end of Register 11. Apparently, these two registers were originally combined in a single volume but were split when the church registers were rebound.]

348. LOUIS GASSION CYRIAQUE RACHAL (s)
#2-1837 ANAÏS PALMIRE COMPÈRE (s)
23 January 1837. 1 ban.
Groom: minor and legitimate son of Sylvestre Rachal and Marie Rose Zorich. Bride: minor and legitimate daughter of Pierre Sébastien Compère and of Marie Lolette Rachal. Dispensation granted from impediment of consanguinity in third degree. All parties are residents of this parish of Natchitoches. Witnesses: S^{tre} Rachal (s); D^{me} S^{tre} Rachal *née* Zoriche (s); P. S. Compère (s); L. Rachal (s); Jean François Hertzog (s); B^{min} Metoyer (s). Priest: D'haund.

349. FRANÇOIS LATTIER (s)
#3-1837 MARIE ATHÉNAIS DESLOUCHE (s)
26 January 1837. 0 bans.
Groom: major and legitimate son of François Lattier and Marie Pelagie Chelettre, widower from his first nuptials with Marie Françoise Plaisance. Bride: minor and legitimate daughter of Pierre Deslouche and Marie Felicité Pommier. All parties are residents of this parish of Natchitoches. Witnesses: B^{noite} Laurents (s); Clément Rachal (s); V. Bouis (s); Thomas A. Morgan (s); E. D. Rachal (s); T. Chaler (s). Priest: D'haund.

350. LUDGER LANGLOIS (s)
#4-1837 MARIE LOUISE McTYER (s)
6 February 1837. 3 bans.

Groom: widower in first nuptials with Marie Louise Adelé, major and legitimate son of Auguste Langlois and Marie Celeste Verger. Bride: major and legitimate daughter of George McTyer and Marie Louise Mayou. All are residents of this parish of Natchitoches. Witnesses: A. B. Sompayrac (s); George H. Barlow (s); Sam'l. P. Russell (s); William Gallien (x). Priest: Français.

351. PIERRE PELLI (s)
#5-1837 LOUISE VICTOIRE STEPHANIE FOURNIER (s)
6 February 1837
Groom: major and legitimate son of Benoit Pelli and Catherine Bareta, a native of Tessin [Ticino] in Switzerland. Bride: major and legitimate daughter of Jean Baptiste Fournier and of Catherine Galluchat. All parties [both spouses?] are residents of this parish of Natchitoches. Witnesses: Fournier (s); E. Sanglier (s); D. Bossier (s); J. V. Bossier (s); J. B. O. Buard (s); C. G. Ochmichen (s); Lemée (s). Priest: D'haund.

352. FRANÇOIS IBARBO (x)
#6-1837 MARIE NICOLASA LONGORIA (x)
25 February 1837
Groom: major and legitimate son of José Ibarbo and of Maria Anastasia Mansola. Bride: major and legitimate daughter of Ignacio Longoria and of Maria Antonia Cortinez, and the widow in second nuptials of Francisco San Miguel. All parties are residents of this parish of Natchitoches. Witnesses: Chrysostomé Pena (x); Joseph Dorlon (s); B. F. Shattuck (s). Priest: D'haund.

353. ADONIS ISIDORE [HISSOURA *dit*] PANTALEON (s)
#7-1837 MARIE AIMÉE BARBEROUSSE (s)
9 March 1837
Groom: major and legitimate son of Bernard Isour de Pantaleon and Marie Marguerite Grillet. Bride: major and legitimate daughter of Michel Barberousse and Marie Anette Gagnié, widow in first nuptials with Louis Jerome Rachall. All are residents of this parish of Natchitoches. Dispensation given from prohibition against marriage during forbidden

period of Church calendar. Witnesses: Ml. Barberousse (s); A. Grilliet (s); C. E. Greneaux (s); Saml. P. Russell (s). Priest: D'haund.

354. #8-1837

FRANÇOIS ROUQUIER (s)
THÉRÈSE ANNE LONGINO (x)
9 March 1837
Groom: widower in first nuptials with Marie Elisabeth Buard, legitimate and major son of François Rouquier and Marie Louise Prudhomme. Bride: minor and legitimate daughter of John Thomas Longino and Apley Luis. All are residents of this parish of Natchitoches. Dispensation from prohibition against marriage during forbidden period of Church calendar. Witnesses: C. Pavie (s); J. F. Cortés (s); E. O. Blanchard (s); D. Slim Burnet (s); Sam'l P. Russell (s); B. V. Cortes (s); G. W. Reeve? (s); W. L. Cockerille (s); Prudhomme (s); P. Petrovich (s); Thomas P. Jones (s); Charles Emile Sompayrac (s); Samuel M. Crawford (s). Priest: D'haund.

355. #9-1837

LOUIS FRANÇOIS NEUVILLE VIENNE (s)
MARIE CÉLIMA PEROT (s)
16 March 1837
Groom: minor and legitimate son of François Vienne and Marianne Buard. Bride: major and legitimate daughter of Faustin Perot and Marie Celeste Bordelon, widow in first nuptials of Jean Baptiste Fonteneau. Dispensation from prohibition against marriage during forbidden period of Church calendar. Witnesses: S. Bordelon (s); Cesaire Fontenau (s); Hyte. Bordelon (s); Jn. Prat (s); Michael Boyce (s). Priest: D'haund.

356. #10-1837

JEAN PHILIPPE BREDA (s)
MARIE HELMINA DRANGUET (s)
17 March 1837
Groom: major and legitimate son of Jean Philippe Breda and Marie Barbe Cholet, native of Verdun, department of Meuse, France. Bride: minor and legitimate daughter of Benjamin Dranguet and Marie Celeste Tauzin. All are residents of this parish of Natchitoches. Dispensation from prohibition against marriage during forbidden period of Church calendar. Witnesses: Thomas M. Linnard (s); A. L. Deblieux (s); T. E. Tauzin (s); J. B. Trezzini (s); F. Williams (s); F. C. Tauzin (s); M. Haurut (s); Mlin Tauzin (s). Priest: D'haund.

357. JOSEPH RAMOS (s)
#11-1837 MARIA EDOUARDA SAN MIGUEL (s)
19 April 1837. 3 bans.
Groom: major and legitimate son of Joseph Ramos and Antonia Billa Morine, natives of Galice in Spain. Bride: minor and legitimate daughter of Joseph San Miguel and Maria Padilla. All are residents of Natchitoches Parish. Witnesses: Joseph San Miguel (x); F^{co} Negrevernis (s); Ignatio Ratio (x); Michel Fontana (s). Groom signed as Josef Ramos. Priest: Français.

358. PIERRE CYR LA BOME (s)
#12-1837 MARIE LOUISE DAVID (x)
1 May 1837. 2 bans.
Groom: major and legitimate son of Joseph La Bome [de La Baume] and Marie Louise Couturier. Bride: major daughter of Magdeleine Grappe [and Louis David]. All are residents of Natchitoches Parish and all [with exception of the fathers of the two spouses] are free people of color. Witnesses: Noël Mezieres (s); Louis Lamate (x); Charles Watts (s); José de La Baume (s). Groom signed as Pedro de La Baume. Priest: D'haund.

[Ed. note: For parental data on bride see note accompanying Entry 157.]

359. SYLVESTRE BOSSIER (s)
#13-1837 HENRIETTE MATHILDE PANNELL(s)
11 May 1837. 1 ban.
Groom: major and legitimate son of Sylvestre Bossier and Susanne Collins, widower in first nuptials with Marie Lacroix. Bride: minor and legitimate daughter of Alexander W. Pannell and Henriette Hodgen Winter. All are residents of Natchitoches Parish. Witnesses: P. A. Morse (s); C. E. Greneaux (s); D. Bossier (s); T. E. Tauzin (s); W. L. Cockerille (s); L. A. Buard (s); Harriet W. Petrovic (s); Charles E. Sompayrac (s); P. Petrovic (s); J. H. Campbell (s); David F. Taber (s); Virginia Sompayrac (s); A. Sompayrac (s); C. G. Ochmichen (s); S. P. Sachell (s); J. V. Bossier (s); M. V. Handy (s). Priest: D'haund.

360. PEABODY ATKINSON MORSE (s)
#14-1837 VIRGINIA SOMPAYRAC (s)
16 May 1837.
Groom: major and lawful son of Bryan? Morse and Susanna Stevens of New Hampshire. Bride: minor and lawful daughter of Ambroise Sompayrac and Josephine Desirée Briant of this parish of Natchitoches. Witnesses: A. Sompayrac (s); Briant Sompayrac (s); Narcisse Prudhomme (s); H. Tauzin (s); F. C. Tauzin (s); V. Sompayrac (s); Prudhomme (s); E. O. Blanchard (s); W. L. Cockerille (s); J. V. Bossier (s); J. Campbell

(s); William Stansburg?, M.D. (s); M^c^. Sompayrac (s); Daniel H. Vail (s); B. V. Cortes (s); V. Rossuy? (s). Priest: D'haund.

361a. [NARCISSE] ANTOINE SERAPHIN RACHAL (s)
#15-1837 BARBE ZELIA BROSSET (s)
16 May 1837. 3 bans.
Groom: minor and legitimate son of Narcisse Rachal and Marie Maneta Rachal. Bride: minor and legitimate daughter of Athanase Brosset and Marie Celeste Baudouin. All are residents of Natchitoches Parish. Witnesses: Sylvestre Rachal (s); C^hs^. F. Benoist (s); Lucien Jarreau (s); P. S. Compère (s). Priest: Français. [cf. Reg. 8.]

361b. GASPARITE LA COURT [LA COUR]
#16-1837 EUSEBIE JARREAU
16 May 1837.
Ratification of marriage contracted before Hoverton, a justice of the peace in the Parish of Rapides. Groom: major and legitimate son of Gasparite La Court and Marie Félicité Brevelle. Bride: major and legitimate daughter of Jean Jarreau and Lucine Tournoir. Witnesses: C^hs^. F. Benoist (s); Pierre Michel (s); Clément Rachal (s); Lucien Jarreau (s). Priest: Français. [cf. Reg. 8.]

362. JOSEPH LESTAGE (x)
#17-1837 MARIE JOSEPHINE RACHAL (x)
5 June 1837. 3 bans.
Groom: major and legitimate son of Barthelemy Lestage and Marie Pelagie Féderic. Bride: minor and legitimate daughter of Jean Baptiste Rachal and Marie Rosette Derbanne. All are residents of Natchitoches Parish. Witnesses: Denis Chelette (s); Thomas Thompson (s); Ludger Rachal (s). Priest: Français. [cf. Reg. 8.]

363. JEAN BAPTISTE OVIDE BUARD (s)
#18-1837 MARIE DÉSIRÉE HERTZOG (s)
20 June 1837. 1 ban.
Groom: minor and legitimate son of Jean Baptiste Buard and Marie Aspasie Bossier. Bride: minor and legitimate daughter of Jean François Hertzog and Marie Anne Prudhomme, all residents of Natchitoches Parish. Dispensation from impediment of consanguinity in fourth degree. Witnesses: François Dassise Bossier (s); J. F. Hertzog (s); J^n^. B^te^. Valsin Lambre (s); P. E. Bossier (s); J. B. Bossier (s); Désirée Hertzog *né[e]* Prudhomme (s); A. Buard (s); Janin, M.D. (s). Priest: D'haund.

364. JAMES LAWRENCE HAUGHTELING (s)
#19-1837 ROSALIE ZULMINA ADLÉ (s)
10 July 1837
Groom: major and lawful son of James H. [*sic*] and Ernestine Dezong?, born in Ontario County, State of New York. Bride: minor and lawful daughter of Antoine Adlé and Louisa Greneaux, native of this parish. Witnesses: C. E. Greneau (s); François Dacise Bossier (s); Pierre Evariste Bossier (s); George J. Florance (s); J. V. Bossier (s); Janin, M.D. (s). Priest: D'haund.

365. NOËL DE MÉSIÈRE (s)
#20-1837 MARIE ODISE TRICHELL (x)
25 July 1837. 2 bans.
Groom: major son of Marijeanne de Mésière, widower in first nuptials with Deloise Perrot. Bride: minor daughter of Marie Joseph[e] Gráppe [and Pierre André Athanase Trichel]. All parties [except bride's father] are free people of color and residents of Natchitoches Parish. Witnesses: F. Bertille Trichell (s); Elisha Parker (s); Joseph de Mésière (s); Antoine Vaca (s). Priest: Français.

[Ed. note: For parental identity of bride see Succ. Bk. 10, pp. 260-64, 459-61; Succ. Bk. 12, pp.12-16, and *Heirs of Pierre Trichel* v. *Cesaire Fonteneau et al*, Microcopy VS.6 (1837), Natchitoches Parish Courthouse. Additional background is to be found in Mills, "(De) Mézières-Trichel-Grappe," *op. cit.*]

366. JUAN JOSÉ MARTINEZ (x)
#21-1837 MARIA MAURICIA CHIRINO (x)
3 August 1837. 0 bans.
Groom: minor and legitimate son of Manuel Martinez and Maria Ignacia De Soto. Bride: minor and legitimate daughter of Juan Bautista Chirino and Maria Merced Sanchez. All are native of this parish of Natchitoches. Witnesses: Miguel Torrez (s); James McKey (s); D. Veulement (s). Priest: D'haund.

367. JOSEPH SOLDINI (s)
#22-1837 MARIE MODESTE GONIN (x)
29 August 1837
Groom: major and legitimate son of Jean Antoine Soldini and Marie Celeste Sciolli, native of Ponte Tresa, Kingdom of Lombard Venitien [Lombardy and Venetia, in Italy]. Bride: major and legitimate daughter of François Xavier Gonin and Marie Barbe Frederic, natives of this parish of Natchitoches. Witnesses: Pierre Pelli (s); François dacise Bossier (s); Jules Victor Bossier (s); P.E. Bossiesr (s); C. E. Greneaux (s). Priest: D'haund.

368. McKENDRICK MOSES
#23-1837 MARIE HÉLÈNE ST. GERMAIN
6 September 1837
Ratification of marriage contracted before a civil magistrate. Groom: lawful and major son of Henry Moses and Priscilla Jones of North Carolina. Bride; minor and lawful daughter of François St. Germaine and Marie Adrienne St. André. Renewal of vows at home of Fçois St. Germaine at Cloutierville. Witnesses: François Marie Normand (s); Jean Ulisse Carrier(s); Thomas A. Morgan (s). Priest: D'haund.

369. PETER TERRY HICKMAN (s)
#24-1837 LOUISE DÉSIRÉE GAIENNIÉ (s)
4 October 1837
Groom: major and lawful son of William Hickman and Mary Webster of the state of Tennessee. Bride: minor and lawful daughter of François Gainnié and Louise Désirée Lalande Ferrier, "all residing in this parish." Witnesses: W. P. Hickman (s); Fçois Gaiennié (s); Fçois Metoyer (s); Thomas J. Hickman (s); F. M. Normand (s); L. Desirée Gaiennié *née* Lalande Ferrière (s); Phanor Prudhomme (s); V. Archinard (s); Valery Gaiennié (s); Benjamin Metoyer (s); C? Ducotel? (s). Priest: D'haund.

370. NICOLAS LA COUR (s)
#25-1837 MAGDELEINE EUPHÉMIE LA COUR (s)
7 November 1837. 3 bans.
Marriage at Rapides Parish home of Mr. Gilbert La Cour. Groom: major and legitimate son of Jean Marie La Cour and Josephine Gillard. Bride: minor and legitimate daughter of Gilbert La Cour and Hélène Geoffrion. All are residents of Rapides Parish. License issued by judge of the parish of Rapides. Witnesses: Bret La Cour (s); Gilbert La Cour (s); Volizard De Blanc (s). Priest: D'haund.

371. JEAN BAPTISTE JERÔME DE BLANC (s)
#26-1837 MARGUERITE IRMA GAILLARD (s)
8 November 1837
Groom: major and legitimate son of Joseph De Blanc and Marguerite Fanny La Cour. Bride: widow in first nuptials of Sylvère Baillio, legitimate and major daughter of Joseph Gillard and Petronille La Cour. License issued by judge of Rapides and dispensation given from the announcement of bans and the impediment of consanguinity and affinity in second degree. All parties are residents of the parish of Rapides. Witnesses: Joseph Gillard (s); Jean Marie LaCour (s); Edouard Jh. Gillard (s); Bret La Cour (s); J. B. M? Gillard (s). Priest: D'haund.

372. JOSEPH TOOLE ROBINSON (s)
#27-1837 HENRIETTE (HARRIET) WINTER CABLE (s)
8 November 1837. 2 bans.
Groom: major and legitimate son of Joseph Toole Robinson and Marie Robinson, natives of Dublin in Ireland, widower in first nuptials with Arsene Trichell. Bride: minor and legitimate daughter of Jared Cable and Caroline Winter. All are residents of this parish of Natchitoches. Witnesses: D. R. Hopkins (s); J. W. Butler (s); J. G. Campbell (s); C. E. Greneaux (s); Ch^{les} E. Sompayrac (s); Jared Cable (s) Priest: Français. [cf. Reg. 8.]

[Ed. note: Bride signed as Harriet. In the French registration of the entry, Register 12, the priest gave the name as Henriette.]

373. THÉODORE ANDRÉ SANSON (s)
#28-1837 HENRIETTE CARASCO (x)
9 November 1837
Groom: major and legitimate son of André Sanson and of Marie [Epron *dit*] Renois. Bride: minor and legitimate daughter of Ilario Carasco and Celeste Walter. All are residents of the parish of Rapides. Witnesses: André Renoy (s); Nicola Gracia (s); Jacques Ninta (s/ Jayme Minta); L. Jarreau (s). Priest: D'haund.

374. NERES PIERRE METOYER (s)
#29-1837 MARIE ELISE ROQUES (s)
13 November 1837
Groom: minor and legitimate son of deceased Pierre Metoyer and Marie Henriette Cloutier. Bride: minor and legitimate daughter of Charles Nerestan Roques and of Marie Pompose Metoyer. All are free people of color and residents of the parish of Natchitoches. Dispensation granted from impediment of consanguinity in third and second degrees. Witnesses: Charles Nerestan Roques (s); J^{n}. B^{te}. Louis Metoyer (s); Jean B^{te}. Augustin Metoyer (s); Louis Morin (s); F. Conant (s); H^{y}. O^{ve}. Deronce (s). Priest: D'haund.

375. CYRIAQUE MONET (x)
#30-1837 MARIE MARGUERITE LECOMTE (x)
28 November 1837
Groom: major son of Baltazar Monet [Jean Baptiste Baltazar] and of Dorothée Monete. Bride: major daughter of Magdeleine Le Comte. All are free people of color and residents of this parish of Natchitoches. Witnesses: Louis Morin (s); Charles Nerestan Roques (s); Jean Baptiste Metoyer *fils* Augustin (s). Priest: D'haund. [cf. Reg. 8.]

[Ed. note: At the close of the original entry in Register 8, there appears the following, barely-legible list which seems to name children being legitimized: "Marie Elina, born September 1830 (1835?) Godparents: Octave Deronce and Lise? Roques; Marie Lise?, born October 1836, Godparents: Louis Morin and Suzette Metoyer; Bte. [illegible] 9 years."

376. CHARLES EMILE SOMPAYRAC (s)
#31-1837 MARIE CLARISSE PRUDHOMME (s)
30 November 1837. 1 ban.
Groom: major and legitimate son of Ambroise Sompayrac and Josephine Désirée Bryant. Bride: minor and legitimate daughter of Narcisse Prudhomme and Marie Thérèse Elisabeth Metoyer. All reside in Natchitoches Parish. Witnesses: Ambroise Sompayrac (s); Narcisse Prudhomme (s); Marie T. Elisabeth Metoyer (s); A. B. Sompayrac (s); Jean Joseph Alexander Plauché (s); Victorin Metoyer (s); Lestan Prudhomme (s); M^c. Sompayrac. Priest: Français.

377. CLÉMENT RACHAL (s)
#32-1837 MARIE HENRIETTE ANTY (s)
27 December 1837. 3 bans.
Groom: major and legitimate son of deceased Barthelemy Louis Rachal and Marie Françoise Grillet. Bride: minor and legitimate daughter of deceased Ignace Anty and Marie Louise Latier. All are residents of Natchitoches Parish. License issued 7 December. Witnesses: Honoré Fredieu (s); Thomas A. Morgan (s); Louis Chevalier (s); Sévere Latier (s); F. Chaler (s). Priest: Français. [cf. Reg. 8.]

378. JEAN BAPTISTE PERROT (s)
#1-1838 CELESTE LAFITTE (x)
6 January 1838
Groom: major and legitimate son of François Perrot and Marie Louise Labairie, widower in first nuptials with Marie Felicité Trichell. Bride: major and legitimate daughter of Paul Boëte Lafitte and Marie Anne De Soto, widow in second nuptials with François Flamming. Dispensation from prohibition against marriage during forbidden period of Church calendar. License dated 2 January. All are residents of Natchitoches Parish. Witnesses: Hyppolite Bordelon (s); Cesaire Fonteneau (s); L^s. O. Perrot (s); Hylaire Bordelon (s). Priest: Français. [cf. Reg. 8.]

379. PIERRE WALAS
* ARTHEMISE PRUDHOMME
7 January 1838

----

* Past this point, annual numbers are not assigned to the entries.

Rehabilitation of marriage contracted about one month earlier. Groom: minor and legitimate son of deceased Pierre Walas and Maria Vacila Grande. Bride: minor and legitimate daughter of Jean Baptiste Prudhomme and Marie Louise Ybarbe. Ceremony at Grande Cannes, district of Bayou Pierre, parish of Natchitoches. Witnesses: Pierre Laffitte; Charles Rambin; Cesaire Prudhomme. Priest: V. Jarney.

380. SYLVESTRE POISSOT
MARIE JOSEPH EUPHEMIE HESSER
8 January 1838
Rehabilitation of civil marriage contracted several years before. Groom: major and legitimate son of Athanase Poissot and Marie Emanuele Soto. Bride: major daughter of deceased Christian Hesser and Adelaïde Rambin. All are residents of Natchitoches Parish. Ceremony at Grande Cannes, district of Bayou Pierre, parish of Natchitoches. Witnesses: Louis Damase Bossier, Pedro Chrisostomé Flores, Pierre Barton. Priest: Jarney.

381. FREDERIC FELIX HESSER
MARIE LOUISE LAFFITTE
8 January 1838
Rehabilitation of marriage contracted civilly several years before. Groom: major and legitimate son of Christian Hesser and Marie Françoise Adelaïde Rambin. Bride: major and legitimate daughter of Louis Laffitte and Marie Antoine Flores. All are residents of Bayou Pierre, Natchitoches Parish. Ceremony at Grande Cannes, Bayou Pierre. Witnesses: Louis Laffitte, Emmanuel Laffitte, François Prudhomme. Priest: Jarney.

382. AMBROISE BERNARD THEOPHILE SOMPAYRAC (s)
MARIE ARMELINE SOMPAYRAC (s)
15 January 1838. 2 bans.
Groom: major and legitimate son of Ambroise Sompayrac and Josephine Desirée Bryant. Bride: minor and legitimate daughter of Marc Sompayrac and Marie Zeline Cloutier. All are residents of this parish of Natchitoches. Dispensation from impediment of consanguinity in second degree. Witnesses: Victor Sompayrac (s); P. A. Morse (s); Abel Sers (s); Charles Émile Sompayrac (s). Priest: Jarney. [cf. Reg. 8.]

383. FRANÇOIS VAN SCHONBROECK
ISABELLA DEHERT
21 January 1838. 3 bans.
Groom: major and legitimate son of Henri van Schonbrook and Jeanne Veulemans. Bride: legitimate and

major daughter of Guillaume Dehert and Catherine De Nef, widow in first nuptials of Pierre Van Melder. All are natives of Belgium; the spouses reside in the parish of Natchitoches. Witnesses: Louis Pietermans, Louis Van Schoenbroeck, Pierre Croes, Matthieu Baecken. Priest: Han? (Wm?) De Veldes.

384. J. CHRISOSTOMÉ VASCOCU
MARIE TELESPHOR FLORES
20 January 1838. 2 bans.
Groom: major and legitimate son of Jean Louis Vascocu and Marie Magdelaine Perrot, widower in first nuptials of Marie Marcelite Ris. Bride: major and legitimate daughter of Joseph Flores and Stephanie Huaisse [Equis]. Witnesses: J. B.te Vascocu; Dassise Bossier; François Rond; Victor Bréchon. Priest: Jarney.

385. GERRY R. WATERS (s)
MARIE ANTOINETTE ADELÉ (s)
23 January 1838. 2 bans.
Groom: major son of Mastin Waters and Sarah Read, natives of the county of Washington, state of Vermont. Bride: minor daughter of Antoine Adelé and Louise Greneaux, residents of this parish of Natchitoches. License issued 2 January. Witnesses: C. E. Greneaux (s); A. Lecomte (s); J. B. Trichell (s); L. Alexandre Buard (s). Priest: Français. [cf. Reg. 8.]

386. DERZELIN DERBANE (s)
CELESTE FERRIER (x)
25 January 1838. 3 bans.
Groom: major and legitimate son of Emmanuel Derbanne and Margueritte Denys. Bride: minor and legitimate daughter of deceased Jean Baptiste Ferrier and Pelagie Lemoine. License issued 12 January. Witnesses: Alexandre Pinçon (s); Joseph Martineau (s); Joseph Perrot (s). Priest: Jarney. [cf. Reg. 8.]

387. CHRISANTO DE ODIARDI (s)
MARIE CELINA TRICHELE (s)
20 February 1838. 2 bans.
Groom: major and legitimate son of Jean Baptiste Odiardi and deceased Claire Belleyancha?, all three of the department of la Corse [Corsica] France. The groom is now residing in Natchitoches Parish. Bride: major and legitimate daughter of deceased Emmanuel Trichele and Marie Euphrosine Prudhomme. License issued 10 February. Witnesses: Remi Perrot (s); Joseph T. Robinson (s); Jn. Prat (s). Groom signed as Trisanto or Visanto de Odiardi. Priest: Jarney. [cf. Reg. 8.]

388. JHON MEARS (s)
MARIE ALIDA COMPÈRE (s)
26 February 1838. 1 ban.
Groom: native of New York, actually residing in this parish, major and legitimate son of James P. Mears and Lucinda Hamilton. Bride: minor and legitimate daughter of Pierre Sebastien Compère and Marie Lolette Rachal, of this parish. License issued 12 February. Witnesses: Silvestre Rachal (s); Cyriaque Rachal (s); Jean Baptiste Dejean (s); Joseph Compère (s); Ls. Compère (s). Groom signed as Jno. H. Mears. Priest: Jarney. [cf. Reg. 8.]

389. LUCIEN COINDET (s)
MARIE ZELINE RACHAL (METOYER) (x)
27 February 1838. 2 bans.
Groom: natural son of Antoine Coindet and Rose Metoyer. Bride: minor and legitimate daughter of Jean Baptiste Rachal and Marie Suzanne Metoyer. All are free people of color [with exception of groom's deceased father] and residents of this parish of Natchitoches. License issued 14 February. Dispensation from impediment of consanguinity in third degree. Witnesses: Charles Sers (s); Jean Baptiste Grandchamp (s); Jean Fabre (s). Priest: Jarney. [cf. Reg. 8.]

[Ed. note: For ethnic identification of groom's father, see *Coindet v. Metoyer*, District Court Suit No. 942, Natchitoches Parish.]

390. REMY CASIMIR PERROT (s)
JULIA LAMBRE (s)
27 February 1838. 1 ban.
Groom: major and legitimate son of Casimir Perrot and Delphine Poissot, widower of Julia Flemming. Bride: minor and legitimate daughter of Jean Jacques Lambre and Marie Luce Cloutier. All are residents of Natchitoches Parish. Witnesses: Jean Laplace (s); J. W. Butler (s); E. O. Blanchard (s); Jean Prat (s); Chs. Noyrit (s): J. Bte. Cloutier (s). Priest: François. [cf. Reg. 8.]

391. FRANÇOIS EUGENE D'ORTOLAND (s)
MARIE URSULE DAGOBERT (x)
1 March 1838. 1 ban.
Groom: minor and legitimate [*sic*] son of Remon d'Ortolant and Madeleine Perrot, a free woman of color. Bride: minor daughter of Suzette Grappe, a free woman of color. Dispensation granted from prohibition against marriage during forbidden period of church calendar. Witnesses: Cesaire Fontenau (s); J. Bte. Perot (s); François Bertille Trichell (s). Priest: François. [cf. Reg. 8.]

[Ed. note: Marriage between the parents of the groom would not have been legal under Louisiana law; however, the parents do appear as man and wife on several of the censuses of Nacogdoches, Texas. If a legitimate marriage occurred, it should have taken place in that province; but Nacogdoches church records for the period of the groom's birth are not extant.]

392. EMMANUEL BREVEL (x)
MARIE CLARISSE CHLETRE (x)
13 March 1838. 0 bans.
Groom: major and legitimate son of Balthazar Brevel and Marie Louise Granderote?. Bride: major and legitimate daughter of Jean Pierre Chletre and Eulalie Soulange [Bossier]. Witnesses: Balthazar Brevill (s); Pierre Metoyer (s); Jerome Sarpy, Jr. (s). Priest: Jarney.

393. AGAPITE HELY (s)
MARCELITTE PLAISANCE (s)
19 March 1838. 0 bans.
Groom: major and legitimate son of Célestin Hely and Marie Celizie Trichell. Bride: major and legitimate daughter of Jean Baptiste Plaisance and Marie Joseph Palvado. License issued 17 March. Dispensation from prohibition against marriage during forbidden period of Church calendar. Witnesses: Benjamin G? Fonteneaux (s); Siboir Perrot; Pierre Ternier (s); J. Bte. Plaisance (s). Priest: Français. [cf. Reg. 8.]

394. JACKSON FREEMAN (s)
ELISA McTYER (x)
19 March 1838. 0 bans.
Groom: major son of John Freeman and Mary Kipson [Gibson?]. Bride: major and legitimate daughter of George Mctyer and Marie Mayou of this parish. Dispensation from prohibition against marriage during forbidden period of Church calendar. Witnesses: Dr. Samuel P. Russel (s); Jno. W. Risher (s); Remy Perrot (s); Jean François Rouquier (s). Priest: Français. [cf. Reg. 8.]

395. BELIZAIRE LORENS (s)
MARIE DENEIGES EZILDA DUPRE (s)
19 March 1838. 0 bans.
Groom: minor and legitimate son of Seraphin Lorens and Marie Aspazie Metoyer. Bride: minor and legitimate daughter of Valsin Dupré and Marie Doralize Derbanne. All are free people of color. Witnesses: Jean Baptiste Louis Metoyer (s); Nerestan Roques (s); J. Bte. Metoyer (s); E. Dupre (s). Groom signed as Belisaire Llorens; bride signed as Denige L. Dupré. Priest: Jarney. [cf. Reg. 8.]

396. ST. CYR METOYER
MARIE ROSALIE
19 April 1838. 0 bans.
Groom: son of Rozalie. Bride: daughter of Marie Jeanne. All are free people of color and residents of this parish of Natchitoches. Witnesses: Joseph Metoyer (s); J. Metoyer, Jr.; Eduard Dupres (s). Priest: Jarney. [cf. Reg. 8.]

397. JEAN BAPTISTE LENOIR
JOSEPHINE VERCHERE
19 April 1838. 0 bans.
Groom: major and legitimate son of Antoine Lenoir and Marie Desneige Derbanne. Bride: minor and legitimate daughter of Jaques Verchere and Euprosine Gallien. Witnesses: Louis Emmanuel Gallien (x); Isidore R. Plaisance (s); Thomas Alexandre Morgan (s). Priest: Jarney.

398. FRANCES JOHNSON (s)
MARIE LOUISE EVELINA BLUDWORTH (s)
24 April 1838. 1 ban.
Groom: major and legitimate son of Joseph Johonson and Catherine Bonneau, a native of Charleston now residing in this parish. Bride: minor and legitimate daughter of James Bludworth and Marie Aimée Rouquier. Witnesses: Edouard O. Blanchard (s); John Carr (s); and Benjamin Valcourt Cortes (s). Priest: Jarney. [cf. Reg. 8.]

399. JESUS FLORES (s)
MARIE CANUTI BARBE [Y BARBO] (x)
4 May 1838. 0 bans.
Groom: major and legitimate son of Vital Flores and Gertrude More. Bride: major and legitimate daughter of Pedro Ibarbe and Jeanne de la Garce. All are residents of Texas. Witnesses: Remy Totin (x); Pedro Flores (s); Remy Ibarbe (x). Priest: Français.

400. JEAN BAPTISTE (x)
SUZETTE ROUQUIER (x)
5 May 1838. 0 bans.
Groom: a free negro. Bride: a free mulatress. Witnesses: Michel Torbayas (s); Antoine Aubuchon (x); Antoine Cotonmais (x). Priest: Français.

401. JEAN BAPTISTE AARNAUD (x)
MARIE DESNEIGES BADIN
7 May 1838. 1 ban.

Groom: [no information given]. Bride: Widow of John Baker. All are free people of color living in this parish. Witnesses: François Bertille Trichell (s); Victor Le Brun (x); Manuel Celestin Ely (x); Joseph Mesière (s). Priest: Français.

402. JOACHIM DELOUCHE (x)
SUZANNE RACHAL (s)
15 May 1838. 2 bans.
Groom: major and legitimate son of Julien Delouche and Osive [Osite] Dupré. Bride: widow of Chrisostomé Perrot, major and legitimate daughter of Dominique Rachal and Rosalie Vercher. All are residents of the parish of Natchitoches. Witnesses: J. Baptiste Trichell (s); Honoré Frédieu (s); Breville Perrot (s). Priest: Français. [cf. Reg. 8.]

403. LOUIS CLÉMENT VICTOR MARY
MARIE MANETTE FONTENEAUX
16 May 1838. 1 ban.
Groom: major and legitimate son of Clément Casimire Marey and Marie Louise Jeanne Charbot, natives of Paris, France. Bride; widow of François Perot, major and legitimate daughter of Louis Fonteneaux and Marie Pelagie Grappe. Widow: Jean Baptiste Perrot (s); Louis Perrot (s); Remy Perrot (s); Spire Bordelon (s); Jean Prat (s). License issued 2 May. Priest: Français. [cf. Reg. 8.]

404. AZENOR THEODULE LA COUR (s)
ELIZABETH ROSELIA DETERVILLE (s)
15 May 1838. No bans.
Groom: major and legitimate son of Leandre La Cour and Marie Louise Gillard. Bride: minor and legitimate daughter of deceased Théodore Deterville and Marie Rose Socié. License issued by judge of Rapides Parish. Witnesses: Jn. Gillard, Sr. (s); Joseph Gillard, Jr. (s/ E. Joseph Gillard); Volizard Deblanc (s); A. La Cour (s); Leandre La Cour (s). Priest: Jarney. [cf. Reg. 8.]

405. FRANÇOIS (EMANUEL) DAVION (x)
ADELAIDE BRICOU
16 May 1838
Ratification, at Cloutierville, of civil marriage contracted several years before. Witnesses: Antoine Barthelemy Rachal (s); Luc Poché (s). Priest: Jarney (s). [cf. Reg. 8.]

[Ed. note: original document in Reg. 8 gives groom's name as Emanuel. Copy recorded in Reg. 12 gives the name as François.]

406. LOUIS BARTHELEMY LECOUR (s)
MARIE LOUISE METOYER (x)
17 May 1838. 3 bans.
Groom: major and legitimate [*sic*] son of Barthelemy Le Cour[t] and Adelaíde Mariote. Bride: minor and legitimate daughter of Dominique Metoyer and Marguerite Le Comte. All are free people of color [with exception of groom's father] and residents of this parish of Natchitoches. Witnesses: Joseph Metoyer, Jr. (s); Emanuel Dupré (s); Emanuel Llorens (s); Lucien Condet (s). Priest: Jarney.

[Ed. note: Rev. Jarney has erred with regard to the inferred marriage of the groom's parents. His father, Barthelemy Le Court, was the son of a French nobleman by a Natchitoches Creole wife of French parentage. The groom's mother, Adelaïde, was a freed slave. Marriage was not possible under Louisiana law. The baptismal entry for Louis Toussaint Barthelemy Le Court correctly identifies him as the "natural son" of Barthelemy and Adelaïde. See Mills, *Natchitoches 1800-1826*, entry 2560.]

407. LOUIS LAMOTE
CELESTE PERROT
1 May 1838
Ratification, at Campti, of civil marriage contracted several years earlier. Legitimatation of children: Louis, Marguerite, Celeste? and Marie Florentine. Witnesses: Jean Githory? and Nicolas Furlong. Priest: Jarney.

408. JEAN BAPTISTE XANDRE VASCOCU (x)
MARIE LOUISE LEFEVRE (x)
21 May 1838
Ratification of civil marriage. Witnesses: Mathieu Bachen (s); Michel Torbeyns (s). Priest: Français.

409. LOUIS MULLON (s)
MARIE SUZETTE COTONMAÏS (x)
20 May 1838. 3 bans.
Groom: major and legitimate son of François Mullon and Marie Louise Metoyer. Bride: minor and legitimate daughter of Antoine Cotonmaïs and Marie Louis Bellepeche. All are free people of color and residents of this parish. Witnesses: Joseph Augustin Metoyer (s); François Metoyer, Jr. (s); Leopold Cadet (s). Priest: Jarney.

410. JOSEPH CHARLES SIMON LAROUILLE (x)
MARIE REINE CLERINE MESIÈRE (x)
29 May 1838. 1 ban.
Groom: major and legitimate son of Charles Simon

Larouille and Marie Lucinte [Vicente] Peres. Bride: minor daughter of Marie Rose Mesière. All are free people of color and residents of this parish of Natchitoches. Witnesses: Antoine Vaca (x); Louis Lamate (x); Jean Baptiste Neisen (s); José Mesières (s). Priest: Français.

411. ANDREW HAMILTON (s)
PHELOE ADELÉ (x)
7 June 1838. 0 bans.
Groom: major and legitimate son of deceased Andrew Hamilton and Loisanie? Allan. Bride: widow of J[ulius C.] Sanders, major and legitimate daughter of Valentin Adlè and Elize [Celisie] Brosset. Witnesses: Jean Baptiste Grandchampt (s); Isidore Champenoir (s); Alver [Albert? Alvin?] M. Day (s); Bte. Adlè (s). Priest: Jarney. [cf. Reg. 8.]

412. JOSEPH LECOUBICHE (x)
MARIE JOSEPH LAFFITTE (s)
30 June 1838. 0 bans.
Groom: major and legitimate son of Joseph Lecoubiche and Mauritia More of the parish of Cadeaux. Bride: minor and legitimate daughter of Emmanuel Laffitte and Marie Salomé Procella of the same parish. License issued in Caddo Parish. Witnesses: Aimé Mauro (s); Gregoire Ybarbe (s); Cesaire Flores (s). Priest: Jarney.

413. CESAIRE PRUDHOMME (x)
MARIE LOUISE LAFFITTE (s)
30 June 1838. 0 bans.
Groom: major and legitimate son of Jean Baptiste Prudhomme and Marie Joseph Ybarbe of the Parish of Caddo. Bride: minor and legitimate daughter of Emmanuel Laffitte and Marie Salomé Procella, of the same parish. Witnesses: Aimé Mauro (s); Gregoire Ybarbe (s); Cesaire Flores (s). License issued in Caddo. Priest: Jarney.

414. JOSEPH GARCIE (x)
MARIE POMPOSE RAMBIN (x)
30 June 1838. 0 bans.
Groom: major and legitimate son of deceased François Garcie and Marie Nolsem of Caddo Parish. Bride: minor and legitimate daughter of Michel Rambin and Fany? Baulieu. License issued in Caddo Parish. Witnesses: Aimé Mauro (s); Gregoire Ybarbe (s); Cesaire Flores (s). Priest: Jarney. [cf. Reg. 8.]

415. MAXIMIN VERCHER (x)
MARIE CELINA FREDIEU (s)
6 July 1838. 2 Bans.
Groom: major and legitimate son of deceased A. Belony

Vercher and Marie Orezite Gallien of this parish. Bride: minor and legitimate daughter of Honoré Fredieu and Suzanne Plaisance, also of this parish. Witnesses: Adonis Isidore Pantaléon (s); Pierre Ternier (s); François J. Levasseur (s). Priest: Jarney. License dated 30 June 1838. [cf. Reg. 8.]

416. JEAN BAPTISTE AUGUSTIN (x)
MARIE MANON (x)
25 July 1838. 0 bans.
Groom: major son of Marie Françoise. Bride: major daughter of Catherine. All are free people of color and residents of this parish. Witnesses: Rev. Français (s); Anatole Jarney (s) Michel Torbeyn (s). Officiating priest: V. Jarney.

417. IRA CARTER ASH (s)
AMANDA JOHONSTON (x)
28 July 1838. 3 bans.
Groom: native of Cheshire County, state of New Hampshire, major and legitimate son of Ebenezer Ash and Anna Watkins, actually residing now in this parish. Bride: widow of Pierre Baulos, major and legitimate daughter of Johon Johnston and Françoise Greneaux of this parish. License dated 10 July. Witnesses: Abel Sers (s); Jean Puiraveau (s); Charles Sers (s). Priest: Jarney. [cf. Reg. 8.]

418. OZMIN PIERRE DERBANNE (x)
ZULMA VERCHERE (x)
30 July 1838. 3 bans.
Groom: minor and legitimate son of deceased Pierre Derbanne and Marie Anastasie Davion, his wife. Bride: minor and legitimate daughter of Jaque Verchere and Rozine Gallien. All are residents of this parish. Witnesses: J. B. Neuville Gallien (s); Jules Trotraut (s/ J. Trotreau); Pierre La Cour (x). Priest: Jarney. [cf. Reg. 8.]

419. PIERRE MATHIEU BACKEN (s)
CELINE VASCOCU (s)
17 September 1838. 1 ban.
Groom: major and legitimate son of Gerard Backen and Marie Elisabeth Kenysemere (Kempemers?), native of the diocese of Malines in Belgium. Bride: minor and legitimate daughter of Jean Baptiste Vascocu and Aspasie Ries of this parish. Witnesses: Victor Bréchon (s); Louis Pietermans (s); John Davidson (s). Priest: Français.

420. JOSEPH PERROT
MARIE CÉPHALIDE BAUDRY
24 September 1838. 1 ban.

Groom: legitimate son of Joseph Perrot and Marie Olympe Fredieu. Bride: legitimate daughter of François Baudry and Marie Victoire St. André. All are residents of this parish. Witnesses: Victor Rachal (s); Seraphin Rachal (s); Landry Carsco (s). Priest: Jarney.

421. ATHANAZE BARTHELEMY LECOUR (x)
ADELE THIERY [QUERRY] (x)
9 November 1838
Groom: major son of Barthelemy Lecour[t] and Marie [blank -- should be Ursulle]. Bride: major daughter of Jean Baptiste [Pierre] Thierry and Françoise [blank -- should be Marie Rosalie Frederic]. The contractants have cohabited for several years. Witnesses: Jean Thomas Morgan (s/ J. Th. Morgan); Pierre Metoyer (s); Joseph Metoyer, Jr. (s). Priest: Jarney.

[Ed. note: For parental data on Jean Baptiste Athanase Barthelemy Le Court see his baptismal entry, Mills, *Natchitoches, 1729-1803*, No. 2932. For parental data on Marie Adeline "Adele" Thiery/Querry, see her baptismal entry, Mills, *Natchitoches, 1800-1826*, No. 157.]

422. DAVID DENISTON (s)
EUPHROSINE ASEMIA DRANGUET (s)
2 October 1838. 2 bans.
Groom: major son of Alexandre Deniston and Phanie Morelle, natives of Arlington County [*sic*], state of Carolina. Bride: minor and legitimate daughter of Benjamin Dranguet and Marie Celeste Tauzin. Witnesses: Theophile E. Tauzin (s); Benjamin Valcour Cortes (s); John Adolphe de Russy (s). Priest: Français.

[Ed. note: Neither North Carolina nor South Carolina has had a county named Arlington. There is a town called Arlington in Wilkes County, NC, but the entry clearly reads "Arlington *Comte*." The reference is probably to Darlington in South Carolina which was variously a county and a district.]

423. JEAN BAPTISTE DERBANNE (x)
DENISSE POISSOT (x)
23 October, 1838.
Ratification of civil marriage contracted two years earlier. Groom: major and legitimate son of Jean Baptiste Gasparite Derbanne and Pompose Plaisance. Bride: major and legitimate daughter of Paul Poissot and Marie Louise Anty. Witness: B. Despallier (x). Priest: Jarney.

424. JEAN BAPTISTE NEUVILLE GALLIEN (s)
MARIE EUPHEMIE GALLIEN (s)
20 November 1838. 0 bans.

Groom: minor son of Neuville Gallien and Eloïze Latier. Bride: daughter of Louis Manuel Gallien and Marie Françoise Thomassie. All are residents of this parish. Dispensation from impediment of consanguinity in second degree. Witnesses: Isaac Plaisance (s); Richard Woods (s); Louis Gallien (s). Priest: Français. [cf. Reg. 8.]

425. REMY McTIRE (x)
MARIE JULIEN GALLIEN (x)
18 Dec 1838. 0 bans.
Groom: major and legitimate son of deceased George McTire and Marie Louise Mayou. Bride: minor and legitimate daughter of Neuville Gallien and Marie Heloïze Lattier. All are residents of this parish. Witnesses: Jacques Vercher (s); Luc Poché (s); Ludger Langlois (s). Priest: Jarney. [cf. Reg. 8.]

426. JOSEPH ANTONIO IBARBO (x)
MARIA ANTONIA HERRERA (x)
20 December 1838. 0 bans.
Groom: major and legitimate son of Joseph Ibarbo and Maria Carle. Bride: daughter of Maria Ruis. All are residents of this parish. Dispensation from the prohibition of marriage during a forbidden period of Church calendar. Witnesses: Francisco Ibarbo (x); Anastasio Barrela (x); Jean Langoria (x). Priest: Français.

427. AUGUSTIN PRUDANS METOYER (s)
FLORENTINE CONANT (s)
8 January 1839.
Groom: minor and legitimate son of Jean Baptiste Metoyer and Suzanne Anty. Bride: minor and legitimate daughter of Florentin Conand and deceased Marie Louise Metoyer. All are free people of color and residents of this parish. Dispensation granted from impediment of consanguinity in second degree and from the announcement of bans. Witnesses: Joseph Augustin Metoyer (s); Joseph Metoyer, *fils* (s); Louis Morin (s). Priest: Jarney. [cf. Reg. 8.]

428. VINCENT (CAUBARREAUX) CABARUS (s)
MARIE DOLORES (x)
15 January 1839. 0 bans.
Groom: major and legitimate son of Pierre Cabarus and Margueritte Lavie. Bride: daughter of Ignatia Dolores. All are residents of this parish. Witnesses: Honoré Fredieu (s); Antoine Fredieu (s); Manuel Derbanne (s). Groom signed as Veincent Canbarreux. Priest: Français. [cf. Reg. 8.]

429. LOUIS GALLIEN (s)
MARIE AZELIE LATTIER (x)
15 January 1839
Groom: minor and legitimate son of Noël Gallien and Marie Françoise Lattier. Bride: minor and legitimate daughter of deceased Joseph Lattier and Marie Adeline Gallien. Dispensation from impediment of consanguinity in second degree and from announcement of 3 bans. Witnesses: Firmin Lattier (s); Jean Baptiste Neuville Gallien (s); Sévère Lattier (s). Priest: Jarney. [cf. Reg. 8.]

430. THOMAS A. MORGAN (s)
AZELIE BROSSET (s)
22 January 1839. 0 bans.
Groom: major son of Raphaelle Morgan and M.ie Shirlitiff. Bride: minor daughter of Athanasse Brosset and Celeste Baudoin. All are residents of this parish. Ceremony at Rivière aux Cannes residence of Philippe Brosset. Witnesses: Elisė Julien Rachal (s/ Elysee J. Rachal); Victor Julien Rachal (s); Oliver Brosset (s). Priest: Français. [cf. Reg. 8.]

431. PIERRE TERNIER (s)
BARBE AZELIE FREDIEU (s)
5 March 1839. 0 bans.
Groom: major and legitimate son of Pierre Ternier and Marie Rozeline Gainié. Bride: minor and legitimate daughter of Honoré Fredieu and Suzanne Plaisance. All are residents of this parish. Witnesses: Jean Louis Perrot (s); Henry F. Trichel (s); B. Olivier Rouquier (s). Priest: Jarney. [cf. Reg. 8.]

432. JEAN JOSEPH ALVAREZ DARIO (x)
MARIA APPOLLONIA DE L'INCARNATION ALEMONE (BARRERO) (x)
10 March 1839. 3 bans.
Groom: son of Bazile Alvares and Jeanne Savaldo (Palvado?). Bride: daughter of Philippe Barrero and Jeanne Gertrude Alemane. Witnesses: Paul Cassanova (s/ Paul Cazenave); Manuel Estrade (x); Joseph Aucle Sanchez (s). Priest: Français. [cf. Reg. 8.]

[Ed. note: Groom is identified in marginal notation as Jean Joseph Alvarez and in text of both the original and the recorded copy as Jean Joseph Alvarez Dario. The bride is identified in text of both original and the copy and in the margin of the copy by her mother's surname, Alemane, and not by the surname of her father, Barrero.]

433. ADOUT BASQUES (x)
MARIE CLARISSE CHOLETTE [CHELETTRE] (x)
9 March 1839. 0 bans.

Groom: major and legitimate son of Mariano Basques and Conceptione Morina. Bride: daughter of Arzene Cholette. Parties have already lived together for several years. Witnesses: Athanase La Cerda (s); Athanase Troquillio (s); Luc Poché (s). Priest: Jarney.

434. THOMAS BASQUES (x)
MARIE PROCELLA (x)
9 March 1839. 0 bans.
Groom: major and legitimate son of Mariano Basques and Conceptione Morina. Bride: minor and legitimate daughter of Leonire? Procella and Marie Padia. Witnesses: Athanase La Cerda (s); Athanase Troquillio (s); Luc Poché (s). Priest: Jarney.

435. JEAN BAPTISTE BONETTE
CATHERINE CHOLETTE
9 March 1839. 0 bans.
Groom: major and legitimate son of Jean Baptiste Bonette and Euphrosine Deny. Bride: major and legitimate daughter of Pierre Cholette and Julia La Violette. Witness: Athanaze La Cerda (s); Athanasio Troquillio (s); Luc Poché (s). Priest: Jarney.

436. GABINE LOUCOUBICHE
MARIE CELINE
9 April 1839
Couple has already been living together for several years. Witnesses: Emmanuel Laffitte; Charles Rambin; Lestan Rambin. Priest: Jarney.

437. ABLIN BROSSET (x)
CELINA LENOIR (x)
15 March 1839. 0 bans.
Groom: major son of Pierre Brosset and Marie Louise Le Cour[t]. Bride: minor and legitimate daughter of Antoine Lenoir and Marie Deneige Derbanne. All are residents of this parish. Witnesses: Tranquillin Le Comte (s); Edouard Murphy (s); Pierre Ternier (s). Priest: Jarney.

438. JEAN VICTOR L'HERISSON (s)
MADELEINE VASCOCU (s)
15 April 1839. 2 bans.
Groom: major son of Dominique L'Herison and Francise Laborde, native of Mauvizanie, department of Gers, France. Bride: minor daughter of Jean Baptiste André Vascocu and Marie Faustine Cherino. All are residents of this parish. Witnesses: Victor Bréchon (s); Antoine Grillet (s); Antoine St? Vigne (s). Priest: Français.

439. GILBERT LACOUR (s)
AURELIA PETRONIE LACOUR (s)
22 April 1839. 0 bans.
Groom: minor and legitimate son of Gilbert Lacour and Hélène Geofriant. Bride: minor and legitimate daughter of Leandre Lacour and Marie Louise Gillard. All are residents of the parish of Rapides. Married at home of Mr. Leandre Lacour after obtaining license from the judge of Rapides parish and after dispensation from impediment of consanguinity in second degree. Witnesses: Bret Lacour (s); Jean Baptiste Gillard (s); Joseph Gillard (s). Priest: Français.
[cf. Reg. 8.]

440. RICHARD WOODS (s)
MARIE CLEMENTINE RACHAL (x)
24 April 1839. 2 bans.
Groom: major son of Richard Woods and Rebeca Willson, natives of Kentucky. Bride: minor daughter of Manuel Rachal and Marie Lise La Cour, residents of this parish. Witnesses: Vallery Gainnié (s); Victor Rachal (s); Louis Gallien (s). Priest: Français.

441. BERESFORD JOHN CARR (s)
MARIE ANNE ADELE CORTEZ (s)
7 May 1839. 1 ban.
Groom: major and legitimate son of deceased Johon Charles Carr and Henriette Rouquier. Bride: minor and legitimate daughter of deceased Jean Cortez and Marie Josephine Marcelete Rouquier. All are residents of this parish. Dispensation from impediment of consanguinity in second degree. Witnesses: Patrick Barry (s); Aaron H. Pierson (s); Siereon E. Carr (s/ C.E. Carr). Priest: Jarney.

442. JEAN SIMON (x)
MARIE JEANNE CORDOVA (x)
29 April 1839
Groom: major and legitimate son of Charles Simon and Marie Vicente Peres. Bride: minor and legitimate daughter of Charles Cordovant and Marie Procella. Witnesses: Noël Condet (s); Noël Mézière (x); Joseph Mézières (x). Priest: Jarney.

443. ISAAC GOURINAT (s)
HELOISE VASCOCU (s)
14 May 1839. 3 bans.
Groom: major and legitimate son of Pierre Gourinate and Rose Derbanne. Bride: minor and legitimate daughter of deceased Louis Vascocu and Celeste Rice. All are residents of this parish. Witnesses: Victor Bréchon (s); P. Mathieu Backen (s); Louis Clerval (s). Priest: Jarney.

444. WILLIAM FLEURY (s)
MARIE NATALIE BUARD (s)
10 June 1839. 0 bans.
Groom: major son of Paul Aimé Fleury and Clara Yong. Bride: daughter of Jean Baptiste Buard and Marie Aspasie Bossier, residents of this parish. Witnesses: P. Evariste Bossier (s); J. Victor Bossier (s). Bride signed as Nathalie Buard. Priest: Français. [cf. Reg. 8.]

445. PIERRE EVARISTE BOSSIER (s)
MATHILDE BLAIR (s)
10 July 1839
Ratification of civil marriage contracted 24 December 1837. Witnesses: Ambroise Lecomte (s); J. Victor Bossier (s). Priest: Jarney. [cf. Reg. 8.]

446. ALFRED JEAN GEORGE HUBNER (s)
MARIE CELINA LEVASSEUR (s)
19 August 1839. 1 ban.
Groom: major and legitimate son of Jean George Hubner and Eliza Gaetz. Bride: major and legitimate daughter of Jean François Levasseur and Marie Françoise Trichell. All are residents of this parish. Witnesses: Theophile E. Tauzin (s); Ambroise Sompayrac (s); Marcelin Tauzin (s); A. L. Deblieux (s). Priest: Français. [cf. Reg. 8.]

447. JOSEPH GAUTIER (s)
MARIE ADELIZE MORANTINE (s)
7 August 1839. 0 bans.
Groom: major and legitimate son of Pierre Gautier and Marie Bernelot. Bride: major and legitimate daughter of Jean Baptiste Morantin and deceased Marie Euphrosine Frederic. All are residents of this parish. Witnesses: Laurent Lacoste (s); François Dhuont (s/ Drohon); Jean François Jarry (s). Priest: Jarney. [cf. Reg. 8.]

448. ELISÉE JULIEN RACHAL (s)
FELONISE DEJEAN (s)
8 August 1839. 3 bans.
Groom: major and legitimate son of Julien Rachal and Malinie Lavespère. Bride: major and legitimate daughter of Jean Baptiste Dejean and Marie Geothier of the parish of St. Landry des Oppelousas. Witnesses: John B. Charleville (s); Armand Lacour (s); Joseph Maximin Compère (s). Priest: Jarney. [cf. Reg. 8.]

449. JOSEPH MARCOLLI (s)
ELMINA HANZELMAN (x)
10 September 1839. 1 ban.
Groom: major and legitimate son of Laurent Marcolli and Pascoalina Roguelli, natives of Canton Tozin [Ticino] in Switzerland. Bride: major and legitimate daughter of Charles Hanzelman, both natives of Germany. The spouses are now residents of this parish.

450. NICOLAS (COLIN) DE BLANC (s)
THEODOZIA GILLARD (s)
10 September 1839. 0 bans.
Groom: minor and legitimate son of deceased Joseph De Blanc and Margueritte La Cour. Bride: minor and legitimate daughter of Jean Baptiste Gillard and Cecile La Cour. All are residents of the parish of Rapides. License issued in Rapides; dispensation granted from impediment of consanguinity in second degree. Witnesses: Bret La Cour (s); Joseph Gillard (s); Appolinaire Baillio (s). Priest: Jarney.

451. LEANDRE LA COUR (s)
MARIE ZOË DE BLANC (s)
16 September 1839. 0 bans.
Groom: major and legitimate son of Leandre La Cour and Marie Louise Gillard. Bride: major and legitimate daughter of Charles Dorsino De Blanc and Marie Eugenie Poché. License issued in Rapides; dispensation granted from impediment of consanguinity in third degree. Witnesses: Jean Baptiste Cezer? (Auger?) Gillard (s); Nicolas De Blanc (s); Numa Gillard (s). Priest: Jarney.

452. SIMON DE SOTO (s)
PHELONISE TESSIER (x)
28 September 1839. 0 bans.
Groom: major and legitimate son of deceased Joseph Antoine Marcel De Soto and Marianne Baillot. Bride: major and legitimate daughter of Pierre Tessier and Madeleine Cidre. Witnesses: Victor Bossier (s); Auguste Fauvelle (x); Chrisostomé Vascocu (s). Priest: Jarney.

453. ANTOINE ST. VIGNE (s)
CELIMENE LAFFITTE (x)
2 October 1839. 3 bans.
Groom: major and legitimate son of Louis St. Vigne and Jeanne Marie Pougeot of this parish. Bride: minor and legitimate daughter of Louis Laffitte and Marie Antoinette Flores, also of this parish. Witnesses: Victor L'herisson (s); Auguste Fauvelle (s); Philippe Denis? (s). Priest: Jarney.

454. JOSEPH LEROUX (s)
MARIE HENRIETTE RACHAL (s)
30 April 1839. 3 bans.
Groom: major son of Jean Baptiste Leroux and Marie Louise Hurseaux. Bride: minor daughter of Solastie Rachal and Marie Louise St. André of the parish of Natchitoches. Witnesses: Syriac Rachal (s/ L. G. Cyriaque Rachal); Charles François Benoist (s); Vallery Gaiennié (s). Priest: Français. [cf. Reg. 8.]

455. GILBERT GILLARD (s)
AZELIE CECILE LA COUR (s)
3 June 1839. 0 bans.
Groom: minor and legitimate son of Joseph Gillard and Petronie La Cour. Bride: minor and legitimate daughter of Gilbert La Cour and Héleine Geoffriant. All reside in Rapides Parish, Dispensation for third degree consanguinity. Witnesses: Gilbert La Cour, Jr. (s); Leandre La Cour, Jr. (s); Colin La Cour (s). Priest: Français. [cf. Reg. 8.]

456. JAMES MOORE (s)
LYDIA ECTOR [HECTOR?]
16 July 1839. 0 bans.
Groom: major son of James More and Heleine McLaskee. Bride: minor daughter of James Ector and Pauly Ustry. All are from this parish of Natchitoches; license issued at Natchitoches 6 July. Witnesses: Manuel Hernandez (x); Joseph Mortinau (s/ Jh. Martineau); J. S. M. Perry (s). Priest: Français. [cf. Reg. 8.]

457. JEAN BAPTISTE PLAISANCE (s)
ELISA RENOY (s)
16 December 1839. 1 ban.
Groom: major and legitimate son of Jean Baptiste Plaisance and Marie Joseph Palvado. Bride: minor daughter of Epron Renoy and Rose Massipe. Dispensation from prohibition against marriage during forbidden period of church calendar. Witnesses: Marcelin Tauzin (s); Edouard Orlando Blanchard (s); Tranquillin Lecomte (s). Priests: Jarney and Français.

458. BENJAMIN GRAPPE (s)
EMELIA VASCOCU (s)
6 January 1840. 2 bans.
Groom: minor son of Jean Pierre Grappe and Felicité Perrot. Bride: minor daughter of Vital Vascocu and Felicité Sorelle. Witnesses: François Fermin Rachal (s); Jean Baptiste Perrot (s); Jean Baptiste Grappe. Priest: Français.

459. JOSEPH METOYER (s)
LODOISKA LLORENS (s)
30 January 1840. 3 bans.
Groom: major and legitimate son of Joseph Metoyer and Pelagie Le Cour[t]. Bride: minor and legitimate daughter of Manuel Llorens and Arsene Anty. Witnesses: Seraphin Llorens (s); Bernard Dauphin (s); Florival Metoyer (s); Firmin Christophe (s). Priest: Français.

460. JEAN BAPTISTE BOSSIER (x)
MARIE LOUISE ORPHILIE LA RENAUDIÈRE (x)
6 January 1840. 3 bans.
Groom: widower in first nuptials of Marie Aurore Gonin, major son of Soulange Bossier and Eleonore Hymel. Bride: major and legitimate daughter of Jean Baptiste La Renaudière and Françoise Beaudoin. All are residents of this parish. Witnesses: Louis Derbanne (s); Louis Emmanuel Gallien (s); Eleuther Brosset (s). Priest: Français.

461. STEPHAN GRANT (s)
MARIE CELINA ARMAND (s)
6 February 1840. 3 bans.
Groom: major and legitimate son of Stephen Grant and Marie Rose Sidec. Bride: minor and legitimate daughter of Jean Baptiste Armand and Louise Adelaīde Noffrey. All are residents of this parish. Witnesses: Edouard Armand (s); Joseph Rachal (s); François Hubert Frederic (s). Priest: Jarney.

462. BARDET ASHTON TERRELL (s)
MARIANNE BLUDWORTH (s)
6 February 1840. 0 bans.
Groom: captain-quartermaster in the United States Army, lawful son of George Hunter Terrell and Hannah Butler Ashton. Bride: lawful daughter of James Bludworth and Marie Aimé Rouquier. Witnesses: E. O. Blanchard (s); Colonel Many; Laiut. [Lieut.] Barba (s/ P. N.? Barbour). Priest: Français. [cf. Reg. 8.]

463. SILVER DELOUCHE (s)
MARIE LISE DELOUCHE (s)
13 February 1840. 1 ban.
Groom: major and legitimate son of deceased John Louis Delouche and Marie Heloīze Dupre. Bride: minor and legitimate daughter of Pierre Derbanne and Felicité Paumier. Dispensation from impediment of consanguinity in second degree. Witnesses: John B. Charleville (s); François Chaler (s); Français Lattier, Jr. (s). Priest: Jarney.

464. JEAN LOUIS PERROT (s)
MARIE HELOÏSE FREDERICK (s)
30 March 1840. 0 bans.
Groom: major and legitimate son of Jean Chrisostomé Perrot and Marie Louise Salvant, widower of Marie Odisse Ternier. Bride: major daughter of François Frederick and Felicité Lavespère, widow of Edouard Plaisance. Witnesses: C. E. Greneaux (s); Severin Trichell (s); Pierre Ternier (s). Groom signed as J^{n}. Ls. Perot, bride as Eloise Frederic. Priest: Français. [cf. Reg. 8.]

465. ALEXANDRE DEBLIEUX (s)
MARIE MARZÉLINE SOMPAYRAC (s)
2 May 1840. 1 ban.
Groom: legitimate son of Alexander Louis Deblieux and Euphrosine Tauzin. Bride: legitimate daughter of Ambroise Sompayrac and Josephine Briant. All are residents of this parish. Witnesses: Hubner (s); P. A. Morse (s); R. Castanedo (s); T. E. Tauzin (s); C. E. Sompayrac (s). Priest: P. Chaudy.

466. PIERRE ADOLPHE LAFARGUE (s)
MARIE ZEPHERINE MICHEL ZORICHE (s)
7 May 1840. 0 bans.
Groom: native of Othez, department of Basse-Pyrenées, France, legitimate son of Arnould Lafargue and of Marie Hengar. Bride: legitimate daughter of Pierre Michel Zoriche and Adelle Rachal. Witnesses: Joseph Leroux (s); Henry Daron de las Mountagnes (s); Oscar Roubieu (s). Priest: Chaudy. [cf. Reg. 8.]

467. ATHANAZE TRUQUILLIO
MARIA [DE LA] SERDA
18 May 1840. 0 bans.
Groom: legitimate son of Gasinto Truquillo and Maria Ramona Savaille, native of Sn. Luis de Potosi, Mexico, and now living in this parish. Bride: legitimate daughter of Athanasio Serda and Maria l'infans Symes, native of Nakodoche, Texas, also living now in this parish. Witnesses: François Davion (x); Gosé Morion [José Morin] (x); I. R. Plaisance (s). Priest: Chaudy. [cf. Reg. 8.]

468. J. VALCOUR METOYER (s)
MARIE EUPHROSIE SARPY (s)
11 June 1840. 3 bans.
Groom: legitimate son of Maxille Metoyer and Aspasie Anty. Bride: legitimate daughter of Jerome Sarpy and Marie Adelle Metoyer. Dispensation from impediment of consanguinity in third and fourth degrees. Witnesses: Jerome Sarpy (s); H. O^{ve}. Deronce (s); J. B^{te}.

Metoyer, *fils* Aug^{tin} (s); Louis Morin (s). Priest: P. J. Doutreluigne. [cf. Reg. 8.]

469.
(472)* FRANÇOIS LATTIER, JR. (s)
MARIE ELISA RACHALE (s)
29 June 1840. 2 bans.
Groom: widower in first nuptials of Marie Plaisance and in second of Adelaïde Deloye [Delouche]. Bride: legitimate daughter of Cyprien Rachal and Marie Azelie Rachal. Witnesses: Cyprien Rachal (s); P. E. Frederic (s); Amedée Rachal (s); E. D. Rachal (s): Melice Anty (s); Joseph Rachal (s); John B. Charleville (s). Priest: P. J. Doutreluigne.

470.
(469)* JEROME MESSI (s)
MARIE AGLAË ESSOURD PANTALEON (s)
2 July 1840. 3 bans.
Groom: legitimate son of Antoine Messi and Chaterine Endemini. Bride: legitimate daughter of Eusepe Essourd *dit* Pańtaleon and Marie Aimée Baccocu [Vascocu]. Witnesses: F^{s}. Negreverni (s); J^{h}. Marcolli (s); Sev. Trichel (s). Priest: Doutreluigne. [cf. Reg. 8.]

471.
(470)* WILLIAM DONOVAN
MARIE C. NORISSE
25 July 1840.
Ratification of marriage contracted in Texas 10 October 1836. Groom: son of Amos Donovan and Marie Thomson of Rapides. Bride: daughter of Nathaniel Norrisse and June [Jeanne] Poirier. Priest: Doutreluigne.

472.
(471)* MIGUEL MARIA BASQUEZ
MARIA DOROTEA CORTES
11 August 1840. 0 bans.
Ratification of marriage contracted civilly. The contractant [female] is ill. Witnesses: Ignace Villegar (s); Joseph Miró; Clement Cortes (s). Priest: T. Alabau. [cf. Reg. 8.]

473. CLEMENT CORTES
MARIE JULIANE PEREZ
11 August 1840. 0 bans.
Ratification of civil marriage [date illegible]. Witnesses: Ignace Villegar and Joseph Miró. Priest: Alabau. [cf. Req. 8.]

474. JOSEPH FECOND AGUSTERA
MARIE DES ANGES TOBAL
11 August 1840. 0 bans.
Bride is widow of Macedonio Permonio. Witnesses:

----

*These four entries in Register 12 are numbered out of sequence. The first number shown for each represents the order in which they appear. The number in parentheses represents the number given to them in the register.

Clement Cortés and Joseph Miró. Priest: T. Alabau. [cf. Reg. 8.]

475. LUC POCHÉ (s)
MARIE ASELINA BROSSET (x)
1 September 1840. 2 bans.
Groom: legitimate son of François Pauché and Celeste Chainot. Bride: legitimate daughter of Pierre Brosset and Marie Le Cour[t]. All are residents of this parish. Witnesses: J. B. C. Rachal (s); J. Knight (s); Isaac Plaisance (s); Gallien (s). Priest: Giustiniani. [cf. Reg. 8.]

476. ELEUTHER BROSSET (s)
ELOIDE NEUVILLE GALLIEN (x)
17 September 1840. 2 bans.
Groom: legitimate and major son of Philippe Brosset and Marie Breuvelle. Bride: minor and legitimate daughter of Neuville Gallien and Eloide Baptiste Laquait [Marie Eloïse Lattier]. All are residents of this parish. Married at home of Neuville Gallien. Witnesses: J. Knight (s); J. B. Gallien (s); J. B. Morantine (s); Luc Poché (s); J. P. Gauthier (s); Marin C. Brosset (s). Priest: Giustiniani. [cf. Reg. 8.]

477. ARTHUR CHALER (s)
MARIE HENRIETTE ANTY (s)
24 September 1840. 3 bans.
Groom: minor and legitimate son of Ursin Chaler and Margherita Chaveau? (Charreau?). Bride: Widow of Clement Rachal. All are residents of this parish. Witnesses: F. Lattier (s); P. E. Frederic (s); Villere Rachal (s); L. M. (A?) Rachal (s). Priest: Guistiniani. [cf. Reg. 8.]

478. VICTOR LE BRUN [DAGOBERT]
DAMASE DORTOLAN (s)
29 October 1840
Groom: son of Susette Grap, a free woman of color. Bride: minor and legitimate [*sic*] daughter of Remond Dortoland and Magdalaine Perot. Dispensation from impediment of consanguinity in third degree. Witnesses: François Bertil Trichel (s); Alexis Le Brun (x). Priest: Guistiniani.

[Ed. note: Groom's nameis given in text as Victor Le Brun; in the cleric's copy of his signature, the name is written as Victor Le Brun DORTOLAND, with the last name being smeared. In the marginal notation he appears as Victor Le Brun Dortoland. However, the Reg. 12 entry is not the original and the copied signature and marginal notation err. The *dit* of the Le Bruns *de couleur* and their white father was

Dagobert. See, for example, Mills, *Natchitoches, 1800-1826*, Nos. 735, 1194, and 2617.

With regard to the inferred marriage of Remond d'Ortoland, white, to his cousin Magdeleine Perot, a free woman of color, see editorial note accompanying No. 391 of the present volume.]

479. CHARLES NERESTAN ROQUES, JR. (s)
MARIE ANAÏSE METOYER (s)
8 November 1840. 3 bans.
Groom: legitimate and minor son of Charles Nerestan Roques and Marie Pompose Metoyer. Bride: minor and legitimate daughter of Maxile Metoyer and Marie Aspasie Anty. Married at chapel on Isle Breuville, after dispensation from impediment of consanguinity in second degree. Witnesses: C. N. Roques (s); J. B. Metoyer, *fils* Aug^{tin} (s); B^{d} Dauphin. [cf. Reg. 8.]

[Ed. note: According to the request for dispensation submitted for this couple by Father Guistiniani, Charles and Marie Anaïse were already married by a civil judge and sought ratification of that marriage. See Rev. Joseph Guistiani to Bishop Antoine Blanc, 15 October 1840, New Orleans Papers, University of Notre Dame Archives, Notre Dame, Indiana.]

480. VICTOR POISSOT (x)
MARIE LOLETTE FREDERIC (x)
9 November 1840
Groom: legitimate son of Paul Poissot and Marie Louise Anty. Bride: legitimate daughter of François Frederic and Felicité Lavespère. Witnesses: Gabriel Perot (s). Pr Frederic (s). Priest: Guistiniani. [cf. Reg. 8.]

481. AMBROISE CHASTAN DOMINIQUE METOYER (x)
MARIE OSINE LABAUME (x)
23 November 1840. 3 bans.
Groom: legitimate and major son of deceased Dominique Metoyer and Marie Margherite Le Conte. Bride: minor daughter of Valere Labaume and Osine David. All are [free people of color and] residents of this parish. Witnesses: E. Dupré (s); C. N. Roques (s); G. Herriman (s); Jh. A^{tin} Metoyer (s). Priest: Guistiniani.

482. JOSEPH NUMA DEBLIEUX (s)
MARIE HELOÏSE TREZZINI (s)
6 January 1841. 1 ban.
Groom: legitimate and major son of Alexandre Louis Deblieux and Marie Euprosine Tauzin. Bride: legitimate and minor daughter of Jean Baptiste Trezzini and

Artemise Chamard. All are residents of this parish. Dispensation from impediment of consanguinity in third degree. Witnesses: A. L. Deblieux (s); J. B. Trezzini (s); C. E. Greneaux (s); J. B. Breda (s); N. (W?) Canotte (s); Narcisse Prudhomme (s). Priest: Guistiniani.

483. MAXIMIN METOYER (s)
CELINA METOYER (x)
9 January 1841. 3 bans.
Groom: major and legitimate son of Maxile Metoyer and Aspasi Anty. Bride: legitimate and minor daughter of Joseph Metoyer and Pelagie Le Cour[t]. Dispensation from impediment of consanguinity in third degree. Witnesses: Bernard Dauphin; Durent G. Herriman; F. Florival Metoyer. Priest: R. Pascual.

[Ed. note: The original of the above entry is not to be found in either Reg. 8 or Reg. 12. The entry from which this abstract was made (that in Reg. 12) is only a copy.]

484. JUAN BAUTISTA MANSOLA (x)
MARIA ADELINA PEREYROT (x)
13 January 1841. 3 bans.
Witnesses: H. T. Trichel (s); M. T. Handy (s). Priest: Alabau. [cf. Reg. 8.]

[Ed. note: Original entry in Reg. 8 spells bride's name Pereyro.]

485. FREDERIC MONTIER (s)
MARIE AIMÉE VASCOCU (s)
27 January 1841. 3 bans.
Groom: legitimate son of deceased Bernard Montier and deceased Anne Elisabeth Courchere, native of Bollegne in Normandie, France. Bride: legitimate and minor daughter of J. B. Andrée Vascocu and Marie Faustine Cheriny. Witnesses: V. T. L'Herisson (s); Joseph Dellro [Del Rio] (s); Gautier (s). Priest: R. Pascual.

[Ed. note: The original of the above entry is not to be found in either Reg. 8 or Reg. 12.]

486. FLORIVAL METOYER (s)
M[ARIE] T[HÉRÈSE] ASPASIE PRUDHOMME (s)
3 February 1841. 3 bans.
Groom: legitimate and minor son of Jean Baptiste Augustin Metoyer and Marie Susette Anty. Bride: minor daughter of Mr. J. B. Prudhomme and Marie Pompose. All are free people of color [with exception of bride's father] and residents of this parish. Witnesses: Prudhomme, *fils* (s); J. B^{te}. Metoyer *fils* Aug^{tin}. (s); N^{s}. Charles Leroy (s); Aug^{te}. Metoyer (s); F. Conant (s); C. N. Roques (s); L. Figuera (s); F. Dauphin (s);

Severin Prudhomme [fmc] (s); A. P. Metoyer (s). Priest: Guistiniani.

[Ed. note: For a more complete name for the bride see her baptismal entry in Reg. 6, 3 November 1826, baptism of Marie Thérèse, "petite Mulatresse de 3 anos," born of Marie Pompos, slave of Mr. J. B. Prudhomme.]

487. FRANÇOIS BERNARD DAUPHINE (s)
MARIE BARBE MELUISSINE METOYER (s)
4 February 1841. 3 bans.
Groom: major son of François Dominique Dauphin and deceased Marie Olive Clementine Chaulotte. Bride: legitimate and minor daughter of Jean Baptiste Augustine Metoyer and Marie Susette Anty. All are [free people of color] and residents of this parish. Witnesses: J. B^{te}. Metoyer, *fils* Aug^{tin} (s); C. N. Roques (s); Prudhomme, *fils* (s); F. Conant (s); N. P. Metoyer (s); Aug^{te}. Metoyer (s); A. P. Metoyer (s); N^{s}. Charles Leroy (s). Priest: Guistiniani.

488. URSIN DERBANNE (x)
MADAME HELENA PEROT JARREAUX (s)
15 February 1841. 3 bans.
Groom: legitimate son of Jean Baptiste Derbanne and Marcelite Dupré. Bride: legitimate daughter of Jean Jarreaux and Lucile Tournoir. Witnesses: Gasparite La Cour (s); J. Knight (s); A^{ne}. B^{my}. Rachal (s). Priest: R. Pascual.

489. JACOB KNIGHT (s)
CLESELIA RACHAL (s)
18 February 1841. 2 bans.
Groom: legitimate son of deceased Guillom [William] Knight and deceased Catherine Rose. Bride: legitimate and minor daughter of deceased Manuel Rachal and deceased Lise La Cour. Witnesses: J? Goulain (s); F. Lattier (s); Elysée J. Rachal (s); J. B. C. Rachal (s); G. Lacour, *fils* (s). Priest: Pascual.

490. THOMAS J. HICKMAN (s)
J? EMMA GAIENNIE (s)
22 February 1841. 1 ban.
Groom: lawful son of Mr. William Hickman and Mary Webster. Bride: Lawful daughter of François Gaiennié and Louise Désirée Lalande Ferrière. Dispensation from impediment resulting from difference in faiths. Witnesses: Vve. Frç^{ois} Gaiennié (s); B^{min}. Metoyer (s); John H. Ransdell (s); P. T. Hickman (s); Valery Gaiennié (s). Priest: Pascual.

491. WILLIAM MIDDLETON (s)
MARIE DELPHINE DERBANNE (x)
20 February 1841.
Groom: son of Isaac S (J?) Middleton and Ann Werley. Bride: legitimate daughter of Jean Baptiste Derbanne and Marie Merceli Dupres. Dispensation from impediment arising from difference in faiths. Witnesses: Victor Rachal (s); A^{ne}. B^{my}. Rachal (s); L. M. Titus (s); A. Bey (s). Priest: Pascual.

492. NORBERT LESTAGE (s)
ELMINA LANGLOIS (s)
23 February 1841. 1 ban.
Groom: legitimate son of Jean Baptiste Lestage and Leocadie Bossier. Bride: legitimate daughter of Lestan Langlois and Josephine Armand. Witnesses: François Hubert Frederic (s); J. Puiraveau (s); P. E. Frederic (s); J? R. Frederic (s); E. D. Rachal (s). Priest: Pascual.

493. JUAN JOSÉ MARTINEZ (x)
MARÍA TIBURCÍA GUERRERO (x)
23 February 1841. 3 bans.
Groom: widower of María Mauricia Chirino. Bride: single, minor, and legitimate daughter of Don Patricio Guerrero, deceased, and Doña María Rita Hernandéz. Witnesses: Francisco Treviño (s); José San Miguel (x) José Míro (s). Priest: Alabau.

494. PIERRE LARNAUDIÈRE (x)
MARIE TRANQUILLINE BOSSIER (s)
15 March 1841. 3 bans.
Groom: legitimate son of deceased Jean Baptiste Larnaudière and Marie Françoise Badoin. Bride: legitimate daughter of Jean Baptiste Bossier and Marie Aurore Gonin. Witnesses: Louis Larnaudière (x); Charles Melançon (x); Jean Baptiste Bossier (x). Priest: Pascual.

495. ANTONIO LAZARINO (x)
TIBURCIA CASTILLO (s)
28 March 1841. 3 bans.
Groom: legitimate son of Juan Lazarin and Josefa Bega. Bride: legitimate daughter of Polinario Castillo and Maria Giminez? Witnesses: D. F. Ja_s (s); I? Longori (x); A. Cortiñez (s). Priest: Alabau.

496. ANTOINE NERESTAN RACHAL (s)
MARIE ALPHONSINE LE COMTE (s)
24 April 1841. 3 bans.
Groom: son of Marie Françoise [and Jean Baptiste Louis Rachal]. Bride: daughter of Marie Marguerite [former slave of Ambroise Le Comte]. Witnesses: Manuel Couty (s);

Emil Colson (s); P. Dubreuil (s). Priest: Ant. Peneo.

[Ed. note: For fuller parental data on spouses see their baptismal entries in Mills, *Natchitoches, 1800-1826*, Nos. 1550 and 2511.]

497. JEROME SARPY, JR. (s)
MARIE SILVANIE ROQUES (s)
26 April 1841. 3 bans.
Groom: legitimate son of Mr. Jerome Sarpy and Dame Adèle Metoyer. Bride: legitimate daughter of Mr. Charles Nerestan Roques and Pompose Metoyer. All are free people of color and residents of this parish. Dispensation granted from impediment of consanguinity in third degree. Witnesses: Charles Nerestan Roques (s); Jerome Sarpy (s); N^{s}. Charles Leroy (s); Charles Nerestan Roques, Jr. (s); Manuel Llorens (s); N.P. Metoyer (s); Brd. Dauphin (s); F. Florival Metoyer (s). Priest: Guistiniani.

498. LEONARD TRICHEL (s)
ZELIA PEROT (s)
26 April 1841. 2 bans.
Groom: legitimate and major son of deceased Emanuel Trichel and Dame Emanuel Trichel. Bride: legitimate and minor daughter of deceased Faustin Perot and deceased Marie Celeste Bordelon. Witnesses: B. G. Fonteneaux (s); L. Perot (s); L. Trichel (s); Cyriaque Perot (s); L. Genty (s); E. B. Fleming (s); Jules Luvini (s); J. B. O. Roquier (s). Priest: Guistiniani. [cf. Reg. 8.]

499. JOSHUA BEAL JESSUP (s)
ADELAÏDE BASILISSE DRANGUET (s)
29 April 1841
Groom: lawful son of Jonathan Jessup and M^{e}. Green. Bride: lawful daughter of Benjamin Dranguet and Victoire Celeste Tauzin. Witnesses: J. P. Breda (s); A^{e} Chamard (s); J. B. Trezzini (s); D. H. Boullt (s); Chas. H. Penkerton? (s); B. St. Amans (s); Simon H. Peche (s); F. C. Tauzin (s). Priest: Guistiniani.

500. LOUIS NARCISSE PRUDHOMME, JR. (s)
MARIE CAROLINE NOIRET (s)
16 June 1841. 1 ban.
Groom: legitimate son of Louis Narcisse Prudhomme and Marie Thérese Elisabeth Metoyer. Bride: legitimate daughter of Charles Noyrit and Marie Azelie Lambre. Witnesses: Prudhomme, *fils* (s); Lestan Prudhomme (s); N^{s}. Charles Leroy (s); Phanor Prudhomme (s); C. Noyrit (s); Narcisse Prudhomme (s); Priest: Peneo.

501. ANTONIO PERINI (s)
LOUISE (ELIZA) RIVERS (s)
23 May 1841. 2 bans.
Groom: son of Severino Perrini and Maria Mad^{ne}. Gargole. Bride: daughter of William Rivers and Elizabeth Case. Both parties are residents of this parish. Witnesses: Adolfo Stucchi (s); Angelo Giannani? (s). Priest: Peneo.

[Ed. note: Bride signed as Louise Rivers and her names appears as such in the marginal notation. Text of entry gives her name as Eliza.]

502. ISAAC C. BIRTT (s)
ELOÏSA DAVID MATURIN (x)
6 July 1841. 2 bans.
Groom: son of Johon Birt and Peniy Manna?. Bride: daughter of Andrés David and Elisabeth David Maturin. Both parties are residents of this parish. Witnesses: Washington Bastian (s); Jno? H. Hazelton (s); Norbert Lestage (s); Poissot (s); Ls Chamard (s); G. H. Barlow (s); Fiorenne?. Priest: Guistiniani.

[Ed. note: Almost surely, the name of the bride's father is given in error. Her baptismal entry identifies her as "Marie Pelagie Eloise David . . . daughter of Elisabeth David and a father unknown" (see Mills, *Natchitoches, 1800-1826*, No. 24). Elisabeth was, herself, the daughter of Andres David, variously called Maturin David, a church *chantre* who died some fourteen months before the conception of Eloïse. See Mills, *Natchitoches, 1729-1803*, 957, 1035, 1604, 1726, and 3071.]

503. IPOLITE BORDELON (s)
EUGENIE MACTAIRE (x)
15 July 1841. 3 bans.
Groom: son of Ipolite Bordelon and Marie Terese Trichel. Bride: daughter of George Mactaire and Marie Mayou. All are residents of this parish. Witnesses: C. E. Greneaux (s); L. Marey (s); Leonard Trichel (s). Priest: Pascual.

504. JULES TROTREAU (s)
MARIE CEPHISE BROSSET (s)
26 July 1841. 3 bans.
Groom: major son of François Trotreaux and Henriette Richard. Bride: legitimate daughter of Philippe Brosset and Marie Thérèse Bruvelle, widow of Louis Solastie Rachal. Witnesses: Philippe Brosset (x); Séraphin Rachal (s); Marin C. Brosset (s); Mc Sompayrac (s); Louis Trouvat (s). Priest: Guistiniani.

505. SEVERIN TRICHEL (s)
MARCELITE LANDREAUX (s)
2 August 1841. 1 ban.
Groom: legitimate and major son of deceased Jean Baptiste Trichel and Marie Modeste Fonteneau. Bride: legitimate and minor daughter of deceased François Landreaux and Marie Marcelite Poissot. Witnesses: C. E. Greneaux (s); Jules Luvini (s); J. B. Rouquier (s); Henry Hertzog (s); J. Puiriveau (s); L. Perot (s); E. V. Deblieux (s); L. A. Buard (s). Priest: Guistiniani.

506. MARCELIN VERCHER (x)
MARIE HENRIETTE GALLIEN (x)
15 September 1841. 0 bans.
Groom: major son of Jaques Vercher and Marie Euprosine Gallien. Bride: major daughter of Louis Gallien and Marie Celeste Anty. Dispensation from impediment of consanguinity in second degree. Witnesses: L. Gallien (s); J. B. Gonain (s); Louis Vercher (s). Priest: Guistiniani.

507. HONORÉ FREDIEU (s)
MARIE LOUISE HANSELMANS (s)
12 October 1841. 1 ban.
Groom: major and legitimate son of Augustin Fredieu and Marie Jeanne Sorel, both deceased, widower in first nuptials of deceased Suzanne Plaisance. Bride: major and legitimate daughter of Conrad Hanselmans and Catherine Hanselmans, also deceased; widow in first nuptials of deceased Joseph Derbanne. All are residents of this parish. Witnesses: J. B. Lafon (s); Theophile Prudhomme (s); P. Amon (s); J. B. Rouquier (s); F. Lattier (s); Sev. Trichel (s); Lestan Prudhomme (s). Priest: Guistiniani.

508. JOSEPH FRANÇOIS METOYER (s)
MARGHERITE CECILE (x)
14 October 1841. 3 bans.
Groom: major son of François Metoyer and deceased Arthemise Dupart. Bride: minor and natural daughter of deceased Celeste Cecile. All are [free people of color and] residents of this parish. Witnesses: François Metoyer, Jr. (s); Emile Dupart (s); Joseph Metoyer (s); F. C. Christophe (s). Priest: Guistiniani

509. PETER HARTMAN (s)
VIRGINY CALAHAM (s)
21 October 1841. 3 bans.
Groom: son of John Hartman and Marian Conts. Bride: daughter of James Calahan and Mary Louisa Lefevre. Both parties have attained the required age for

marriage and are residents of this parish. Witnesses: V. Bréchon (s); B. V. Lefevre (s); Augustus Lefebre (s); John F. Payne (s); F. Montir? (s). Priest: N. Stehlé.

510. THEOPHILE TAUZIN (s)
MARY VICTOIRE DURST (s)
22 October 1841. 0 bans.
Groom: major and legitimate son of deceased Joseph Tauzin and deceased Marie Chamarge. Bride: legitimate and major daughter of Jacob Dust and Marie Charter? (widow of deceased Antoine Woolf). Witnesses: Narcisse Prudhomme (s); A. Lecomte (s). Priest: Guistiniani.

511. PIERRE SIMPHORIEN DERBANNE (s)
MARIE LOUISE DESIRÉ RACHAL (x)
3 November 1841. 0 bans.
Ratification of civil marriage contracted before "Lenard, Justice of the Peace of this parish." Groom: legitimate son of deceased Pierre Derbanne and Marie Tasite [Anastasie] Davion. Bride: legitimate daughter of Jean Baptiste Barthelemy Rachal and Marie Pelagie Breuville. Dispensation from impediment of consanguinity in third degree. Witnesses: V. P. Bossier (s); Manette Lestride [Manette Rachal, wife of Samuel Reid] (s); Marie Emelie Narcisse Rachal (s). Priest: Guistiniani.

[Ed. note: The bride's name is erroneously given in marginal notation as Marie Tasite Davion. Text of entry properly identifies Davion as mother of the groom and Rachal as the bride.]

512. VICENTE MICHELI (s)
BIBIANA CARMON (x)
19 November 1841. 1 ban.
Groom: legitimate son of Vicente Micheli and Marie Cortes (widower of deceased Marie Procella). Bride: legitimate daughter of Macedonia Carmon and Maria Angel Tobar. Witnesses: Antonio Menchaca (s); Maria Feliciana Sanches (x); J. T. Buvens (s). Priest: Guistiniani.

513. THOMAS JEFFERSON QUISENBERRY (s)
ZÉLINE GEOFFROIS (x)
13 January 1842. 3 bans.
Groom: son of Henry Quisenberry and Nerey Quisenberry. Bride: daughter of Louis Geoffrois and Maria Theresa Davion. Both parties have attained the required age for marriage. Dispensation granted for the impediment of different faiths. Witnesses: Athanase Ely (s); Cyriaque Perot (s); Nicolas Furlong (s); Priest: N. Stehlé.

514. FRANÇOIS DES POIRIER (x)
MARIE LOUISE VALENTIN (x)
14 October 1841. 0 bans.
Groom: legitimate son of Jean Baptiste Poirier and Elisabeth Davion. Bride: legitimate daughter of Joseph Valentin and Marie Thérèse Prudhomme. Legitimation of the following children: Marie Elisabeth, Joseph, Marie Zelia, Marie Chaterine, Marie Jeane Olina, Louise, Marie Laisa Selvina. Witnesses: Samuel Norris (s); A. Maesro (Moreau?) (s); Ives Moreno (s). Priest: Pascual.

[Ed. note: The original of this entry is not to be found in this Register 12 or in Register 8. The "signatures" on the above entry represent the cleric's copy of the original signatures. The second witness is undoubtedly the same An. Moreau who witnessed, that same day, the other Poirier-Valentin marriage. See entry 517 below.]

515. AUGUSTE DORESTAN METOYER (s)
SERAPHINE LLORENS (x)
11 November? 1841. 3 bans.
Groom: major and legitimate son of Pierre Metoyer and Henriette Cloutier. Bride: minor and legitimate daughter of Séraphin Llorens and Aspasie Metoyer. Married at Isle Brevelle chapel after dispensation from impediment of consanguinity in third degree. Witnesses: N. P. Metoyer (s). J. Valcour Metoyer (s); B$^{r.d}$ Dauphin (s); C. N. Roques, *fils* (s); J. L. Metoyer (s); F. C. Christophe (s); Suzanne Llorens (s); Arcine Llorens (s). Priest: Stehlé.

516. DENIS CASENEUVE (x)
MARIE JULIANA DE SOSA (x)
26 October 1841. 0 bans.
Groom: legitimate son of Michel Case Neuve and M. Risse. Bride: daughter of Miguel Sosa and Maria Antonia y Barbo. Witnesses: Andrés M. Rambin (s); Marie Emée Case Neuve (s). Priest: Pascual.

517. URSIN POIRIER (x)
MARIE MAGDELENE VALENTIN (s)
14 October 1841. 0 bans.
Groom: legitimate son of François Poirier and Marie Thérèse [illegible]. Bride: legitimate daughter of Joseph Valentin and Marie Thérèse Prudhomme. Witness: F. Lattier (s); An. Moreau (s); Michel Lattier (s). Priest: Pascual.

518. FREDERIÇ E. FEARING (s)
FELICITE CHAMARD (s)
3 February 1842.

Groom: legitimate son of Martin Fearing and Abey Martin. Bride: legitimate and major daughter of André Chamard and Felicité Sociët. Dispensation from impediment of differing faiths. Witnesses: A. Chamard (s); Martin Fearing (s); B. St. Amans (s); L. G. De Russy (s); Abby M. Fearing (s); A. Chamard, Jr. (s); J. P. Breda (s); J. B. Jessup (s); J. W. A. De Russy (s); Ls. Chamard (s); ?. D. Martin? (s). Priest: Guistiniani.

519. SAMUEL S. SIMONS (s)
MARIE ANNE COMBS (s)
16 June 1842
Groom: legitimate and major son of deceased William Simons and deceased Bedah Simpy. Bride: legitimate and minor daughter of deceased Robert D? Coombs and Henriette Winter. Dispensation from impediment of differing faiths. Witnesses: B. B. Breazeale (s); R. M. Campbell (s); John Patton (s); Benj. Bullitt (s); Henriette Bossier (s); T. Torchson? (s); D. Hopkins (s); C. Coombs (s); P. Petrovic (s); H. M. Petrovic (s); S. Bossier (s). Priest: Guistiniani.

520. ARMAND BIOSSAT (s)
ABBY A. ALLEN (s)
8 February 1842.
Groom: minor son of Antoine Biossat and Marie Louise Rossignol. Bride: minor daughter of the late Noah H. Allen and the late Harriette Martin. Dispensation from impediment of differing faiths. Witnesses: Martin Fearing (s); S. W. H__?__ (s); L. G. De Russy, Jr. (s); Abby M. Fearing (s); Marie Louise Biossat (s); B. St. Amand (s); J. W. A. De Russy (s). Priest: Pascual.

521. MARTIN CHARLES HAURUT (s)
MARIE LUCE RACHAL (s)
19 March 1842
Groom: legitimate son of François Haurut and Marguerite Hugonin, native of France, department of Gironde. Bride: legitimate daughter of Ls. Barthelemy Rachal and Françoise Grillet, and a widow of Alexis Cloutier. Both parties are residents of this parish. Witnesses: Valery Gaiennié (s); A^{ne} B^{my} Rachal (s); J. B. Chopin (s); C. Bertrand (s). Priest: Guistiniani.

522. GUILLOM HOY (x)
LOUISE MAGDONELLE (x)
25 October 1842. 0 bans.
Groom: legitimate son of Guillom Hoy and Marianne Le Mêtre. Bride: legitimate daughter of Luc? Magdonnell and Nanette Olivier. Witnesses: Andres Mª Rambin (s): Marie Emée Caseneuve (s). Priest: Pascual.

523. EUSEVIO DAVIS (x)
MARIE ADELAÏDE DUBOIS (x)
24 October 1842. 0 bans.
Groom: legitimate son of John Davis and [blank -- possibly Nancy Harmon]. Bride: legitimate daughter of Zédoinne Dubois and Marie Antoinette Malige. License issued by Judge of Caddo Parish. Legitimation of three children: Joseph, Pierre Olivier, Marie Pompose. Witnesses: Andrés Rambin (s); Auguste Rambin (s). Priest: Pascual.

524. PIERRE PERIAC POIRIER (x)
CARMELITE PRUDHOME (x)
13 October 1841. 0 bans.
Groom: legitimate son of François Poirier and Marie Teresa Anastasia [no surname given]. Bride: legitimate daughter of Jean B. Prudhome and Maria Eusebia [no surname shown]. Witnesses: Nathaniel Norris (s); A. Moro (s); J. T. Norris (s); Louis Poirier (s). Priest: Pascual.

525. ONORE RAUBELO (x)
MARIE PELAGIE RECIA NORRIS (s)
15 October 1841. 0 bans.
Groom: legitimate son of Pierre Robelo and Marie Magdelene Prudhomme. Bride: legitimate daughter of Nathaniel Norris and Jeanne Poirier. Legitimation of children: Marie Cephalide, Augustin, Pierre Ceser. Witnesses: A. Mauro (s); J. T. Norris (s); Nathaniel Norris (s). Priest: R. Pascual.

526. YVES MORENO (s)
MARIE MARCELITE RACHAL (x)
14 October 1841. 0 bans.
Groom: legitimate son of Joseph Maria Moreno and Trinidad Balboa. Bride: daughter of François Rachal and Marie Poirier. Legitimation of one child, Marie Artemise. Witnesses: F^{s} Latier (s); A. Mauro (s); J. T. Norris (s).

527. CHARLES BERTRAND (s)
MARIE FLORENTINE RACHAL (s)
3 March 1842. 0 bans.
Groom: legitimate son of Charles Beninne Bertrand and Marie Jeanne Gaudrio. Bride: legitimate daughter of Louis [illegible] Rachal and Marie [illegible] St. André. Witnesses: Valery Gaiennie (s); J. B. Chopin (s); F^{s} Benoist (s); F^{s} Goulin (s).

528. JOSEPH VERGERE [VERCHER] (x)
MARIE ELMINA DENIS (x)
29 March 1842. 0 bans.
Groom: legitimate son of Jacque Verger and Marie

Frosine Gallien. Bride: legitimate daughter of Athanase Denis and Marie Modeste Bodoin. Witnesses: François Denis (x); Valsin Vergere (x); L. Gallien (s). Priest: Pascual.

529. THOMAS EDWARD DERUSSY (s)
MARIE AMELIE EULODIE ST. AMANS (s)
4 May 1842. 1 ban.
Groom: legitimate and minor son of Louis Gustave De Russy and deceased Elisabeth Claire Boerum. Bride: legitimate and minor daughter of Joseph Guillaume Bouvard de St. Amans and Marie Victoire Poissot. Witnesses: Louis G. De Russy (s); B. St. Amans (s); Lewis G. De Russy, Jr. (s); F. Warksmut? (s); T. McConnell (s); William De Russy (s). Amans B^{d}. St. Amans. Priest: Guistiniani.

530. SIBOIRE PEROT (s)
MARIE EMELIE RACHAL (s)
30 May 1842. 1 ban.
Groom: legitimate son of J. Baptiste Perot and Marie Felicité Trichel. Bride: minor and legitimate daughter of Narcisse Rachal and Marie Louise Desiré Rachal. All are residents of this parish. Witnesses: C. E. Greneaux (s); H^{re}. Fredieu (s); E. B. Fleming (s); J. B. Perot (s); J. B. O. Rouquier (s); Isaac Plaisance (s). Priest: Guistiniani.

531. JEAN BAPTISTE OSCAR DUBREUIL (s)
MARIE CELINA RACHAL (s)
27 June 1842. 3 bans.
Groom: son of Louis Dubreuil and Julia Talon. Bride: legitimate and minor daughter of Jean Baptiste l'Espalier Rachal and Marie Susanne Metoyer. All are free people of color and residents of this parish. Witnesses: J^{n}. B^{te}. Rachal (s); J^{h}. A^{tin}. Metoyer (s); F. C. Christophe (s); Aug. D^{tant}. Metoyer (s); St. Cir Metoyer (s); T^{e}. L. P. Murphy (s). Priest: [no signature; entry is recorded in handwriting of Guistiniani.]

532. JEAN BAPTISTE CHOPIN (s)
JULIA BENOIST (s)
18 July 1842. 2 bans.
Groom: legitimate and major son of Antoine Chopin and Marie Thérèse Everard, native of Jouaignes, department of l'Aisne, France. Bride: legitimate and minor daughter of Charles François Benoist and Susette Rachal. Witnesses: Ch. F^{s}. Benoist (s); Suzette Benoist (s); M^{c}. Sompayrac (s); Jules Sompayrac (s); Victor Rachal (s); J. B. C. Rachal (s); B^{noits}. Laurents (s). Priest: Guistiniani.

533. PATRICK SHELLY (s)
MARGARET HEWITT (s)
16 August 1842. 0 bans.
Groom: lawful son of William Shelly and Ann Ryan. Bride: widow of J. Fallon, lawful daughter of Johon Hawyett and Ann Matcalf. Witnesses: John Shely (s); Edward Brenan? (s); John Patterson (s); John Molony (s); William Def[undecipherable] (s); James Fallon (s); Catherine M[undecipherable]; Anne Brady (s). Priest: Guistiniani.

[Ed. note: Bride's name is written in text as Margherite Hawyett; she signed as Margaret Hewitt.]

534. JOSEPH EDOUARD ARMAND (s)
MARIE SUSETTE RACHAL (s)
26 July 1842. 2 bans.
Groom: legitimate son of Jean B. Armand, Sr., and deceased Marie Catherine Frederique. Bride: daughter of Louis Barthelemi Rachal and Marie Louise Chelete. Dispensation from impediment of consanguinity in third degree. Witnesses: Villere Rachal (s); Amedée Rachal (s); J. Lattier (s); I? Rachal (s); N. Lestage (s). Priest: Pascual.

535. RAMON VILLAREAL (s)
MARIA GUADALUPE CORTES (s)
13 October 1842. 0 bans.
Groom: legitimate son of Domingo Villa Real and Maria Olaya Gonzalez. Bride: legitimate daughter of Juan Cortes and Maria Cruz Rodriguez. Witnesses: José Miró (x); José San Miguel (x). Priest: Pascual.

536. ANSELMO CORTINAS (x)
MARIA RAFAEL (x)
21 May 1842. 0 bans.
Groom: son of Ignacio Cortinas and Ursina Carmon. Bride: daughter of Maria Sabina Diaz. Witnesses: José Bastian Basquez (s); Guerra (s); Manuel Ybarbo (s). Priest: Pascual.

537. ENCARNACION PROCELLA (x)
MARIA ANTONIA (x)
22 May 1842. 0 bans.
Groom: legitimate son of Manuel Procella and Maria Apolinaria Egene [Eguis]. Bride: daughter of Maria Fernandez. Witnesses: Andres Gonzalez (x); Miguel Torres (x); Phelipe Procella (x). Priest: Pascual.

538. ANDRES ISAAC ESSER (x)
MARIE GENEVIÈVE ADLÉE (x)
27 May 1842. 0 bans.
Groom: legitimate son of Cristian Esser and Adelaïde

Rambin. Bride: legitimate daughter of Jean B. Timotee Adlée and Marie Thérese Denege Prudhomme. Dispensation from impediment of consanguinity in third degree. Witnesses: François Rambin (s); Auguste Fauvelle (s); D. Chamard (s). Priest: Pascual.

539. LOUIS GASPARD DERBANNE (x)
MARCELITE JOSEPHINE ARMAND (s)
3 November 1842. 3 bans.
Groom: legitimate son of J. B. Gaspard Derbanne and Marie Elenne Breuvelle. Bride: legitimate daughter of J. B. Armand and Marie Chatherine Frederic. Witnesses: Fr. Lattier (s); Victor Rachal (s); J. B[t] Armant, *fils* (s); Villeré Rachal (s); J. B[te] Frederic (s). Priest: Pascual.

540. GEORGE W. DUNCAN (s)
MARIE FELICITÉE SANGLIER (s)
10? November 1842.
Groom: son of Alexander Duncan and Françoise [no last name]. Bride: daughter of Mele South[er]land [free woman of color]. Dispensation for disparity of faith. Witnesses: W. P. [illegible--possibly Vaughn] (s); Adolph Sompayrac (s); W. S. Wals (s). Priest: Pascual.

541. EMILE DUPART (s)
ANRIETTE CLOUTIER (x)
14 November 1842. 3 bans.
Groom: son of Charles Dupart and Victoire Mulon. Bride: daughter of Derotée [Monet]. [Both parties are free people of color.] Witnesses: C. N. Roques, *fils* (s); Peeter Veleumans (s). Priest: Pascual.

542. JEAN BENJAMIN MORANTIN (s)
MARIE SUZETTE MICHEL (s)
14 November 1842. 2 bans.
Groom: legitimate son of J. Morantine and Marie Eufroisen Frederic. Bride: legitimate daughter of Pierre Michel Zorich and Marie Adel Rachal. Witnesses: L. A. Charleville (s); Aristide Mery (s). Priest: Pascual.

543. JOSEPH MÉZIERE (s)
CELESTINE DAVID (x)
26 December 1842. 0 bans.
Groom: son of Phanie Mézière. Bride: daughter of Felicité Castro. Witnesses: Noël Mézieres (s); Lebrun Dagobert (s). Priest: R. Pascual.

[Ed. note: The Register 12 entry from which this abstract was taken is ostensibly the original. Yet it appears to err with its identification of the surname of bride's mother. All other Davids *de couleur* in the parish were children of Felicité GRAPPE by Sr. Louis

David. No Felicité CASTRO has yet been found in the parish in this era. On the population schedule of the 1850 federal census, Celestine David and husband appear as No. 694; No. 695 is his mother Fanny De Mézières; No. 696 is Marie Claire GRAPPE Silvie (a proven daughter of Felicité GRAPPE, together with Marie Louise David Le Baume, another proven daughter of Felicité GRAPPE. No. 693 is the widow François GRAPPE. No Castros are in that part of the parish. At the 1848 baptism of Marie Angela, born to Celestine David and Joseph (De) Mezières (Reg. 10, p. 93) the godmother was Susette GRAPPE, sister of Felicité. All points considered, the editor concludes that the surname of the bride's mother in the foregoing marriage record should be GRAPPE rather than Castro.]

544. JOSEPH RACHAL (s)
SEBERINE LE COUR (x)
2 January 1843.
Groom: legitimate son of Pierre Rachal and Perine Dominique Metoyer. Bride: legitimate daughter of Vallery Le Cour[t] and Marie Sylvie Dominique Metoyer. All are free people of color and residents of this parish. Witnesses: Emile Colson (s); Ambroise Metoyer (s); Thanasite Metoyer (s); O^{me}. D^{que}. Metoyer (s). Dispensation from impediment of consanguinity in second degree. Priest: Guistiniani.

545. AMBROISE BERNARDIN THEOPHILE SOMPAYRAC (s)
MARIE ROSELINE DEBLIEUX (s)
4 January 1843. 1 ban.
Groom: widower of Armeline Sompayrac, legitimate son of Ambroise Sompayrac and Josephine Briant. Bride: legitimate and minor daughter of Alexandre Louis Deblieux and Marie Eufrasine Tausin. All are residents of this parish. Witnesses: A. Sompaÿrac (s); A. L. Deblieux (s); M^{c}. Sompayrac (s); J. B. Trezzini (s); P. A. Morse (s); D. Deniston (s); F. C. Tauzin (s); Ale. Prudhomme (s); T. E. Tauzin (s); Virginia Morse (s); Briant Sompayrac (s); C. E. Carr (s); Desirée Bossier (s). Priest: Guistiniani.

546. GERVAIS FONTENOT (s)
PRUDENCE ADLÉ (s)
1[illegible] January 1843. 1 ban.
Groom: legitimate son of Louis Fontenot and deceased Brigitte Gradenigo. Bride: legitimate and minor daughter of Baptiste Adlé and deceased Marie Denise Dolé. Witnesses: B^{te}. Adlé (s); J. B^{te}. Cloutier (s); Suzette Cloutier (s); J. B. Lafon (s); Valery Gaiennié (s); Prudhomme, *fils* (s); Heloïse Metoyer (s); Amanda Gaiennie (s). Priest: Guistiniani.

546(bis) GUILMA PEROT (s)
JULIA PLAISANCE (s)
15 January 1849
Groom: legitimate son of François Perot and Manette Fonteneaux. Bride: legitimate daughter of Jean B. Plaisance and Marie Joseph Palvado. Dispensation from impediment of consanguinity in third degree. Witnesses: Marin C. Brosset (s); Mme. J. Bte Perot (s); Emérante Derbane (s). Priest: Pascual.

[Ed. note: This is an original document, on a loose sheet of paper, which has been inserted into the register (and filmed) at the wrong chronological point. A copy of this document appears as No. 660 of this register, dated 15 January 1849. On that original, the 9 is written in such a manner as to be misread as 3, hence its filing out of sequence by an unwary clerk.]

547. WILLIAM PATRICK REYBURN (s)
HENRIETTE SIBLEY (s)
17 January 1843.
Groom: legitimate son of James Reyburn and Mary Gullaen. Bride: widow of B. F. Chapman, daughter of John Sibley and Eulalie Malige. Witnesses: M. C. Dunn (s); Michael Boyce (s); E. O. Blanchard (s); H. H. Sibley (s); S. M. Hyams (s); Helene Kimball (s); R. A. Sibley (s). Dispensation from impediment resulting from disparity in faiths. Priest: Guistiniani.

548. NICOLAS KIFFER (s)
MARGUERITHE BOLLENDER (s)
25 January 1843
Groom: son of Nicolas Kiffer and Elisabeth Fual, widower of Magdeleine Schifler. Bride: legitimate daughter of François Bollender and Anne Veiss, widow of Jaque Brian. Both of the parties are French. Witnesses: Martiney Blanka (s); Ae Chamard (s). Priest: Guistiniani.

549. JACQUES LECOURT
MARIE ZÉLINE ANDRÉ RACHAL
20 May 1843.
Ratification of civil marriage contracted 14 months earlier. Witnesses: Joseph Augustin Metoyer; Severin Bodiaud; Saint-Cyr Metoyer. Priest: J. M. Hignard.

550. J. B. OLIVIER ROUQUIER (s)
EMELIE GENTY (s)
1 February 1843. 1 ban.
Groom: legitimate son of François Rouquier and deceased Elisabeth Buard. Bride: legitimate and minor

daughter of Louis Genty and Marie Delphine Poissot. Dispensation from impediment of consanguinity in third degree. Witnesses: E. O. Blanchard (s); Ale. (Ah?) Prudhomme (s); W. P. Morrow (s); P. Bludworth (s); Lestan Prudhomme (s); Narcisse Prudhomme, *fils* (s); F. B. Sherburne (s); A. Chategnier (s). Priest: Guistiniani.

551. FLORENTIN CONANT, JR. (s)
MARIE TERESINE CARLES (s)
9 February 1843. 3 bans.
Groom: legitimate son of Florentin Conan and of Marie Louise Metoyer. Bride: daughter of Rose Metoyer [and Dr. Jean André Zepherin Carles]. Dispensation from impediment of consanguinity in third degree. Witnesses: L. Figari (s); J. E. Roques (s); A. P. Metoyer (s). Priest: Pascual.

[Ed. note: For identity of the bride's father, see her baptismal registration dated 20 December 1826, unnumbered entry in Register 7.

552. FIRMIN CAPPELOT CRISTOPHE (s)
MARIE JULIA METOYER (s)
16? February 1843. 3 bans.
Groom: legitimate son of Firmin Cristophe and Marie Françoise Mayou. Bride: legitimate daughter of Jean B. Augustin Metoyer and Susete Anty. Witnesses: Severin Prudhomme (s); F. Florival Metoyer (s); François Forcel (x). Priest: Pascual.

553. TEOPHIL LOUIS METOYER (s)
ELINA METOYER (x)
23 February 1843. 3 bans.
Groom: legitimate son of deceased Jean Baptiste Louis Metoyer and Marie Susette Metoyer. Bride: legitimate daughter of deceased Joseph Metoyer and Marie Pelagie Le Curt. Dispensation from impediment of consanguinity in third degree. Witnesses: P[re]. Metoyer (s); Aug. D[tant]. Metoyer (s); Seraphin Llorens (s). Priest: Pascual.

554. CLEMENT ODUHIGG LAVESPERE (s)
MARIE FROISINE SUSETTE BROSSET (s)
26 March 1843. 0 bans.
Groom: legitimate son of Yler [Hilaire] Lavespère and Agatte Rachal; bride: legitimate daughter of Felipe Brosset and Marie Terese Breuvelle. Witnesses: Victor Rachal (s); J[s]. Trotreau (s); L. A. Rachal (s); H. B. Lavespère. Dispensation from impediment of consanguinity in third degree. Priest: Pascual.

555. (copy) CHARLES DORSINO DEBLANC (s)
MARIE ELISA DERBANNE (x)
18 April 1843. 2 bans.
Groom: legitimate son of Charles Dorsino Deblanc and Marie Eugenie Porche. Bride: legitimate daughter of Lastie Derbanne and Elenne Lemoine. Witnesses: C. F? Rachal (s); L. M. Titus (s); C[les]. D. De Blanc (s). Priest: Pascual.

556. JOSEPH XIMENES (s)
MARTINAS CADENA (x)
31 May 1843. 2 bans.
Groom: son of Domingo Zimenes and Joseph Gonzales. Bride: daughter of Francisco Cadena and Maria Juanna Bargas. Both parties are residents of this parish. Witnesses: Fran[co]. Ybarbo (s); Jas. Fallon (s); Francisco Ybalbo (x).

[Ed. note: There is no signature for the officiating minister, although the entry appears to be recorded in the hand of Guistiniani. The family name of the groom is spelled also as "Hymenes" in text.]

557. ANTONIO LACASAS (x)
LISE BREVELLE (x)
25 July 1843
Groom: son of deceased Antoine Lacasas and deceased Marie Louise Ardoin. Bride: daughter of deceased Baltasar Breuvelle and Marie Louise Masilde. Witnesses: Baltasar Breuvelle, Jr. (x). Priest: Guistiniani.

558. (copy) JUAN JOSÉ YBARBO (x)
MARIA ALFONSO FLORES (x)
17 May 1843.
Groom: legitimate son of Juan Josė Ybarbo and Maria Arcoria Garcia. Bride: legitimate daughter of Vital Flores and Getrudes Mora. Dispensation from impediment of consanguinity in third degree. Witnesses: Charles Rambin (x); Gregorio Ybarbo (s). Priest: Pascual.

559. (copy) MANUEL GUTIERREZ (s)
FROISINE POISSOT (x)
18 May 1843
Groom: widower of Isabel Mededin. Bride: widow of Michel Sac. Witnesses: Charles Rambin (x); Gregorio Ybarbo (s). Priest; Pascual.

560. (copy) GUILLOM BÉBÉ (x)
MARIA LUISA PROCELLA (x)
8 June 1843. 0 bans.
Groom: legitimate son of Guillom Bébé and Maria Bustamente. Bride: daughter of Maria Procella.

Witnesses: Ventura Guerra (s); Juan Maria Martinez (s); J. Vicente Michely (s). Priest: Pascual.

561. (copy) GUILLOM ARISON [WILLIAM HARRISON] (x)
MARIE CELINE BOLIEN (x)
14 June 1843. 0 bans.
Groom: legitimate son of John Arison and Maria Macfierson [MacPherson?]. Bride: legitimate daughter of Edouard Bolien and Marie Morin. Dispensation from impediment created by differing faiths. Witnesses: François Rambin (s); Em^{ell} Laphite (s). Priest: Pascual.

562. (copy) CIRIAQUE FLORES (s)
MARIE LOUISE INOCENTE ESSERT [HESSER] (s)
17 June 1843. 0 bans.
Groom: legitimate son of Pedro Crisostomé Flores and Marie Magdelene Laphite. Bride: legitimate daughter of Antoine Essert and Marie Louise Gaigné. Dispensation from impediment of consanguinity in the third degree. Witnesses: Ceser Flores (s); Pedro Flores (s); James Welche (s). Priest: Pascual.

[Ed. note: Bride's surname is also spelled Essedr in text.]

563. FRANÇOIS GRAPPE (x)
MARIE JULIENNE TRICHEL (x)
9 November 1843. 3 bans.
Groom: legitimate son of Jacques Grappe and Marie Rose La Serru [De la Cerda]. Bride: legitimate daughter of Simeon Trichele and Damassene Simon. [All, except groom's mother, are free people of color.] Ceremony at Campti. Witnesses: Gabriel Grappe (s); Antoine Poissot (x); Louis David (x); Eugene Dortolin (x). Priest: Mignard.

564. HENRY WHITE (s)
MRS. MARY McGOWN (x)
30 October 1843. 0 bans.
Groom: legitimate son of Andrew White and Elisabeth Byrnes, a native of Dublin, Ireland. Bride: legitimate daughter of James McGown and Mary Sheridan, a native of Edenderry, Ireland. Witnesses: Matthew O'Connor (s); James Fallon (s). Priest: Guistiniani.

565. VALERY GAIENNIÉ (s)
HELOISE METOYER (s)
27 January 1844. 1 ban.
Groom: legitimate son of François Gaiennié and Louise Desiré Lalande Ferrière. Bride: legitimate daughter of Benjamin Metoyer and Aurore Lambre. Witnesses: C. E. Greneaux (s); B. Metoyer, Sr? (Jr?) (s); F^{s} Archinard (s); V. Lambre (s); F. B. Sher-

burne (s). Priest: Pascual.

566. EDOUARD FLEMING (s)
JULIA BORDELON
30 January 1844. 1 ban.
Groom: legitimate son of deceased Barthelemy Fleming and Constance Fonteneau. Bride: legitimate daughter of Ipolite Bordelon and deceased Marie Dene Fonteneau. Dispensation from impediment of consanguinity in third degree. Witnesses: Michael Boyce (s); Jules Luvini (s); Alex Denniston (s); J. W. McDonald (s). Priest: Guistiniani.

567. J. G. CAMPBELL (s)
ADELINE SOMPAYRAC (s)
15 February 1844.
Groom: "The Honorable . . . Judge of this Parish, bachelor of age, not a member of the Catholic Church." Bride: "Catholic maiden under age, lawful daughter of Mr. Ambrose Sompayrac and Mrs. Josephine Briant of this parish." "The Honorable J. G. Campbell having satisfied to the requisitions of the Church provided in such as case, as consigned in the First Decree of the Fourth Provincial Council of Baltimore, of which he has taken cognisance," a dispensation has been given to the couple because of their differing faiths. Witnesses: Mc Sompayrac (s); P. A. Morse (s); V. Sompayrac (s); M. C. Dunn (s); A. Sompaÿrac (s); Briant Sompayrac (s); Alexander Deblieux (s). Priest: Guistiniani.

568. FRANCIS M. HARTMAN
MARY CATHERINE DOUGHERTY
18 February 1844
Witnesses: John D. Hartman; Mary Isham; Anna Hartman. Priest: Chartier.

569. (copy) PIERRE OSCAR CHALER (s)
CELINE ANTY (s)
19 February 1844. 3 bans.
Groom: legitimate son of deceased Ursin Chaler and Margherite Chauveau. Bride: legitimate daughter of deceased Ignace Anty and Marie Louise Lattier. Dispensation granted from impediment of consanguinity. Degree of relationship not given. Witnesses: T. Lattier (s); U. Chaler (s); Art Chaler (s). Priest; Guistiniani.

570 (copy) TEODORO QUINTERO (x)
MARIA JESUSA BARGAS (x)
22 November 1843. 0 bans.
Groom: widower of Maria Ignacia Rosales. Bride: daughter of Juan Bargas and Celeste Lonnes? Witnesses:

Juan Maria Martinez (x); Candido Sanchez (x); Vicente Micheli (x). Priest: Pascual.

571. (copy) ISAAC PERROT (x)
ARMELINE PHREDIEU [FREDERIC] (x)
8 September 1843. 0 bans.
Groom: legitimate son of Joseph Perrot and Marie Phredieu [Fredieu]. Bride: legitimate daughter of François Phredieu [Frederic] and Felicité Lavespère. Witnesses: Etienne Davion (s); Avit Davion (s); Antoine Fredieu (x). Priest: Pascual.

572. BENTURA GUERRA (s)
MARIA JESUSA CALDERON (s)
22 November 1843. 0 bans.
Groom: legitimate son of Don Alexandro Guerra and Doña Luzgarda Garcia. Bride: legitimate daughter of Juan José Calderon and Maria Nieves Curvela. Witnesses: Juan Maria Martinez (s); Candido Sanchez (x); Vicente Michely (s). Priest: Pascual.

*573. ANDRES BERMELLA (s)
MARIA BRIGIDA YBARBO (x)
20 February 1844. 0 bans.
Groom: widower of Juana Cadena. Bride: legitimate daughter of Manuel Ybarbo and Dna. Maria Getrudes Calderon. Witnesses: Fran.co Negrevernis (s); Ventura Guerra. Priest: Pascual.

*574. (copy) JUAN PRADO (x)
MARIE EMEE DORSINO RACHAL (x)
18 March 1844. 0 bans.
Groom: legitimate son of Martin Prado and Getrudes Soto. Bride: legitimate daughter of Dorsino Rachal and of Adel. License issued in Sabine Parish. Witnesses: Maximilien Arcia (x); Gillom Bébé (x). Priest: Pascual.

[Ed. note: Fr. Pascual makes an erroneous assumption regarding the marital status of the bride's parents. Fuller parental identity is provided in the baptismal entry of the bride's brother, Francois Ursin. (See Mills, *Natchitoches, 1800-1825*, No. 1272). The bride's mother, as a free woman of color, could not legally marry Rachal, who was her cousin but of French parentage. For the baptism of the bride's mother see *Ibid.*, No. 69.]

*575. (copy) JOSEPH BÉBÉ (x)
MARIA JUANA SEPULVEDA (x)
18 March 1844. 0 bans.
Groom: legitimate son of Gillom Bébé and Maria Josefa Charna. Bride: legitimate daughter of José Antonio Sepulveda and Maria Guadalupe Chabana. Witnesses: Maximilien

Arcia (x); Gillom Bébé (x). License issued in Sabine. Priest: Pascual.

576. VALCIN METOYER
LISE RACHAL
6 April 1844
Blessing of civil marriage performed 8 months earlier. Groom: legitimate son of Jean Baptiste Metoyer and Adelaide Rachal. Bride: legitimate daughter of Mission Rachal and Perine Metoyer. Witnesses: "I have not put the names of the witnesses since I do not recall their names." Priest: Mignard.

577. M. M. ROBINSON (s)
MARGUERITTE GAYOSO (s)
2 May 1844. 1 ban.
Groom: born in Virginia, major and legitimate son of deceased M. Robinson and Ane H. Nicolas, a non-Catholic who has met necessary qualifications for marriage in the church. Bride: minor and legitimate daughter of deceased Fernando Gayoso and the living Lodoïska Perez, a Catholic by birth. Witnesses: L. Gayoso (s); Henry Hertzog (s); P. A. Morse (s); J. C. Carr (s); J. G. Campbell (s); C. E. Carr (s); W. P. Reyburn (s); Fernando Geyoso (s); Adolphe Lemee (s). Priest: Mignard.

578. MICHEL BOYCE (s)
LUCINDA ROUBIEU (s)
[Day and month illegible] 1844
Groom: legitimate son of deceased Pierre [Peter] Boyce and Mme. Frances Gilbert. Bride: legitimate daughter of François Roubieu and Ozitte Rachal. Witnesses: L^{s}. Chevalier (s); S. D'Anglais (s); Ch^{s}. F. Benoist (s); W. P. Reyburn (s). Priest: Mignard.

579. JEAN BAPTISTE ANTY (s)
MARIE AGLAE RACHAL (x)
30 January 1844. 3 bans.
Groom: legitimate son of Ignace Anty and Marie Louise Lattier. Bride: legitimate daughter of Louis Barthelemy Rachal and of Marie Louise Cheletre. Witnesses: A^{n}. Chaler (s); F. Lattier (s); L. A.? Rachal (s). Priest: Mignard.

580. ATHANASE ELY (s)
MARIE CELINA PEROT (s)
29 June 1844. 1 ban
Groom: legitimate son of Celestin Ely and of deceased Celesie Triche. Bride: legitimate daughter of Jean Louis Perot and deceased Marie Arcise Ternier. Witnesses: Ciriaque Perot (s); Pierre Ternier (s); Sev. Trichel (s); J. L^{s}. Perot (s). Priest: [not shown].

----

*These four entries are omitted from the NSU film.

581. WILLIAM P. CANNON (s)
MARIE SUZETTE RACHAL (s)
21 January 1844. 0 bans.
Groom: legitimate son of Jean Cannon and Adeline Lesard [Layssard]. Bride: legitimate daughter of Manuel Ilaire Rachal and Felicie Emilie Rachal. Witnesses: J. B. Anty (s); F. C. Christoph (s); Ambroise A. Metoyer (s). Priest: Mignard.

[Ed. note: Although the record does not indicate the church in which the marriage ceremony took place, the presence of Metoyer and Christophe (his in-law) as official witnesses suggest that the event occurred at the Metoyer family chapel on Isle Brevelle (St. Augustine). This church was widely used by white families of the Isle in that era.]

582. FIRMIN LATTIER
VICTORINE RACHAL
30 April 1844. 3 bans.
Groom: major and legitimate son of François Lattier and Marie Chelettre. Bride: legitimate daughter of deceased Victor Rachal and Marie Henriette Armant. Witnesses and priest: [not shown].

583. PIERRE RACHAL (x)
MARIE ATANASIE LEMEL (x)
27 January 1844. 0 bans.
Groom: son of deceased Pierre Rachal and Perine Metoyer. Bride: daughter of Lemel and Marie N. Witnesses: Ambroise A. Métoyer (s); F. C. Christophe (s); William P. Cannon (s). Priest: Mignard.

584. PIERRE WALLACE (s)
SUZETTE LALLANDE (x)
27 May 1844
Ratification, at Campti chapel, of marriage contracted some fifteen days earlier. Witnesses: A^d Lauve (s); Athanasite Ely (s). Priest: Mignard.

585. JEAN MARCOLI (s)
AURORE MICHAMPS (s)
27 May 1844. 3 bans.
Groom: legitimate son of Laurent Marcoli and Pascaline Richelli. Bride: legitimate daughter of Jean Eugene Michamps and Catherine Miller. Witnesses: Alex Dennston (s); Jules Luvini (s); W. T. Handy (s); T. J. Flanner (s). Priest: Mignard.

586. FRANÇOIS FLORIVAL METOYER (s)
MARIE THÉRÈSE ROQUES (s)
4 June 1844
Groom: major and legitimate son of J. Baptiste Metoyer and Marie Susanne Anty. Bride: legitimate and

minor daughter of Charles Nerestan Roques and Marie Pompose Metoyer. All are free people of color and residents of this parish. Dispensation from impediment of consanguinity in second degree. Witnesses: Hypolyte Metoyer (s); H^{y} O^{ve} Deronce (s); Aug. D^{tant} Metoyer (s); N^{tant} P^{re} Metoyer (s); A. P. Metoyer (s); L. Figuera (s); F. C. Christophe (s). Priest: Guistiniani.

587. VICENTE IBARBO (x)
JULIANA MARTINEZ (x)
27 June 1844
Groom: legitimate son of deceased José Polonio Ibarbo and deceased Louciana Caro. Bride: legitimate daughter of deceased [Es]meregildo Martinez and Dario Castro. Witnesses: Fran^{co} Ibarbo (s); Joseph Ximines (s); Dionicio y Barbo (s). Priest: Guistiniani.

588. ISAAC PLAISANCE (s)
MARIE CHRISANTE PANTALEON (x)
17 July 1844. 0 bans.
Groom: widower of Marie Zeline Latier, legitimate son of Bertrand Plaisance and Marie Barbe Grillet. Bride: daughter of Eusebe Isour Pantaleon and deceased Marie Aimé Vascocu. Dispensation from impediment of consanguinity in third degree. Witnesses: C. E. Greneaux (s); H^{re} Fredieu (s). Priest: Guistiniani.

589. LUDGER LEVASSEUR (s)
MARIE LOUISE McTIER (s)
19 August 1844. 3 bans.
Groom: major and legitimate son of Emanuel Levasseur and deceased Josette Mercier. Bride: widow in first nuptials of deceased Ludger Langlois, major and legitimate daughter of George McTier and Marie Louise Mailloux. All are residents of this parish. Witnesses: C. E. Greneaux (s); Sev. Trichel (s); J. Freeman (s); L. G. De Russy, Jr. (s). Priest: Guistiniani.

590. (copy) ONOFRE FLORES (x)
MARIE ROBLO (x)
30 June 1844. 0 bans.
Groom: son of José Flores and Estefania Equix. Bride: legitimate daughter of Pierre Robló and Magdeleine Prudhomme. Witnesses: Lougier Deval (s); Pedro Flores (s); Hilaire Flores (s). Priest: Pascual.

591. (copy) VICTOR VALENTIN (x)
IRENE POIRIER (x)
15 July 1844. 0 bans.
Groom: legitimate son of Joseph Valentin and Marie Theresa Prudhomme. Bride: legitimate daughter of

Antoine Poirier and Marcellite Proveau. Witnesses: Nathaniel Norris (s); Samuel T. Norris (s); Joseph V. Norris (s). Priest: Pascual.

592. PIERRE LAPHITE (x)
(copy) MARIE CEPHALIDE ROBLÓ (x)
30 June 1844. 0 bans.
Groom: legitimate son of Ceser Laphite and Elizabeth Leten. Bride: legitimate daughter of Pierre Robló, Jr., and Marie Basile Grande. Witnesses: Joseph Laphite (s); Dionisio Flores (s); Pierre Robló (s). Priest: Pascual.

593. ANDRÉ BEY (s)
MARIE AURORE DUPRÉ (x)
19 November 1844. 0 bans.
Ratification of civil marriage. Groom: native of "Alsace, Strasbourg," son of Conrad Bey. Bride: legitimate daughter of Joseph Dupres and Marie Celina Rachal. W. L. Deslouches (s); Adolphe Rachal (s). Priest: Guistiniani.

594. LEWIS M. TITUS (s)
SEPHIRA DESLOUCHES (s)
19 November 1844. 0 bans.
Groom: native of Pensilvanie, major and legitimate son of Amos Titus and Christine Nongrilper (Nongrisser?). Bride: legitimate and minor daughter of J. Louis Delouche and Marie Eloïse Dupré, both deceased. Witnesses: U. Chaler (s); Julien Deslouches (s); C. E. Greneaux (s). Priest: Guistiniani.

595. JULES SOMPAYRAC (s)
CAROLINE TREZZINI (s)
21 January 1845. 1 ban.
Groom: major and legitimate son of Mark Sompayrac and deceased Zeline Cloutier. Bride: legitimate and minor daughter of J. B. Trezzini and Mme. Arthemise Chamard. Witnesses: A. Sompaÿrac (s); P. A. Morse (s); J. G. Campbell (s); A. L. Deblieux (s); A. B. Sompayrac (s); W. L. Tuomey (s); H. O. Haller (s); D. Denniston (s); Aphe Sompayrac (s); C. E. Greneaux (s). Priest: Guistiniani.

596. SIBOIRE PEROT (s)
MARIE ASELIE FREDIEU (s)
25 February 1845
Groom: legitimate son of J. Baptiste Perot and deceased Marie Felicité Trichel, widower in first nuptials of Emelie Rachal. Bride: legitimate daughter of Honoré Fredieu and deceased Marie Susanne Plesance. Dispensation from impediment of consanguinity in the fourth degree. Witnesses: Hre Fredieu (s); T. E.

Tauzin (s); Sev. Trichel (s). Priest: Guistiniani.

597. JOSEPH SMITH (s)
MARGARET MELONE (s)
6 February 1845. 0 bans.
Groom: son of James Smith and Elisabeth Plomage, a native of London. Bride: daughter of Joseph Jeremy Mellone and Catherine Tillebory?, native of County Cork, Ireland. Dispensation granted since the spouses are of different faiths. Witnesses: David Campbell (s); James McGraw? (s). Priest: Guistiniani.

[Ed. note: Bride's name is spelled Margherite Mallony in text. She signed crudely as Marget Molone.]

598. (copy) BENJAMIN BUILLET (s)
CELINE PEROT (s)
31 March 1845. 1 ban.
Groom: legitimate son of Benjamin Buillet and Marie Forguesson. Bride: legitimate daughter of Crisostomé Perot and Marie Susanne Rachal. Witnesses: John Colton (s); C. Rachal (s); W. H.? De Russy (s). Priest: Pascual.

599. MATIEU FEGUEN (s)
CATHERINE HOREN (x)
2 April 1845
Groom: legitimate son of Tomas Feguen and Catherine Henesi, a native of America. Bride: legitimate daughter of Tomas Horen and Catharine Roiff?, a native of Golwe [Galway, Ireland?]. Witnesses: R. Edwards (s); R. Kennedy (s). Priest: Pascual.

[Ed. note: Groom's name is given in marginal notation as THOMAS FEGUEN. He signed as M. Feguen. Bride's name is given in margin as Catharine HOTIEN.]

600. (copy) JOSÉ SANTOS (x)
FELIPA QUINTERO (x)
3 March 1845. 0 bans.
Groom: legitimate son of José Santos and Clotin Chenevert. Bride: legitimate duaghter of Teodoro Quintero and Conception Navarro Avila. Witnesses: Manuel Ybarbo (x); José Maria Ybarbo (x); Teodoro Quintero (x). Priest: Pascual.

601. LORENZO DE SOTO (s)
MARIE OPHELIA RACHAL (s)
7 January 1845. 0 bans.
Groom: legitimate son of Jean B. De Soto and Feliciane Rodriguez. Bride: legitimate daughter of Jean B. Julien Rachal and Roseline Derbanne. Witnesses: Teophile Prudhomme (s); Firmin Desoto (s); Nicolas Keiffer (s). Priest: Pascual.

602. (copy) FIRMIN LATTIER (s)
VICTORINE RACHAL (s)
29 May 1845.
Groom: legitimate son of François Lattier and Marie Chelette. Bride: legitimate daughter of Victor Rachal and Marie Anrriette Armand. Dispensation from impediment of consanguinity in fourth degree. Witness: Louis Gaspar Derbanne (x). Priest: Pascual.

603. (copy) CLEMENT LORENZE [LLORENS] (s)
ELISA DUPART (x)
2 June 1845
Groom: legitimate son of Serafin Lorenze and Marie Aspasie Metoyer. Bride: legitimate daughter of Emil Dupart and Marie Rose Baltasar. Dispensation from impediment of consanguinity in fourth degree. Witnesses: François Gassion Metoyer (s); Augustin Metoyer (x). Priest: Pascual.

604. AMEDÉE RACHAL (s)
MARIE HENRIETTE POISSOT (x)
19 June 1845. 3 bans.
Groom: legitimate and major son of deceased Cyprien Rachal and deceased Aspasie Rachal. Bride: legitimate and minor daughter of Remis Poissot and Zeline Agaisse. All are residents of this parish. Witnesses: P. O. Chaler (s); V. R? Rachal (s); J. R? Frederic (s); F. Vienne (s). Priest: Guistiniani.

605. (copy) JOSEPH MOREAU (x)
MARIE ROSELIA RACHAL (x)
21 August 1845. 1 ban.
Groom: son of Joseph Moreau and deceased Julie Laviolette. Bride: minor and legitimate daughter of J. Baptiste Rachal and Almire Breuville. Both are residents of this parish. Witnesses: Onesime Chelette (s); Marie Tranquilline Bossier (x); Louis Larnodiere (x). Priest: Guistiniani.

[Ed. note: Although the above entry infers a marriage between the bride's parents, no record of that marriage has been found. The baptismal entry for Marie Roselia identifies her as the "natural infant of Amyre," with no reference to a father. See Reg. 10, No. 28-1833. The presence of entries on this [illegible] *sonnes de couleur et esclaves*, may be attributed to the Indian ancestry of Amire's mother.]

606. [Ed. note: This number appears to have been omitted in the recording of entries within Register 12.]

607. CAYETANO PADIA (x)
PETRA CARAVAJAL
30 August 1845. 1 ban.
Groom: legitimate son of Felipe Padia and Juana Baron. Bride: daughter of Josepa Torres. Witnesses: Bernardo Maricolli (s); José Mora (s); Ignacio Recío (x). Priest: Pascual.

[Ed. note: Marginal notation for the entry reads "Padia & TORRES." However, text identifies bride as "Petra CARAVAJAL, daughter of Josepa [note feminine ending of this name] TORRES." Where the signature of the bride should appear, directly under that of groom, there is found "Josepa Torrez X her mark." The signature or mark of Petra Caravajal does not appear at all. It would seem that in recording the bride's mark, the priest identified her by the name of her mother.]

608. AMBROISE ASINORE METOYER (s)
MARIE LILETTE SARPY (s)
14 October 1845. 1 ban.
Groom: legitimate son of Pierre Metoyer and Marie Deneige Metoyer. Bride: legitimate daughter of Jerome Sarpy and Marie Jeanne Metoyer. Dispensation from impediment of consanguinity in third degree. Witnesses: Jerome Sarpy (s); P[re]. Metoyer (s); F. Conant (s); A. P. Metoyer (s); C. N. Roques, Jr. (s); F. C. Christophe (s); F. Florival Metoyer (s). Priest: Guistiniani.

609. JOSÉ ALEXO DEL RIO (x)
MARIE ANISETTE OMBRERO (x)
25 October 1845.
Groom: son of deceased Felix Del Rio and Juanna Francisca Mansola. Bride: daughter of deceased Victoriano Ombrero and deceased Josepha Monguey. Witnesses: Antonio Vacca (x); Margil Garnac (x); Candelaria Martines (x). Priest: Guistiniani.

609a. (copy) CESER FLORES (s)
MARIE ANTOINETTE GRANDE (s)
14 October 1845
Groom: legitimate son of Pedro Flores and Marie Magdelene Laphite. Bride: legitimate daughter of Julien Grande and Maria Trinidad Flores. Dispenstion for impediment of consanguinity in second degree. License issued in De Soto Parish. Witnesses: Hilaire Flores (s); Andrés Rambin (s). Priest: Pascual.

610. (copy) CLEMENT LAFITTE (s)
MARIA CATARINA CORDOVA (x)
20 October 1845

Groom: legitimate son of Pierre B. Laphite and Essule Gaigné. Bride: legitimate daughter of Manuel Cordova and Maria Equis. License issued in De Soto Parish. Witnesses: A. Moro (s); Em^{el}. Laphite (s); Neuville Rambin (x). Priest: Pascual.

611. CHARLES CHRISTOPHE (s)
MARIE AGNES CONAND (s)
18 November 1845. 2 bans.
Groom: legitimate son of Firmin Christophe and Marie Françoise Maillioux. Bride: legitimate daughter of Florentin Conand and Marie Louise Metoyer. Witnesses: F. Conant (s); Firmin Christophe (s); J. B^{te}. Metoyer, *fils* A^{tin}. Metoyer (s); F. C. Christophe (s). Priest: [not given].

612. ETIENNE DAVION (s)
MELISA OUALETTE (x)
27 November 1845. 1 ban.
Groom: legitimate son of Dominique Davion and Pelagie Gagné, widower of Celine Lafitte. Bride: legitimate daughter of Louis Oualette and Angele Gagné. Dispensation from impediment of consanguinity in second degree. Witnesses: Nicolas Furlong (s); J^{n}. L^{s}. Perot (s); Avit Davion (s); Victor Barberousse (s). Priest: Guistiniani.

613. (copy) THEODORE BUVENS (s)
ELIZABETH DENDY (s)
13 December 1845
Groom: legitimate son of Peter Buvans and deceased Elisabeth Gronl<u>ey?</u>. Bride: legitimate daughter of Thomas Jeferson Dendy and Marie Anne Jones. Witnesses: James Kelly (s); Henry Buvens (s). Priest: Guistiniani.

614. THEODORE J. MOÏSE (s)
MATHILDA VAUGHN (s)
18 December 1845
Groom: "widow[er] of Cecila his first wife, natives of South Caroline, not a member of the Catholic Church." Bride: legitimate daughter of Robert Vaughn and Mary Garner. Dispensation granted after groom satisfied the conditions for marriage in the Church. Witnesses: J. B. Lennard, Capt? (s); J. G. Campbell (s). Priest: Guistiniani.

615. (copy) NEILL McCLEAN (s)
NATIVITY TESSIER (s)
22 January 1846
Groom: native of Georgia, a non-Catholic, legitimate son of Lothland McClean and Sara McClean. Bride:

legitimate daughter of John Tessier and Pelagie Adlé. Groom has met the conditions for marriage within the Church. Witnesses: J. M. Tessier (s); John C. Patton (s). Priest: H. Figari.

616. LEWIS ACOSTA (x)
CESARIA BUSTAMENTE (x)
28 January 1846
Groom: native of Texas, son of Joseph Acosta and Mary Cruz. Bride: native of Texas, daughter of Manuel Bustamente and Mary Louisa Sanches. Witnesses: A. Laurents (s); Raphaela Martinez (x). Priest: Figari.

617. (copy) JOSEPH LEON TREMAUX (s)
MARIE CELINA MARION DE MONTILLY (s)
5 February 1846
Groom: legitimate son of deceased François Etienne Tremaux and Aimé Àdelaïde Lebrun. Bride: legitimate daughter of Victor Marion de Montilly and Francinne Anne l'Evêque, and widow in first nuptials of Louis Schmitt. Witnesses: P. A. Morse (s); V. Sompayrac (s); J. Lacoste (s); George Morse (s); E. Montilly (s). Priest: Guistiniani.

618. AMBROISE LECOMTE (s)
LOUISE VICTOIRE DESIRÉE SOMPAYRAC (s)
10 February 1846. 1 ban.
Groom: major and legitimate son of Jean Baptiste Lecomte and Dame Cephalide Lambre, widower in first nuptials of Julia Buard. Bride: major and legitimate daughter of Ambroise Sompayrac and Dame Josephine Briant, widower in first nuptials of Victor Bossier. Dispensation granted for impediment of affinity. Witnesses: A. Sompaÿrac (s); A. L. Deblieux (s); Phanor Prudhomme (s); J^{n}. Rogueol (s); P. A. Morse (s); V. Lambre (s); J. B^{te}. Cloutier (s); A. B. Sompayrac (s); Alexandre Deblieux (s); T. E. Tauzin (s); A^{phe}. Sompayrac (s); James Kelly (s); J. P.? Lambre (s); C. E. Sompayrac (s). Priest: Guistiniani.

619. (copy) ONESIME PLAISANCE (s)
MARIE EMMA PEROT (s)
18 January 1846. 2 bans.
Groom: son of Faustin Plaisance and Genevieve Almeïde Levasseur. Bride: daughter of François Perot and Marie Manette Fonteneau. Witnesses: M. T. Handy (s); F^{tin}. Plaisance (s); A? Hubner (s); L. Marey? (s). Priest: Figari.

620. ANTOINE BALZARETTI (s)
ADÈLE MICHAMPS (x)
12 March 1846. 1 ban.
Groom: legitimate son of Pierre Balzaretti and Anna Soldoti, native of Italy. Bride: legitimate daughter of Jean Eugene Michamps and Anna Catherine Müller. Witnesses: J^{n}. E^{gne} Michamps (s); F. Eugene Bossier (s); Aurellia Dugas (s); Théophile Bossier (s). Priest: Figari.

621. JULES BMY. BRETEL (s)
MARIE DENISE POISOT (x)
26 May 1846. 2 bans.
Groom: native of Cherbourg, department of La Manche, France, legitimate son of Luc Ermeland Bretel and Susanne Luce Lamour. Bride: widow of deceased Manuel Phonde, a resident of this parish, legitimate daughter of Paul Poissot and Marie Louise Anty. Witnesses: J. R. Frederic (s); G? Bossier (s); J. O. Rachal (s). Priest: Guistiniani.

622. CARLES GALLIEN (s)
AGNES AGLAË TOMASSI (x)
16 April 1846
Groom: legitimate son of Louis Gallien and Marie Celeste Anty. Bride: legitimate daughter of Jerome Thomassi and Marie Adeline Gallien. Witnesses: Adolphe Gallien (s); J. B. N. Gallien (s). Priest: Figari.

623. EMILE BELISAIRE CHEVALIER (s)
SUSANNE LLORENS (s)
18 June 1843. 2 bans.
Groom: natural son of Louis Chevalier and Fanny Chevalier. Bride: legitimate daughter of Manuel Llorens and Arsene Anty. All [with exception of groom's father] are free people of color. Witnesses: J^{n}. B^{te}. Metoyer, *fils* Aug^{tin} (s); J. B^{te}. Metoyer (s); F. Florival Metoyer (s); C. N. Roques, Jr. (s). Priest: Guistiniani.

624. PIERRE BROSSET
MARIE EMELIE RACHAL
16 April 1846
Groom: son of Athanase Brosset and Marie Celeste Badoin. Bride: daughter of Louis Julien Rachal and Marie Reine Thomassi. Priest: Figari.

625. FIRMIN JOSEPH LATTIER
MARIE EURANIE GALLIEN
16 April 1846.
Groom: son of Joseph Lattier and Marie Adeline Gallien

Bride: daughter of Louis Emanuel Gallien and Marie Françoise Thomassi. Priest: Figari.

626. JOHN DAVIS (s)
(copy) ELISABETH BUVENS (x)
29 April 1846
Groom: son of Archibald Davis and Lutha Curby. Bride: daughter of Peter Buvens and deceased Anna Elisabet Gronlus. Marriage performed "in the state of Texas." Witnesses: Petrus Buvens (s); P. M. Backen (s); F. G. Buvens (s). Priest: Figari.

627. RAYMONDO HIMENES (x)
BARBARA SANCHEZ (x)
23 May 1846
Groom: son of Francisco Himenes and Andeloisine? Sosa?. Bride: daughter of Ignatio Sanches and Anisetta Ombrera. Witnesses: Juan Ximenes (s); Carlo Garcia (s); Francisco Ximenes (x); Antonio Vacca (x). Priest: Guistiniani.

628. THEOPHILE BOSSIER
CLARA DUGAS
8 June 1846. 1 ban.
Groom: legitimate son of Cesaire Soulange Bossier and Marie Modeste Gonnin. Bride: legitimate daughter of deceased Pierre Dugas and Clarisse Milan. Both parties are residents of this parish. Witnesses: F. Eugène Bossier (s); L. J. Rouquier (s); T. E. Tauzin (s); C. E. Greneaux (s). Priest: Figari.

629. JOSEPH AMBROISE LANDREAUX (s)
(copy) MARIE MELISA PEROT 9s)
16 July 1846
Groom: major and legitimate son of François Landreau and Marcelite Poissot. Bride: legitimate and minor daughter of Crisostomé Perot and Suzette Rachal. Witnesses: Severin Trichel (s); François Vienne (s); B. Perot (s); Prudent Rachal (s); F. Rachal (s). Priest: Guistiniani.

630. VIENNE METOYER (s)
(copy) MELISINE RACHAL (x)
8 August 1846. 3 bans.
Groom: legitimate son of J. B. Dominique Metoyer and Adelaïde Rachal. Bride: legitimate daughter of Pierre Rachal and Perine Metoyer. All are free people of color and residents of this parish. Witnesses: F. C. Christophe (s); Emanuel Dupré (s). O. D^{que} Metoyer (s); B. Metoyer (s); T^{nte} Metoyer (s). Dispensation from impediment of consanguinity in second degree. Priest: Guistiniani.

631. TIMOTHÉE LACOSTE (s)
MARIE OLANDINE FORT (s)
1 September 1846. 1 ban.
Groom: legitimate son of Lorent Lacoste and Marie Emelie Chiasson. Bride: legitimate daughter of Andrée Fort and Marie Eleocadie Himel. Witnesses: J. A. Ducounau (s); L. J. Rouquier (s); T. E. Tauzin (s); J. B. O. Buard (s); [one illegible signature]. Priest: [not shown].

632. VICTOR RENOIS (s)
HELOÏSE MALIGE (s)
29 September 1846. 2 bans.
Groom: legitimate son of deceased Epron Renois and deceased Marie Rose Massip. Bride: legitimate daughter of deceased Noël Malige and Adelaïde Palvado. Both parties are residents of this parish. Witnesses: P. O. Rachal (s); Benjamin Lacase (s); Marin C. Brosset (s). Priest: Guistiniani.

633. LOUIS CASIMIR RACHAL
ZELINE LACOUR [LE COURT]
4 October 1846.
Groom: son of J. Baptiste Palier Rachal and Cesaire [Susanne] Metoyer. Bride: daughter of Barthelemy Lacour [Le Court] and Eulaïde [Adelaïde] Mariotte. Ratification of civil marriage. All are free people of color [except groom's father]. Witnesses: James Kelley; Valsin Metoyer (s). Priest: Guistiniani.

634. JACOB ELISÉE ROQUES (s)
MARGHERITE CELESTINE LAMATE (s)
26 December 1846. 1 ban.
Groom: legitimate and minor son of Charles Nerestan Roques and deceased Marie Pompose Metoyer. Bride: legitimate and minor daughter of Louis Lamate and Celestine Perot. All are free people of color. Witnesses: C. N. Roques (s); J^{n}. B^{te} Metoyer, *fils* Aug^{tin} (s); C. N. Roques, Jr. (s); N^{tant} P^{re} Metoyer (s); L^{s} Lamathe, Jr. (s); F. Florival Metoyer (s); J. Sarpy, Jr. (s). Priest: Guistiniani.

635. MAXIMIN VERCHER
OPHELIA GALLIEN
[illegible]
Groom: son of Beloni Vercher and Marie Auresile Gallien. Bride: daughter of Louis Neuville Gallien and Marie Eloise Lattier. Dispensation from impediment of consanguinity in second degree. Priest: Figari.

636. ANTOINE THEODULE MONETTE (s)
FELICITÉ FLORENTINE METOYER (x)
28 January 1847
Groom: legitimate son of Louis Metoyer and Marie Louise Cottonmaïs. Bride: legitimate daughter of Louis Dominique Metoyer and Marie Theodosia Chagnon. All are free people of color and residents of this parish. Witnesses F. Azénor Metoyer (s); J.h A.tin Metoyer (s); E. Dupré (s). Priest: Figari.

637. THEOPHILE TAUZIN (s)
EMÉE LACOSTE (s)
11 February 1847. 1 ban.
Groom: legitimate son of Joseph Tauzin and Marie Chamard. Bride: legitimate and minor daughter of Lorent Lacoste and deceased Emelie Chiasson. Witnesses: T. Bossier (s); J. Lacoste (s); J. H. Breda (s); H.re Fredieu (s); J? Sompayrac (s); J. N.? Deblieux (s); J. B. Jessup (s); A. Lecomte (s); P. A. Morse (s); A. Sompaÿrac (s); J. E. Tauzin (s); M.lin Tauzin (s). Priest: Guistiniani.

[Ed. note: Bride's name is given in margin as Eimée and in text as Aimé. She signed as Emée.]

638. AUGUSTE ROY (s)
JOSEPHINE MADLEINE TARBY (s)
22 April 1847. 1 ban.
Groom: legitimate son of deceased Pierre Roy and Celestine Ducreux, native of France, department of Doubs. Bride: Widow of Hardy, native of France, same department. Witnesses: C. E. Greneaux (s); A. Sompaÿrac (s); J. A. Ducournau (s); A. Laurents (s); J. E. Tauzin (s). Priest: Guistiniani.

639. WILLIAM PENN MORROW (s)
MARIE MARIANNE AZOLINE VIENNE (s)
29 April 1847. 1 ban.
Groom: legitimate son of deceased Robert Morrow and Emerantinne Greneaux. Bride: legitimate and minor daughter of deceased François Vienne and deceased Marianne Buard. Witnesses: Phanor Prudhomme (s); C. E. Greneaux (s); E. Vienne (s); L. J. Rouquier (s). Priest: Guistiniani.

640. B. V. CORTES (s)
CAROLINE CARR (s)
12 May 1847. 1 ban.
Groom: legitimate daughter of John Carr and Josephine Marcellite Rouquier. Bride: legitimate daughter of John Charles Carr and Henriette Rouquier. Dispensation from impediment of consanguinity in

first degree. Witnesses: Henry Hertzog (s); Alex Denniston (s); A. Prudhomme (s); P. Shulman? (s). Priest: Aloysi Parodi.

[Ed. note: The entry appears to err in its statement of the degree of relationship existing between the bride and groom. Marriages within the FIRST degree are not permitted under Church law; no dispensations for such are granted. The parties were actually first cousins, thereby falling within the second degree of kinship for which a dispensation can be obtained.]

641. (copy) E. O. BLANCHARD (s)
CELESTE CORNELIA DRANGUET (s)
27 May 1847. 1 ban.
Groom: legitimate son of deceased Thomas Blanchard and deceased Aine Newton, widower of Elisa Bloodworth. Bride: legitimate daughter of deceased Benjamin Dranguet and Celeste Tauzin. Witnesses: T. J. Flanner (s); T. N. Taylor (s); B. St. Amans (s); E. V. Deblieux (s). Priest: Guistiniani.

642. LOUIS VAN SCHONBROEK (s)
MARIE SUSANNE SHELBURNE (x)
29 May 1849
Ratification of civil marriage. Groom: legitimate son of Henry Van Schonbroek and Joanna Vulments. Bride: daughter of Silas Shelberun and Margherite Knot. Witnesses: J. Theodore Buvens (s); Elizabeth Buvens (s). Bride signed as Mary Susan Shelburne. Priest: Guistiniani.

643. WILLIAM L. TUOMEY (s)
MARGUERITE ANN HARRISON (s)
16 September 1847. 1 ban.
Groom: lawful son of Patrick O. Tuomey and Honora C. Long. Bride: lawful daughter of James P. Harrison and Ann Keiser. Witnesses: M. C. Dunn (s); J. G. Campbell (s); P. Bludworth (s); Henry Hertzog (s); F. Williams (s); James Taylor (s); Thomas P. Jones (s). Priest: Guistiniani.

644. PIERRE ALCIDE BUARD (s)
MARIE ANTOINETTE IDA LEMÉE (s)
4 October 1847. 1 ban.
Groom: legitimate son of deceased J. Babptiste Buard and Aspasie Bossier. Bride: legitimate daughter of Alexis Lemée and Marie Eugenie Lamarle. Witnesses: A. Lemée (s); Henry Hertzog (s); J. B. O. Buard (s); Octave Metoyer (s); E. Vienne (s). Priest: Guistiniani.

645. FRANÇOIS GASSION METOYER (s)
(copy) PERINE METOYER (s)
30 November 1847
Groom: widower, son of Augustin Metoyer and Marie Agnes Dupré [Poissot]. Bride: legitimate daughter of Pierre Metoyer and Marie Denege Metoyer. Witnesses: Pierre Metoyer (s); J. Bte Metoyer, *fils* Augtin Metoyer (s); C. Roques (s); Jn Augustin Metoyer (s). Priest: Guistiniani.

646. CHARLES NERESTAN ROQUES (s)
(copy) MARIE BARBE MELUISINE METOYER (s)
10 January 1848
Groom: widower of Marie Pompose Metoyer. Bride: widow of Bernard Dophin. Dispensation from impediment of affinity in second degree. Witnesses: J. Bte Metoyer *fils* Augustin (s); A. P. Metoyer (s): C. N. Roques, Jr. (s); Augustin Metoyer (x). Priest: Pascual.

647. FRANÇOIS MERO ESSER
MARIE EMELIA RAMBIN (x)
10 December 1847
Groom: legitimate son of Christian Esser and Adelaïde Rambin. Bride: legitimate daughter of Andrés Michel Rambin and Emée Caseneuve. Dispensation from impediment of consanguinity in second degree. Witnesses: A. M. Rambin (s); Emée Caseneuve (x). Priest: Pascual.

648. CHARLES MELANÇON (x)
MARIE ELODIE ARMANT (x)
28 February 1848
Groom: legitimate son of Charles Melançon and Marie Lousie Bodoin. Bride: legitimate daughter of Baptiste Armant, Jr. and Louise Adelaïde Nafret. Witnesses: Michel U. Melançon (s); Théodore Clément Rachal (s); J. Bte Armant, Jr. (s). Priest: Pascual.

649. LOUIS WALETTE (s)
(copy) ELISA HELY (x)
7 March 1848
Groom: legitimate son of deceased Louis Wallette and Angèle Gagné. Bride: widow of Sylvestre Poissot, legitimate daughter of Pierite Hely and Marie Derbanne. Witnesses: ? Rachal (s); Etienne Davion (s); Pierre Ternier (s); Sylvain Trichel (s). Priest: Guistiniani.

[Ed. note: In this recorded copy of the original, the groom's signature was copied by Father Guistiniani as Louis Woilet.]

650. HENRY HERTZOG (s)
CEPHALIDE LAURA LECOMTE (s)
6 June 1848. 1 ban.
Groom: legitimate son of deceased Jean François Hertzog and Desirée Prudhomme. Bride: legitimate daughter of Ambroise Lecomte and deceased Julia Buard. Dispensation from impediment of consanguinity in fourth degree. Witnesses: A. Lecomte (s); E. O. Deblieux (s); J. A. Ducournau (s); P. Bludworth (s); E. O. Blanchard (s); C. E. Tauzin (s); S. M. Hyams (s); W. L. Tuomey (s); M. C. Dunn (s). Priest: Guistiniani.

651. LOUIS EUGENE MICHAMPS (s)
MARIE LOUISE ROND (x)
18 July 1848
Groom: legitimate son of Julies Eugène Michamps and Anne Catherine Muller. Bride: legitimate daughter of François Rond and Marie Aurore Beçons. Both parties are natives of this parish. Witnesses: J^{n}. E^{gne}. Michamps (s); Fçois Rond (s); O? Rond (s). Priest: Guistiniani.

652. (copy) JULES NOËL CONDÉ, JR. (s)
GENEVIÈVE DEL RIO (x)
7 August 1848
Groom: legitimate son of Noël Condé and Natalie Mezier. Bride: legitimate daughter of Roman del Rio and Marguerite Triche. [All are free people of color.] Dispensation granted from impediment of consanguinity in third degree. Witnesses: Nobert Chatenier (s); Joseph Meziere (s); Toussaint Lebrun (s). Priest: Pascual.

653. (copy) CIRIAQUE PEROT (s)
MARIE ROSELIA BORDELON (s)
29 August 1848. 0 bans.
Groom: legitimate son of deceased Fostin Perot and deceased Marie Celeste Bordelon. Bride: legitimate daughter of deceased Ipolite Bordelon and Marie Denege Celimene Fonteno. Witnesses: Silvin Trichel (s); Cesaire Fonteno (s); J^{n}. L^{s}. Perot (s); Hilaire Bordelon (s); F^{s}. Vienne (s). Dispensation from impediment of consanguinity in second and fourth degrees. Priest: Pascual.

654. JAMES M. B. TUCKER
CALEDONIA C. MARRS
3 November 1848
Groom: lawful son of James B. Tucker and Mary Stone; a non-Catholic. Bride: lawful daughter of John Marrs and Nancy Stone. Groom has met the conditions

for marriage in the Church. Witnesses: John Tucker (s); A. B. Sompayrac (s); J. N. Deblieux (s); J. W. Butler (s); Aphe Sompayrac (s); E. V. Deblieux (s). Priest: Guistiniani.

655. (copy) JEAN BAPTISTE VALIERE RACHAL (x)
MARIE CELESIE DAVION (s)
30 October 1848. 3 bans.
Groom: widower of Catherine Chonet, legitimate son of Jean B. Rachal and Marie Denise Lemoine. Bride: widower of Jean Lalande, legitimate daughter of Jean B. Davion and Pelagie Gaigné. Witnesses: J.L. Perot (s); C. Omer Perot (s); Victor Barberousse (s); Athanasitte Ely (s). Priest: Pascual.

656. WILLIAM LUYSTER (s)
CAROLINE COOMBS (s)
28 September 1848
Groom: lawful son of Abraham R. Luyster and Mary Robinson. Bride: lawful daughter of Robt. L. Coombs and Harriet Winter, present wife of Peter Petrovic, esquire. Witnesses: Charles A. Petrovic (s); Peter Petrovic (s); J. Bossier (s); Bn.? Campbell (s); S.S. Simons (s); Bam. Clark? (s); T. E. Tauzin (s). Parties of different faiths; dispensation granted. Priest: Pascual.

657. ABDA H. CHRISTIAN (s)
SARAH ANN OTIS (s)
20 November 1848
Groom: son of Gabriel Christian and Marvison B. Gilmer; a non-Catholic. Bride: daughter of John Otis and Alice Flamigan his wife. Dispensation for disparity of faiths; groom has satisfied the conditions for marriage in the church. Witnesses: A. S. Grovenor (s); Thos. M. Gilmer (s); P. A. Morse (s); Geo. W. Morse (s); J. Criswell (s). Priest: Guistiniani.

658. WILLIAM WALKER (x)
MARIE MADELEINE VASCOCU (s)
7 December 1848
Groom: lawful son of William Walker and Fevy Huten [Phoebe Houston?]. Bride: lawful daughter of Chrisostomé Vascocu and Marie Marcelite Ries. Witnesses: P. M. Backen (s): S. Vascocu (s); J. B. Vascocu (s). Parties are of different faiths. Dispensation granted. Priest: Pascual.

659. ADOLPHE PRUDHOMME (s)
OCTAVIE METOYER (s)
18 January 1849
Groom: legitimate son of Antoine Prudhomme and Marie

Lambre. Bride: legitimate daughter of Benjamin Metoyer and Aurore Lambre. Dispensation from impediment of consanguinity in third degree. Witnesses: Ch^{s}. W. Hertzog (s); Lestan Prudhomme (s); Valery Gaiennié (s); François Metoyer (s). Priest: Pascual.

660. (copy) GUILMA PEROT (s)
JULIA PLAISAINCE (x)
15 January 1849
Groom: legitimate son of François Perot and Manete Fonteneaux. Bride: legitimate daughter of Jean B. Plaisance and Marie Joseph Palvado. Dispensation from impediment of consanguinity in third degree. Witnesses: Marin C. Brosset (s); Mme. J. B. Perot (x); Emerante Derbanne (s).

[Ed. note: This is a not entirely accurate copy of the original marriage entry filed as number 546 (bis). Spellings of some names on this copy differ slightly from that on the original.]

661. ASUMPTION RAMIREZ (x)
MARIA APOLONIA DEALEMAN (x)
5 February 1849
Groom: son of Gajetain [Cayetano] Ramirez and Maria Josepha Pongez. Bride: daughter of Phelipe Barrera and Juana Gertrude Dealemana. Witnesses: Gualupe Andrada; Carmelita Prou (x); Phelippe Barrera (x). Priest: Guistiniani.

[Ed. note: Marginal notation identifies bride as Maria JOSEPHA PONGEZ, while text identifies this individual as mother of the groom. According to text, bride was Maria APOLONIA DEALEMAN, although text identifies her father as Barrera and her mother as Dealemana. Signature of bride is given as "Apolonia Dealeman X, her ordinary mark." Bride appears to be same individual as that in Entry 432 -- i.e. Maria Appollonia de l'incarnation Alemone, daughter of Philippe Barrero and Jeanne Gertrude Alemone.]

662. MARTIN CHAUSON (TOSSON)
LISA CLINTON
19 February 1849
Groom: son of Marie Jean-Louis. Bride: daughter of Marie Angelie. All are free people of color and residents of this parish. Witnesses: Augustin Cloutier (s); Azenor Vienne (s); Roquie Plaisance (x). Priest: Guistiniani.

[Ed. note: Marginal notation identifies groom as Tosson, text as Chauson.]

663. JEAN ADOLPHE DUCOURNAU (s)
MARIE APPOLINE CASTANEDO (s)
10 April 1849. 1 ban.
Groom: legitimate son of J. Baptiste Ducournau and Marie Rival. Bride: legitimate daughter of Remond Castanedo and Louise Aimé Piver. Witnesses: R. Castanedo (s); A. Castanedo (s); E. V. Deblieux (s); P. A. Castanedo (s); F. Metoyer (s); L. J. Rouquier (s); L. F. Martine (s). Priest: Guistiniani.

664. ALFRED LAURENTS (s)
ELISABETH VALERIE CASTANEDO (s)
10 April 1849. 1 ban.
Groom: legitimate son of Benoist Laurents and Marie Sophie Le Forte. Bride: legitimate daughter of Remond Castanedo and Louise Aimé Piver. Witnesses: R. Castanedo (s); A. Castanedo (s); J. A. Castanedo (s); E. V. Deblieux (s); F. Metoyer (s); L. J. Rouquier (s); L. F. Martine (s). Priest: Guistiniani.

665. JUAN HYMENES (s)
JACOBA SALCEDA (s)
22 April 1849
Groom: legitimate son of Francisco Himenes and Albina Posos. Bride: legitimate daughter of Desiderio Salcedo and Juanna Flores. Witnesses: Desiderio Salceda (x); Seraphine Garcia (s); Joseph Pantaleon (s). Priest: [not given].

[Ed. note: Groom signed as Ximenes.]

666. MARCELIN TAUZIN (s)
MARIE AZELIE PEROT (s)
24 April 1849. 1 ban.
Groom: legitimate son of Joseph Tauzin and M. Catherine Chamard. Bride: legitimate daughter of Faustin Perot and Marie Celeste Bordelon. Witnesses: F. Vienne (s); J. W. Butler (s): J. Sompayrac (s); A. B. Sompayrac (s); E. O. Blanchard (s); J. G. Campbell (s); J. N. Deblieux (s); J. B. O. Rouquier (s). Priest: Guistiniani.

667. SALUSTIANO VASQUEZ
MARIA PEDRA IBARBO
6 May 1849
Witness: Chaurios. Priest: C. Chambodut.

668. (copy) M. T. HANDY (s)
EMERANTE DERBANNE (s)
15 May 1849
Witnesses: Jules Luvini (s); Michael Boys [Boyce] (s); T. Quisinberry (s); Silvain Trichel (s). Priest: A. Verrina.

669. (copy) EUGENE VALERY DEBLIEUX (s)
F. AURORE METOYER (s)
24 May 1849
Witnesses: Aurore Metoyer (s); H. C. Deblieux (s); Lestan Prudhomme (s); F. B. Sherburne (s); J. B. Cloutier (s); J. Roubieux (s); J. N. Deblieux (s); Alex Deblieux (s). Priest: Verrina.

670. (copy) PATRICK JAMES O'DOHERTY
EUGENIA REBECCA SAXON
15 June 1849. 1 ban.
Witnesses: Octave Voorhies (s); Pauline Roubieu (s): A. Chaurios? (s). Priest: Verrina.

671. FELICIEN BENJAMIN METOYER (s)
MARIE LOUISE EUGENIE LEMÉE (s)
19 June 1849. 1 ban.
Groom: legitimate son of François Benjamin Metoyer and Aurore Lambre. Bride: legitimate daughter of Allin Gustave Alexy Lemée and Marie Eugénie Lamarelère. Witnesses: A. Lemée (s); Eugénie Lemée (s); Aurore Metoyer (s); Phanor Prudhomme (s); Valery Gaiennié (s); Ls. Rueg (s); Jean Prudhomme (s). Priest: Verrina.

672. DESIDERIO SALCEDO (x)
MARIA JUSTA LASA (x)
17 September 1849
Groom: legitimate son of Cajetan Salcedo and Therèse de Jesus. Bride: legitimate daughter of José Lasa (Lara? Sosa?) and Maria Bernarda Saīs. Witnesses: José Ximenes (s); James Kelly (s). Priest: A. Andrieu.

673. STEPHEN W. KILE (s)
ELLEN POWER (s)
20 November 1849
Groom: lawful son of Georges Kile and Ann Marshal. Bride: legitimate daughter of William Power and Eliza Bennet. Witnesses: J. Henry (s); J. Moting? (s); James Kelly (s); H. Cosgrove (s). Priest: Andrieu.

674. JOSEPH ROMAN FRÈDERIC (s)
HENRIETTE CORA BOSSIER (s)
13 December 1849. 2 bans.
Groom: legitimate and major son of François Frederic and deceased Felicité Lavespère. Bride: legitimate and minor daughter of Jean B^{te}. Bossier and Marie Aurore Gonin. Witnesses: J. B^{te}. Armant, Jr. (s); J. B. L. Bossier (s); T. Clement Rachal (s); F. H. Frederic (s). Priest: Andrieu.

675. (copy) SIMEON M. HART
MARY ASPASIE LAMBRE
21 January 1850. 1 ban.
Witnesses: J. J. Lambre (s); E. O. Blanchard (s); R. Perot (s); T. J. Flanner (s); J. Somperac (s); F. Williams (s); J. L. Perot (s). Priest: Verrina.

676. (copy) ASHTON G. RUSHING (s)
EMELIE BORDELON (s)
24 January 1850.
Dispensation for disparity of religion. Witnesses: Cleri Grilliet (s); B. Rushing (s); Madison Mobley (s); J. B. Perrot (s). Priest: Verrina.

677. FRANKLIN PHILOGENE ADLÉ (s)
EMILIE DUPRÉ (s)
8 April 1850. 2 bans.
Both parties are natives of this parish. Witnesses: J. M. Tessier (s); Abel Sers, Jr. (s); J. B. Plaisance (s). Priest: Aug. Martin.

678. LEONARD RIVERS (x)
DESIDERIA SAUCERA
13 April 1850. 2 bans.
Witnesses: Joachim Salinas (x); James? Sturges (s); Simon Perés (x). Priest (assistant): Cuny.

[Ed. note: The signature Carron (Larron) Saude appears beside that of the groom.]

APPENDIX A

Register 7: Baptisms, 1826-1831 (Slaves)

[Ed. note: One marriage record from the studied period appears on the last page of this register.]

A-679 JACQUES DUFROIS DERBANNE (x)
MARIE EUPHEMIE ROUBIEU (x)
__ October ______.
Groom: native of Natchitoches Parish, legitimate and major son of J^{n}. B^{te}. Derbanne and Marie Hélène Brevel, all of Rivière aux Cannes. Bride: Born at Riviere aux Cannes, minor and legitimate daughter of deceased Auguste Roubieu and Marie Judith [Le] Vasseur. Dispensation from impediment of kinship in [illegible] degree. Witnesses: L^{s}. Somperat (s); L^{s}. Pierre Levy? (s).

[Ed. note: According to the baptismal entry recorded for the bride in Register 5, dated 22 August 1811 (see Mills, *Natchitoches, 1800-1826*, Entry 327), Euphemie was actually the "natural" daughter of Roubieu and LeVasseur. By the terms of Roubieu's will, dated 27 July 1812, he acknowledged Euphemie as his natural daughter and heir. See Succession Book 1, pp. 81-86, Natchitoches Parish.]

APPENDIX B

Register 8

[Ed. note: Two entries bound now into Register 8 do not duplicate those recorded in Registers 11 and 12 (abstracted in this volume) or Register 5 (previously abstracted in Mills, *Natchitoches, 1800-1826*). Those two entries are:

A-680 [Reg. 8 Sheet 1] JOSÉ LUIS DE LA BEGA (s)
MARIA GUADALUP PRU (x)
2 November 1816.
Ratification of civil marriage contracted in Territory of Nueva ______ [New ______]. Groom: native of San Miguel in Spain, aged [blank], son of [blank] and Maria Dolores de [blank]. Bride: native of San Antonio de Bexar, aged 13 years and 1 month, legitimate daughter of Antonio Pru and Maria Juana Pachero?. Witnesses: James Smith (s); Joseph Carrière (s); B. [illegible] (s); Jose Acosta (s).

A-681 [Reg. 8 Sheet 89] FRANÇOIS BAUDRY (x)
MARIE JOSEPHINE MOREAU (x)
18 September 1839. 0 bans.
Groom: legitimate and major son of deceased François Baudry and of Victoire St. André. Bride: legitimate and major daughter of deceased Pierre Moreau and of Marie Louise St. André. Witnesses: Seraphin Rachal (s); Alexander Moreau (s). Bride and groom are first cousins. Priest: Français.

INDEX

A______, Thomas: 279

Aarnaud, Jean Baptiste: 401

Aco____, José: 14

Acoit *[see Arcoit]*

Acosta,
- José: A-680
- José Ignacio: 32
- Joseph: 330, 616
- Joseph Andres: 62
- Juan Joseph: 62
- Luis: 616
- Marie Eulalia *[see de la Cruz]*

Adams, Maria Antonia (Dña. Santiago Lopez): 88

Adelaïde, f.w.c.: 267 *[see also Mariotte, Adelaïde]*

Adlé (var. Adlet, Adelé),
- Antoine: 291, 385
- Baptiste: 277, 285 *[see also Jean Baptiste]*
- Des Neiges *[see Marie Pelagie des Neiges]*
- François: 159
- Franklin Philogene: 330, 677
- Jean Baptiste: 6, 24, 29, 158, 265, 303, 411?
- Jean Baptiste: 139, 546
- Jean Baptiste Timothé: 263, 538
- Marie Antoinette (Mrs. Gerry R. Waters): 385
- Marie Azelie (Mme. J.B. Grandchampt): 265
- Marie Geneviève (Dña. Narciso Cordova; Mme. Andres Isaac Hesser): 263, 538
- Marie Herzile [?Ursulle] (Mme. Onezime St. André): 29
- Marie Louise (Mme. Ludger Langlois): 139
- Marie Pelagie Des Neiges (Mme. François Royer; Mrs. George Schamp): 178, 291
- Marie Pheloe (Mrs. Julius C. Saunders; Mrs. Andrew Hamilton, II): 206, 411

Adlé (continued)
- Marie Ris?: 263
- Marie Zeline (Mme. Athanase Oliver Brosset): 303
- Pelagie (Mme. Jean Tessier): 615 *[see also Marie Pelagie]*
- Philogene *[see Franklin Philogene]*
- Prudence (Mme. Gervais Fontenot) 546
- Rosalie Zulmina (Mrs. James L. Haughteling): 364
- Valentin, I: 206, 411
- Zulmina *[see Rosalie Zulmina]*

Agaisse (var. Aguesse, Agues),
- François: 335
- Jacques: 315
- Jean Renaud, I: 185, 315, 335
- Jean Renaud, II: 185, 335
- Zeline (Mme. Remy Poissot): 604

Agustera, Joseph Fecond: 473

Ailhaud Ste. Anne, Marie Thérèse Victoire (Mme. J.B. Prudhomme): 168

Airey, George W.: 306, 345(bis)

Alain, Luisiane? (Mrs. Andrew Hamilton, I): 411

Alamillo, Agustina (Dña. Julian Rosales: 26

Aleman (var. Alemone; De Aleman, Dealeman),
- Jeanne Gertrude (Dña. Philippe Barrero): 432, 661
- Maria Apolonia (Dña. Asumption Ramirez): 661
- Marie Charlot (Dña. Joseph Maria Sanches): 61
- Pierre Joseph?: 61

Allen,
- Abby A. (Mme. Armand Biossat): 520
- Noah H.: 520

Alvarez,
- Bazile: 432
- Dario Jean Joseph: 432

Amador, Juana (Dña. Pedro Cruz): 3

Amon, P.: 507

Andrada, Gualupe: 661
Anty,
Arsene (Mme. Emanuel Llorens); f.w.c.: 459, 623
Celine (Mme. Pierre Oscar Chaler); 569
Jean Baptiste I: 64, 170
Jean Baptiste *fils* J. B. Ignace): 579, 581
Jean Baptiste Ignace II: 64, 377, 569, 579
Marie Aspazie (Mme. Maxille Metoyer; Mme. Henry Octave Deronce); f.w.c.: 211, 468, 479, 483
Marie Celeste (Mme. Louis Gallien): 166, 184, 309, 506, 621
Marie Henriette (Mme. Clement Rachal; Mme. Arthur Chaler): 377, 477
Marie Louise (Mme. Paul Poissot): 83, 185, 199, 233, 315, 317, 335, 423, 621
Marie Susanne "Suzette" (Mme. J.B. Augustin Metoyer); f.w.c.: 339, 487, 552, 586
Marie Thérèse Carmelite (Mme. Auguste Metoyer), f.w.c., 172
Melice: 170, 301, 469
Michel: 287
Silvestre: 287, 325
Valerie: 280
Aragon,
Des Neiges (Dña. Nazario Ortis): 155
Juan Bautista: 155
Araino, Antonio: 97
Archinard,
François Xavier: 302, 565
L.: 302
V.: 369
Arcia (de Arze), Maximilien: 574-75
Arcoit,
François: 18
Louis: 18, 192
Ardoin, Marie Louise (Mme. Antoine Lacase I): 557
Armand (var. Armant),
Adele (Mme. Prudent Rachal): 159
Edouard: 461 *[see also Joseph E.]*
Jean Baptiste I: 57, 58, 108, 122, 159, 170, 255?, 282, 534, 539
Jean Baptiste II: 122, 159, 255?, 289, 461, 539, 648, 674
Armand (continued),
Joseph Edouard: 57, 534
Josephine (Mme. Lestan Langlois) 492 *[see also Marcelitte Josephine]*
Marcelitte Josephine (Mme. Ls. Gaspard Derbanne): 539
Marie Celina (Mrs. Stephen Grant): 461
Marie Clara (Mme. Felix Langlois): 282
Marie Elodie (Mme. Charles Melançon II): 648
Marie Henriette (Mme. Victor Damas Rachal; Mme. Melice Anty): 108, 170, 582, 602
Arnaud, Euphrosine (Mme. Sylvestre Cesaire Bossier): 340-341
Aro *[see De Aro & Alvarez Dario]*
Arocha (var. Aroche),
Angela (Dña. Manuel Delgado): 30
José Damian: 91, 119
Josef: 79
Maria Jesus[a] (Dña. Juan Cruz): 119
Maria Juana Leonor (Dña. José Maria Murquiz): 91
Arriola, Maria Josefa (Dña. Bartolo Chirino): 39
Aryand, Marie Magdelaine (Mme. Jacques Antoine Bouis): 197
Ash,
Ebenezer: 417
Ira Carter: 417
Ashton, Hannah Butler (Mrs. George Hunter Terrett): 462
Aubuchon, Antoine: 400
Augustin *[see Jean Baptiste Augustin]*
Avila *[see Navarro Avila]*
Ayala,
José Andres: 89
Nicolas: 89

Ba____, B.: 180
Babet, Marie Orezille Denis (Dña. José Maria Robles): 329
Baccocu *[see Vascocu]*
Backen (var. Baecken),
Gerard: 419
Pierre Mathieu: 383, 408, 419 443, 626, 658

Baden (var. Badin),
    Antoine, f.m.c.: 52
    Marianne, f.w.c.: 52
    Marie Denise, f.w.c. (Mrs. John Baker; Mme. J. B. Aarnaud): 52, 401
Baillio (var. Bayou, Bailloud, Baillot),
    Apollinaire: 243, 450
    Auguste: 23, 236, 305?
    Fs.: 236
    Marie (Mme. Joseph Antonio Marcel de Soto): 49, 256, 452
    Maryanne (Mrs. William Preston Hickman): 236
    Sylvère: 371
Baker,
    John, Jr., fmc.: 52, 401
    John, Sr., fmc.: 52
    Nancy (Mrs. John, Sr.): 52
Balboa, Trinidad (Dna. Joseph Maria Moreno): 526
Baltazar (var. Balthasard),
    Jean Baptiste, f.m.c.: 156, 375
    Louis, f.m.c.: 149, 171
    Marie Rose (Mme. Emile Dupart): 156, 603
Balzaretti,
    Antoine: 620
    Pierre: 620
Bam Clark?: 652
Baptiste *[see Jean Baptiste]*
Barberousse (var. Barberoux),
    Joseph Victor: 239, 292
    Marie Aimeé (Mme. Louis Jerome Rachal; Mme. Adonis Isidore Hissoura *dit* Pantaleon): 353
    Michel: 36, 77, 107, 239, 353
    Victor: 612, 655
Barbour, P. N.?, Lieutenant: 462
Bardon,
    Catherine (Mme. Louis Chamard): 261
    Marianne: 11
Barela (var. Barel, Varela),
    Feliciano Antonio: 14, 19, 98
    Athanasio (Anastasio): 98, 426
    Joseph Felix: 20, 98
    Juana Baptista (Dna. José Manuel Sanchez): 14
Bareta, Catherine (Mme. Pierre Pelli): 351
Bargas,
    Juan: 570
    Maria Jesusa/Juana (Dna. Teodoro Quintero): 570
Barlow, George H.: 350, 502
Barnes *[see Byrnes]*
Baron, Juana (Dna. Felipe Padilla): 607
Barrero (var. Barrera),
    Juan *[see Varrera]*
    Maria Appollonia de l'Incarnation Alemone (Dna. Juan Joseph Alvarez Dario): 432
    Philippe: 432, 661
Barron,
    José Aguino: 3
    José Antonio: 3
    Mary (Mrs. Charles Lewis I): 306
Barry *[see Berry]*
Barton?, Pierre: 380
Basques (var. Basquez, Bask, Basco, Vasquez),
    Adout: 433
    José Bastian: 536
    Mariano: 128, 433-34
    Miguel Maria: 472
    Salustiano: 667
    Thomas: 128, 434
Bastien, Washington: 502
Baudry,
    François I: 420, A-681
    François II: A-681
    Marie Cephalide (Mme. Joseph Perrot): 420
Baulos,
    François: 190
    Pierre: 140, 162, 190, 265, 309, 417
Bauvard de St. Amans, ____: 17, 28, 36, 68
Beance, Belgire de (Mme. Hypolite Rodolphe Carron): 135
Beaudouin (var. Baudoin, Baudouin, Badoin, Bodoin, Beaudoin, Daudoin),
    François: 125
    Marie Aimée (Mme. Louis Emanuel Gallien): 347
    Marie Celeste (Mme. Athanase Brosset): 361, 430, 624
    Marie Elisabeth (Mme. J. B. Denis): 247, 293
    Marie Françoise: 325, 460, 494

Beaudouin (cont'd),
Marie Froisine (Mme. Athanase Denis): 528
Marie Josephe Adelise (Mme. Michel Melançon): 81
Marie Louise (Mme. Charles Melançon): 15, 648
Marie Thérèse (Mme. Pierre Beaulieu): 65
Nicolas: 125
Pierre: 4, 15, 81, 347
Beaulieu,
Marie Phany (Mme. Michel Rambin): 65, 414
Pierre: 65
Bébé (Beebe),
Catherine: 60
Guillaume I: 560, 574-75
Guillaume II: 560
Joseph: 575
Bega *[see Flores]*
Bela,
Nicolas: 235
Pedro: 235
Belanger, Juan: 70
Beler, Barton, f.w.c.: 48
Belknap, Seth E.: 329
Bellegarde? (Belleyancha?), Claire (Mme. J. B. Odiardi); 387
Bellegarde (var. Bergard),
Geneviève (Mme. Antoine Le Moine): 53, 194-95
Maria (Mrs. John Cedars): 53
Bellepeche, Marie Louise (Mme. Antoine Cotonmaïs): 152, 171, 175, 409
Bennet, Eliza (Mrs. William Power): 673
Benoist,
Charles François: 82, 92, 106, 145-46, 161, 183, 209-210, 212, 274, 287, 361a-b, 454, 527, 532, 578
Julia (Mme. J. B. Chopin): 532
Sanguinette Hubert: 158
Bensan *[see Vicente]*
Bermea (var. Bermella),
Andrew: 76, 573
Mathias: 76
Bernar, Marie, f.w.c.: 130
Bernelot, Marie (Mme. Pierre Gautier): 447
Bernot (the elder): 36
Berry,
Patrick: 284, 441
Sylvester: 284
Bertille, François *[see Trichel]*
Bertin, Pierre: 219-20, 223-24, 226, 235, 286, 317, 322, 335
Bertrand,
Benoit: 100
Charles Beninne: 527
Charles Claude: 521, 527
Besson (var. Beçons),
François: 68, 321
Jean Baptiste I: 75, 205, 273
Jean Baptiste II: 205
Julien: 68, 273
Maria Aurore (Mme. Joseph François Rond): 75, 651
Bethel?, François: 200
Bey,
André: 491, 593
Conrad: 593
Biareal *[see Villarea.]*
Biossat,
Antoine: 520
Armand: 520
Marie Louise: 520
Birtt,
Isaac C.: 200, 232, 502
Johon: 502
Blair, Mathilde (Mme. Pierre Evariste Buard): 445
Blanchard,
Edward Orlando: 296, 345, 354, 360, 390, 398, 457, 462, 547, 550, 641, 650, 666, 675
Thomas: 296, 641
Bludworth,
James: 241, 296, 301, 398, 462
Marianne (Mrs. Bardet Ashton Terrell): 462
Marie Elisa (Mrs. Edward Orlando Blanchard): 296
Marie Louise Evalina (Mrs. Francis Johnson): 398
P.: 550, 643, 650
Bodeaud, Severin: 549
Bodoin *[see Beaudouin]*
Boerum, Elisabeth Claire (Mrs. Louis Gustave De Russy): 269, 529
Bohannon, Anne (Mrs. Simeon B. Chapman): 279

Bonneau, Catherine (Mrs. Joseph Johnson): 398
Bolien,
Edouard: 561
Marie Celine (Mrs. William Harrison): 561
Bollender,
François: 548
Marguerithe (Mme. Jacques Brian, Mme. Nicolas Kieffer II): 548
Bonette,
Jean Baptiste I: 435
Jean Baptiste II: 435
Bordelon (var. Bourdelon),
Emelie (Mrs. Ashton G. Rushing): 676
Hillaire *[see Manuel Hillaire]*
Hypolite I: 67, 503
Hypolite II: 102, 111, 113, 189; 315?, 355?, 378, 503, 566, 653
Julia (Mrs. Edward Fleming): 566
Louis Spire: 101-02, 113, 144, 237, 245, 332, 355, 403
Lufroy: 63
Manuel Hillaire: 63, 67, 271, 378, 653
Marie Celeste (Mme. Jean Chrisostomé Faustin Perot): 189, 355, 498, 653, 666
Marie Louise (Mme. Cezaire Fonteneau): 103
Marie Rosalie (Mme. Cyriaque Perot): 653
Spire *[see Louis Spire]*
Bossier (var. Boissier),
_____: 221, 340
Alexandre Soulange: 7, 106, 289, 346, 460
Cezer Soulange: 7, 628
D.: 44, 218-19, 351, 359
Dassise *[see François Placide Dacize]*
Desirée: 545
Eulalie (Mme. Jean Louis Buard): 120, 204, 328
Eulalie *[see also Marie Aimée Eulalie]*
Evariste: 134, 218
Evariste *[see also Pierre Evariste]*
F. Eugene: 620, 628
Bossier (Cont'd),
François Placide Dacize: 135, 253, 328, 363, 367, 384
François Paul: 150, 218, 253
G?: 621
H.: 41, 44
Henriette Cora (Mme. Joseph Roman Frederick): 519, 674
Irena (Mme. Augustin Hartman): 340
J.: 656
J. B. L.: 674
J. D.: 140
J. P.: 207
Jean Baptiste: 460, 494, 674
Jules Victor: 132, 181, 199, 218, 228, 253, 264, 292, 351, 359-60, 363, 367, 444-45, 618
Leocadie (Mme. Jean Baptiste Lestage): 492
Lolitte (Mme. François Massip): 106
Louis Dunoye (Damas?): 150, 199, 380
Marie Aspasie (Mme. Jean Baptiste Buard): 363, 444, 644
Marie Azelie (Mme. Eloy Rachal; Mrs. Peter McDonald): 346
Marie Aimée Eulalie (Mme. Jean Pierre Cheletre; Mme. Baltazar Brevelle, Jr.): 187, 219, 266, 289, 346, 392
Marie Tranquilline (Mme. Pierre La Renaudière): 494, 605
Paul *[see François Paul)*
Pierre Evariste: 120, 199, 218, 253, 328, 363, 367, 444-45
Placide: 120, 190
Placide *[see also François Placide Dacize]*
S.: 519
S. S?: 340
Sophia (Mrs. John L. Ellis): 341
Soulange *[see Alexandre Soulange]*
Sylvestre I: 359
Sylvestre II: 359
Sylvestre Cesaire: 185, 340-41
Thèophile: 620, 628, 637
V. P.: 511
Victoire Emerante (Mme. Emanuel Greneaux): 264
Victor: 134, 452 *[see also Jules]*

Boudrige,
Antoine: 270
Mathieu Léon: 270
Bouis,
Jacques Antoine: 197
Pierre Victor: 197, 349
Boullt, D. H.: 499
Bourg, Marie (Mme. Bernard Mericq, Sr.): 56
Bouvac, Catharina (Mme. Nicolas Du Bois): 31
Boyce (var. Boice, Boys),
Michael: 160, 205, 276, 284, 355, 547, 566, 578, 668
Peter: 578
Brady, Anne: 533
Breazeale, B. B.: 519
Brechon, Victor: 384, 419, 438, 443, 509
Breda,
J. H.: 637
Jean Philippe I: 356
Jean Philippe II: 356, 482, 499, 518
Brenan?, Edward: 533
Bretel,
Jules Barthelemy: 621
Luc Ermelind: 621
Brevel (var. Breuvelle, Breuville, Brevell, Vrevel),
Almire: 605
Baltazard, I: 29, 82, 255, 289, 346 (bis), 392, 557
Baltazard, II (the elder): 289 557?
Baltazard, II (the younger): 255, 557?
Emmanuel: 392
Guillaume: 220
Jean Baptiste II: 255
Jean Baptiste III? ("Batoche"): 170
Lise (Mme. Antoine La Case): 255, 557
Marie Felicité (Mme. Gaspard La Cour): 40, 151, 212, 225, 361
Marie Hélène (Mme. J. B. Gaspard Derbanne): 22, 24, 46, 83, 145, 151, 539, A-679
Marie Louise (Mme. Julien Rachal): 86
Brevel (cont'd),
Marie Pelagie (Mme. J. B. Barthelemy Rachal): 45, 58, 222, 254, 511
Marie Thérèse (Mme. Philippe Brosset): 143, 246, 254, 303, 305, 476, 504, 554
Marie Victoire "Victorine" (Mme. J. B. Adlé): 29, 158, 265, 303
Placide: 346 (bis)
Brian, Jaque: 548
Briant, Josephine Desirée (Mme. Ambroise Sompayrac): 181, 218, 360 376, 382, 465, 545, 567, 618
Bricou, Adelaïde (Mme. François Emanuel Davion): 405
Brosset,
_____: 143
Ablin: 437
Athenaise (Mme. Lucien Jarreau): 305
Athanas: 15, 81, 125, 361a, 430, 624
Athanase Oliver: 303, 307, 430
Azelie (Mrs. Thomas A. Morgan): 430
Barbe Zelia (Mme. Narcisse Seraphin Rachal): 361a
Catherine (Mme. Joseph Derbanne): 186
Cilesie (Mme. Valentin Adlé): 206, 411
Eleuther: 460, 476
Françoise Reine (Mme. Etienne Derzelin Rachal): 254
Marie Aselina (Mme. Luc Poché): 475
Marie Cephise (Mme. Louis Solastie Rachal; Mme. Jules Trotreau): 504
Marie Froisine Susette (Mme. Clement Oduhigg Lavespère): 554
Marie Silvie (Mme. Jacques Le Comte): 240
Marin C.: 476, 504, 546, 632, 660
Oliver *[see Athanase Oliver]*
Philippe: 143, 246, 254, 303, 305, 476, 504, 554
Philipe Cyriaque: 246

Brosset (cont'd)
Pierre, *fils* Athanase: 624
Pierre *[Cesaire]*: 437, 475
Pierre Sepherin "Zephor": 307, 310
Susette *[see Marie Froisine Susette]*
Zephore *[see Pierre Sepherin]*
Brown,
David: 107
John: 20
Scolastique (Mme. Jean Ortolan): 125
Byrnes, Elisabeth (Mrs. Andrew White): 564
Buard,
Adelaïde: 292
Alcide *[see Pierre Alcide]*
Aspasie: 363
E. A.: 218
Jean Baptiste: 44, 363, 444, 644
Jean Baptiste (Widow): 150
Jean Baptiste Ovide: 351, 363, 631, 644
Jean Louis: 120, 204, 328
Jean Louis (Widow): 150
Julia (Mme. Ambroise Le Comte): 120, 618, 650
Louis Alexandre: 187, 204, 292, 328, 359, 385, 505
Marianne (Mme. François Vienne) 355, 639
Marie Elisabeth (Mme. François Rouquier, Jr.): 354, 550
Marie Nathalie (Mrs. William Fleury): 444
Pierre Alcide: 644
Bullard,
Charles A.: 148, 241, 296
Julia Ann (Bludworth): 241
Bullitt (var. Buillet)
Benjamin I: 598
Benjamin II: 519, 598
Bunel?, Dr.: 132
Burgher, Henry: 291
Burnett,
D. Slim: 354
Missoury (Mrs. Michael Colegan): 275
Peter: 275
Burns *[see Byrnes]*
Bussy, Eugenie: 312
Bustamente,
Cesaria (Dña. Luis Acosta): 616
Josef Maria: 91
Manuel: 37, 39, 88, 295, 616
Maria (Mme. Guillaume Bébé I): 560
Butler, J. W.: 372, 390, 666
Buvens,
F. G.: 626
Henry: 613
J. Theodore: 512, 613, 642
Petrus: 613, 626

Cable,
Harriet (Henriette) Winter (Mrs. Joseph Toole Robinson): 372
Jared: 306, 345, 372
Cadena *[see Caldenas]*
Cadet, Leopold: 409
Calaham,
James: 509
Virginy (Mrs. Peter Hartman): 509
Caldenas (var. Cadena),
Francisco: 76, 556
Maria Francesca Juana (Dña. Andres Bermella): 76, 573
Martinas: 556
Calderon,
Juan José: 572
Maria Getrudis (Dña. M. Ybarbo): 573
Maria Jesusa (Dña. Bentura Guerra): 572
Calley, Phillip: 20
Camadi, Marie (Mme. Pier Celestin Trezzini): 13
Campbell,
Bn.: 656
David: 597
J. G.: 359-60, 372, 567, 577, 595; 614, 643, 666
R. M.: 519
Canbarreux (var. Canbarreaux, Canbarus),
Pierre: 428
Vincent: 428
Cannon,
John (Jean): 581
William P.: 581, 583
Canotte, N? W?: 482

Cantona (var. Cantoana, Cantonus),
Maria Antonia (Dña. Pedro Bela): 235
Warline *[Warlupe? Guadalupe?]*: 235
Capelo, José Maria: 25-26
Carasco (var. Carsco, Carrasco),
Henriette (Mme. Theodore André Sansom): 373
Ilario: 35, 373
Landry: 420
Caravajal, Petra (Dña. Cayetano Padilla): 607
Cardenas (var. Cardenes),
Bisente: 226
Francisco: 226
Francisco: 347 (bis)
José Guadalupe: 347 (bis)
Carle (var. Carles),
Eulalie "Lally": 192, 300
Maria (Dña. José y Barbo): 426
Marie Teresine (Mme. Florentin Conant II): 551
Carmon (var. Carmona, Permonia),
Bibiana (Dña. Vicente Micheli II) 512
Francisco: 1
Macedonia: 473, 512
Maria Concepcion (Dña. Andres Galindo): 1
Ursina (Dña. Ygnacio Cortinas): 536
Caro (var. Carro),
José Feliciano: 330
Jossé: 235
Louciana (Dña. José Polonio y Barbo): 587
Maria Josefa (Dña. Feliciano Antonio Barela): 14, 19, 98
Pedro José: 330
Caron *[See Carron.]*
Carr,
Aaron H.: 441
Bereford John: 284, 398, 441
C. E.: 284, 441, 545, 577
Caroline (Mme. B. V. Cortes): 640
J. C.: 577
John II *[see Bereford John]*
John Charles: 17, 148, 284, 313, 441, 640
Marie Emma Herminia (Mrs. Patrick Berry): 284
Carr (cont'd),
Marie Henriette (Mme. Stanislas Etienne D'Anglas): 313
Oscar W.: 284
Siereon (Simeon?): 441
William: 284
Carrasco *[see Carasco]*
Carrier,
Jean Ulisse: 368
Joseph: A-680
Carron (var. Caron),
Aimé: 135, 228
Hypolite Rodolphe: 135
Case, Elizabeth (Mrs. William Rivers) 501
Case? Ease, William: 113
Casenave (var. Caseneuve, Cassenava, Cassanova, Casanave, Cazenave),
_____: 32, 62-63
Denis: 114, 516
Jean Baptiste: 15
Marie Aimée (Mme. Andres Michel Rambin): 36, 516, 522, 647
Michel Denis: 36, 114, 516
Paul: 36, 261-62, 340-41, 432
Castanedo,
A.: 663-64
Elisabeth Valerie (Mme. Alfred Laurents): 664
Marie Appoline (Mme. Jean Adolphe Ducournau): 663
P. A. (J. A.?): 663
Remond: 465, 663-64
Castillo,
Polinario: 495
Tiburcia (Dña. Antonio Lazarino): 495
Castro,
Antonio: 62
Daria (Dña. Esmeregildo Martinez): 587
Felicité: 543
Juan de Diaz: 224
Joseph: 3
Maria Jacinta (Dña. Juan Joseph Acosta): 62
Catherine, f.w.c.: 416
Cavaros? (Cavrio?), Juan José: 90-91
Cavert,
Benjamin: 96
John: 96
Cazenave *[see Casenave]*

Cecile, f.w.c.: 213
Cecile,
Celeste, f.w.c.: 508
Jean Baptiste, f.m.c.: 213
Margherite, f.w.c.: 508
Perine (Metoyer), f.w.c.: 242
Cedars (var. Sidre),
Isabel (Mme. Antoine Le Moine, Jr.): 53
John: 53
[see also Cidre]
Cevallos, Maria de Serai?: 89
Chabana (var. Chabanne, Chavanne),
José Maria: 347 (bis)
Jossé: 272
Lino: 272
Maria Guadalupe (Dña. José Antonia Sepulveda): 575
Martin: 272
Chabot,
Henry: 324
Henry Theodore: 133, 324
Chabus,
Carmelita (Mrs. Lucas Hazleton): 11
François I: 11, 78, 140
François II: 140, 292
Rosemond: 114
Chagnot (var. Chagnau, Chainot),
Marie Theodoze (Mme. Louis Dominique Metoyer): 164, 636
Celeste (Mme. François Poché): 475
Chaler,
Arthur: 477, 569, 579
François Terence: 209-10, 254, 282, 290, 349, 377, 463
Pierre: 106
Pierre Oscar: 569, 604
U.: 569
Ursin: 477, 569, 594
Chamard (var. Chammard),
André I: 7, 12, 49, 149, 180, 197, 234, 295, 311, 314-15, 499, 518
André II: 518
Catherine: 13
D.: 538
Edmond Rozamond: 13, 261
Felicité (Mrs. Frederic E. Fearing); 518
Louis I: 261
Chamard (cont'd),
Louis II: 502, 518
Marie Catherine (Mme. Joseph Tauzin): 180, 193, 510, 637, 666
Marie Adelaÿde (Mme. Remy Marcel de Soto): 49
Marie Arthemise (Mme. J.B. Trezzini): 13, 482, 595
Marie Emelie (Mme. Pierre Victor Bouis): 197
Michel: 13, 49, 54, 77, 88
Rozemond *[see Edmond Rozamond]*
Champenoir, Isidore: 411
Chapman,
Benjamin Franklin: 279
Simeon B.: 279
Charbot, Marie Louise Jeanne (Mme. Clément Casimir Mary): 403
Charleville,
Baptiste, f.m.c., 27
John Baptiste: 92, 210, 254, 448, 463, 469
L. A.: 542
Charna, Maria Josefa (Mme. Guillaume Bébé I): 575
Chategnier (var. Chatenier),
A.: 550
Norbert: 652
Chaugnier (Chatagnier?), A: 75
Chaulotte, Marie Olive Clementine: 487
Chauvios, A.: 667, 670
Chauson (var. Tosson), Martin: 662
Chauveau, Margherita (Mme. Ursin Chaler): 477, 569
Chavanne *[see Chabano]*
Chavis, Barbara (Dña. Lino Chabanne) 272
Cheletre (var. Chelettre, Chelette, Chelete, Chletre, Cholette, Schelettre, Sheletre, Shelettre, Slecttre, Slettre),
Arzene: 433
Catherine *[see Catherine Cholette]*
Denis: 362
Etienne Brevelle: 301
Euphrosine (Mme. François Adlé): 158
Jean Baptiste: 158, 246, 301
Jean Pierre I: 158, 187, 219, 266 289, 346 (bis), 392
Jean Pierre II: 266

Cheletre (cont'd),
Marie Caroline (Mme. Philippe Cyriaque Brosset): 246
Marie Cephalide (Mme. Placide Brevelle): 346 (bis)
Marie Clarisse (Dña. J. B. Francisco Gonzales: Mme. Emanuel Brevel): 219, 392
Marie Clarisse (Dña. Adout Basquez): 433
Marie Clemantine (Mme. Etienne Roi): 187
Marie Emelie (Mme. Jean Pierre Vercher): 290, 307
Marie Françoise (Mme. Joseph Lattier): 23, 290
Marie Louise (Mme. Louis Barthelemy Rachal): 57, 222, 534, 579
Marie Pelagie (Mme. François Lattier): 64, 137, 163, 207, 210, 582, 602
Onesime: 605
Pierre *[see Jean Pierre]*
Pierre *[see Pierre Cholette]*
Rose (Mme. J. B. Dubois): 35, 195
Chenal (Cheval, Chenat), B.: 15, 81, 125
Chenevert, Clotin (Dña. José Santos II): 600
Cherbonnier, V.: 126
Cherbourne *[see Sherburne]*
Cherter(?), Anne (Mrs. Jacob Durst): 510
Cherino *[see Chirino]*
Chevalier,
_____: 41
Emile Belisaire, f.m.c.: 623
Fanny, f.w.c.: 623
Louis: 183, 255, 377, 578, 623
Cheze, Claude: 136
Chiasson, Marie Emelie (Mme. Laurent Lacoste): 631, 637
Chirino (var. Cherino, Cheriny),
Bartolo: 39
Josefa Barbara? (Dña. Cristoval Sota/Sosa?): 69
Joseph Encarnasion: 1, 2, 39
Juan Bautista: 366
Maria Faustina: (Mme. Jean Baptiste André Vascocu): 438, 485
Chirino (cont'd),
Maria Guadaloup (Dña. Manuel de los Santos Coy): 311
Maria Mauricia (Dña. José Martinez): 366
Cholet, Marie Barbe (Mme. Jean P. Breda): 356
Cholette,
Catherine: 435
Pierre: 435
[See also Cheletre, Collet]
Chopa, Maria Concepcion (Dña. José de los Santos Coy): 70
Chopin,
Antoine: 532
Jean Baptiste, Dr.: 52, 527, 532
Choppin,
Claude Antoine: 87, 120, 127, 129
Jean Baptiste: 87,
Christian,
Abda H.: 657
Gabriel: 657
Christophe (var. Cristophe),
Charles, f.m.c.: 611
Firmin Cappelot I, f.m.c.: 339, 459, 508, 515, 531, 552, 611
Firmin Cappelot II, f.m.c.: 552, 581?, 583?, 586?, 608?, 611, 630
Seraphine Elina, f.w.c. (Mme. J.B. Leandre Metoyer): 339
Cidre, Madeleine (Mme. Pierre Tessier?): 452
Cidre *[see also Cedars]*
Clark, Samuel D.: 96
Clerval, Louis: 443
Clinton, Lisa (Mme. Martin Chauson): 662
Closeau, Louis: 75, 104, 193, 205, 245
Cloutier (var. Clouttier),
Alexis: 137, 521
Augustin, f.m.c.: 10, 662
Jean Baptiste: 127, 161, 253, 269, 288, 390, 545, 618, 669
Jean Pierre: 21, 127, 137, 166
Marie Henriette, f.w.c. (Mme. Pierre Metoyer, Jr.; Mme. Emile Dupart): 167, 374, 515, 541
Marie Lise (Mme. Jean Jacques Lambre): 21, 390

Cloutier (cont'd),
Marie Zeline (Mme. Marc Sompayrac): 181, 382, 595
Cobbs, W. T?: 11
Cockerille, Wm. L.: 178, 269, 279, 306, 345, 345 (bis), 354, 359-360
Coe, Aaron: 17
Coindet (var. Coindé, Condé),
Antoine: 31, 389
Jacques, f.m.c.: 196
Jules N., f.m.c.: 652
Lucien, f.m.c.: 389, 406
Marie Antoinette, f.w.c. (Mme. Joseph Metoyer), 165
Marie Dorolyse, f.w.c. (Mme. Joseph Metoyer II): 196
Marie Felonise, f.w.c. (Mme. Valerie Perot): 320
Noel, f.m.c.: 141, 320, 442, 652
Colegan,
John: 275
Michael: 275
Collet,
Jean Baptiste: 343
Marie Josephine: 343
[see also Cholette]
Colson, Emile, f.m.c.: 338, 496, 544
Colton, John: 598
Commache, Trinidad (Dña. F. Flores): 226
Compère,
Anaïs Palmire (Mme. Louis Gassion Cyriaque Rachal): 348
Joseph Maximin: 388, 448
Louis: 388
Marie Alida (Mme. John Mears): 388
Pierre Sebastien: 22, 42, 71, 86-7 92, 112, 183, 231, 253, 302, 329, 361a, 388
Compton, Elisabeth (Mrs. Julius C. Saunders): 206
Conand (var. Conant),
Florentin II, f.m.c.: 551
Florentine (Mme. Augustin Prudans Metoyer), f.w.c.: 427, 608
Jean Baptiste Florentin (I), f.m.c. 6, 244, 338-39, 374, 427, 486-7 551, 611
Marie Agnes, f.w.c. (Mme. Charles Christophe): 611
Condé *[see Coindet]*
Conts (Kons), Mary (Mrs. John Hartman): 340, 509
Coombs,
Caroline (Mrs. Wm. Luyster): 519, 656
Marie Anne (Mrs. Samuel S. Simons): 519
Robert D?: 519, 656
Coranada?, _____ (Dña. Joseph Sanchez): 14
Cordero,
Antoine: 214
Maria Guadalupe (Dña. Precilliano Fuentos; Dña. Joseph Deroque): 214
Cordova (var. Cordovant),
Charles: 442
José: 33-34
Joseph Crisostomo: 33, 347 (bis)
Manuel: 610
Maria Catarina (Mme. Clement Lafitte): 610
Marie: 261
Marie Celezie (Mme. Edmund Rozamond Chamart): 261
Marie Jeanne (Mme. Jean Simon): 442
Narcisse: 263
Pedro: 263
Petra (Dña. José Guadalupe Cardenas): 347 (bis)
Cortes, (var. Cortez),
Adele (Mrs. Beresford John Carr): 441
Benjamin Valcourt: 241, 264, 279, 345, 354, 360, 398, 422, 640
Clement: 472-73
J. W.: 12
Jean: 148, 241, 269, 441, 640
Jean François: 148, 269, 354
Juan: 535
Marcelite (Mme. Guillaume Gille Dupart): 148, 241
Maria Dorotea (Dña. Miguel Maria Basquez): 472
Maria Guadalupe (Dña. Ramon Villa Real): 535
Marie (Dña. Vicente Micheli I): 512
Marie (Mme. Pierre Laplace): 241
Marie Josephine Clara (Mme. Jean Laplace): 241

Cortes (cont'd),
Marie Louise Marcellite: 11
Odille: 241
V. *[possible Veuve (Widow)]*: 269
Cortiñez, A.: 495
Cortinas (var. Cortines, Cortina),
Anselmo: 536
Ignatio: 311, 536
José Dolores: 311
Maria Antonia (Dña. Ignacio Longoria): 30, 352
Cosgrove, H.: 673
Cotonmaïs (var. Cotton-Maÿs, Cotton-Maïs),
Adelayde Arsene, f.w.c. (Mme. Jacques Porter): 175
Antoine, f.m.c.: 118, 152, 171, 175, 400, 409
Antoinette, f.w.c. (Mme. Louis Balthasar): 171
Marie, f.w.c. (Mme. François Metoyer, Jr.): 118
Marie Louise, f.w.c. (Mme. Louis Monet): 152, 636
Marie Suzette, f.w.c. (Mme. Louis Mullon): 409
Couchere, Anne Elisabeth (Mme. Bernard Montier): 485
Courterie, Marie Louise Hortance, f.w.c. (Mme. Joseph de la Baume): 73, 177, 358
Couteret, Gabriele (Mme. Antoine Boudrige): 270
Couty, Manuel: 496
Cowan,
Charlotte H. (Mrs. William Gaugh): 327
Jane E. H. (Mrs. Charles George Lewis): 306
Sarah P?: 327
T? H.: 306
William: 306, 327
Crawford, Samuel W.: 354
Crête, Marie Jeanne: 137
Criswell, Joseph: 275, 657
Croes, Pierre: 383
Crois, Victoire (Mme. Vincent Placide?): 199
Cruz (var. de la Cruz),
Juan: 119
Lumin? (Louis?): 119
Cruz (cont'd),
Maria Cesarea (Dña. José Aguino Barron): 3
Marie Eulalie (Dña. José Feliciano Caro): 330
Maria Ines (Dña. Joseph Quinoñes): 20
Maria Victoriana (Dña. Joseph Acosta): 330, 616
Maria Zarizoga? (Dña. Francisco Elde): 70
Pedro: 3
Cruz *[see also Groes]*
Cuellar *[see de Cuellar]*
Cur?, Wesley: 199
Curby, Lutha (Mrs. Archibald Davis): 626
Curvela, Maria Nieves (Dña. Juan José Calderon): 572

Dagênêt, Marie Joseph (Mme. J. B. Vanier): 278
Dagobert *dit* Le Brun,
_____: 543
Alexis, f.m.c.: 478
Marie Ursule, f.w.c. (Mme. François Eugene Dortoland): 391
Toussaint, f.m.c.: 652
Victor, f.m.c.: 401, 478
D'Anglais,
Etienne: 313
Stanislas Etienne: 313, 578
Daron de las Mountagnos, Henry: 466
Darvon? Duvin?,
Ma___: 69
Torivio: 69
Dauphine (var. Dauphin),
François Bernard) f.m.c.: 338, 459, 479, 483, 486-87, 497, 515, 646
François Dominique: 487
Davenport, Samuel: 38
David,
André Maturin: 502
Catherine, f.w.c. (Mme. Joseph Ozeme Metoyer): 249
Celestine, f.w.c. (Mme. Joseph Mézière): 543
Elisabeth Maturin: 502
Louis: 73, 177, 563
Marie (Mme. Dominiaue Sorel): 205
Marie Cephalide, f.w.c.: 157

David (cont'd)
Marie Louise, f.w.c. (Mme. Pierre St. Cyr de la Baume): 358
Marie Osinne, f.w.c. (Mme. Valery de la Baume): 73, 481
Davidson, John: 419
Davion,
Avit: 176, 612
Elizabeth (Mme. François Poirier), 514
Etienne: 110, 571, 612, 649
François: 467
Francois Emanuel: 405
Jean Baptiste: 77
Jean Baptiste Dominique: 77, 105, 110, 132, 176, 612, 655
Marie Anastasie (Mme. Pierre Derbanne, II): 333, 418, 511
Marie Azoline (Mrs. Nicholas Furlong): 132
Marie Celesie/ Selesine (Mme. Jean Lalande: Mme. J. B. Valière Rachal): 77, 655
Mary Theresa (Mme. Louis Geoffrois): 513
Davis (var. Deves),
Archibald: 626
C.: 142, 148
Eusevio: 523
John I: 88, 96, 523
John II: 88
John (son of Archibald): 626
Joseph: 523
Marie (Dña. Ignacio Lopez): 88
Marie Pompose: 523
Pierre Olivier: 523
Day, Alver M.: 411
de _____, Maria Dolores: A-680
De______enaux, Jos. Crevier: 280
Dealeman *[see Aleman]*
de Aro, Petra (Dña. Andres Ayala): 89
Deb_____, William: 533
De Blanc (var. Deblanc),
Charles Dorsino I: 451, 555
Charles Dorsino II: 555
François Jules: 230
Jean Baptiste Jerome: 371
Joseph: 371, 450
Marie Zoë (Mme. Leandre La Cour II): 451
Nicolas "Colin": 450-51
Rosella Marguerite (Mme. J. B. Auger Gillard): 230
De Blanc (cont'd)
Volizard: 370, 404
Deblieux,
_____, 13, 49
Alexandre Louis I, 7, 13, 126, 183, 264, 292, 356, 446, 465, 482, 545, 595, 618
Alexandre Louis II: 465, 482, 567, 618, 669
Eugene Valery: 505, 641, 650, 654, 663-64, 669
H. C.: 669
Joseph Numa: 482, 637, 654, 666, 669
Marie Rosaline (Mme. A. B. T. Sompayrac): 545
Debrun, _____: 340
de Cuellar, Maria Getrudis (Dña. Francisco Galindo): 1
de G____me, Jeanne (Mme. Jean Gravier): 228
Dehert,
Isabella (Mme. Pierre Van Melder, Mme. Fçois Van Schonbroeck): 383
Guillaume: 383
Dejean,
Felonise (Mme. Elisée Julien Rachal): 448
Jean Baptiste: 448
de la Baume (var. La Baume; La Vombe),
Joseph, I: 73, 177, 358
Joseph II, f.m.c.: 177
Marie Osine, f.w.c. (Mme. Ambroise Chastain Dominique Metoyer): 481
Pierre (Pedro) St. Cyr, f.m.c.: 177, 358
Valerio: f.m.c.: 73, 481
de la Bega, José Luis: A-680
de la Bega *[see also Vega]*
de la Cerda (var. La Cerda, La Serru, Serda),
Ana Maria (Dña. Louis Sarnac): 16
Athanaso: 133-35, 467
Maria (Dña. Athanazo Troquillo): 467
Maria Manuela (Dña. José Maria Procela): 32
Maria Telesfora (Dña. Esteban Morin): 138, 154, 322
Marie Rose (Mme. J. Grappe): 563

de la Cruz *[see Cruz]*
de la Garza (var. de la Garce, de la Garsa),
  Alexandre: 342
  José Ls?: 95
  Marcelino: 95
  Maria Josepha (Dña. Francisco Cardenas): 347 (bis)
  Raphaël: 342
  Refugio (Rev.): 177
de Langla__, Adelaïde (Mme. Etienne D'Anglas): 313
de la Peña, Juan: 89
de la Rue, C.: 72, 336
Delauney (var. Delaunay),
  Pierre I: 233
  Pierre II: 233
de la Vega,
  José Luis: 25-27
  Maria Josefa *[see Flores]*
de Leon,
  Maria de Jesusa (Dña. Joseph Andres Torres): 37
  Valentin: 37
Delgado,
  José Miguel: 30, 39
  Manuel: 30, 39
  Maria Josefa Candida (Dña. José Encarnacion Chirino): 39
del Garde, Gertrude (Dña. Adout Gutieres): 223
Delinsworth, Catherine (Mrs. Josiah Oaks): 291
de los Santos Coy (var. de los S[tos] Coy),
  Ignacio: 16, 20, 25-26, 30, 32-34, 69, 202
  José: 70
  Manuel: 311
  Maria Antonia Ezeckiel (Dña. José Dolores Cortines): 311
  Maria Jesusa (Dña. Ignacio Elde): 70
  Ramon: 34
  [see also Santos]
Delouche (var. Deslouche, Deslouches),
  Jean Louis: 145, 594
  Joachim: 402
  Julien: 23-24, 402, 594
  L.: 593
  Marie Athenais Adelaide (Mme. François Lattier): 349, 469
Delouche (cont'd)
  Marie Lise (Mme. Silvère Delouche): 463
  Pierre: 93, 349, 463
  Sephira (Mrs. Lewis M. Titus): 594
  Silvère: 463
del Rio (var. Del Rio, Delrio, Dellro),
  Faustin: 52, 320
  Felix: 609
  Génèvievè, f.w.c.: 652
  José Alexo: 609
  Joseph: 485
  Manuel: 234
  Pedro: 234
  Roman: 652
  [see also Rivers]
De Luna (var. de Luna),
  Faustino: 34
  Juan: 202, 223
  Juan Joseph: 34
  Pedro: 202
de Marmela, Apolinar: 84-85
De Mézières (var. Demesier, Demesieres, Mésières, Mézières),
  Eulalie (Mme. Bernard Hissoura): 60
  Fanny, f.w.c.: 215, 543
  Jacques, f.m.c.: 60
  Joseph, f.m.c.: 365, 401, 410, 442, 543, 652
  Marie Flavie, f.w.c. (Mme. François Gassion Metoyer): 215
  Marie Jeanne, f.w.c.: 141, 149, 365
  Marie Josephe, f.w.c.: 60
  Marie Reine Clerine, f.w.c. (Mme. Joseph Charles Simon): 410
  Marie Rose, f.w.c.: 410
  Nattalie, f.w.c. (Mme. Noël Coindet): 141, 652
  Noel, f.m.c.: 149, 358, 365, 442, 543
  Zenon, f.m.c.: 130
de Monteziore?, Marie: 224
Dendy,
  Elizabeth: 613, 642
  Thomas Jefferson: 613
De Nef, Catherine (Mme. Guillaume Dehert): 383
Denis (var. Deny, Denys),
  A[ne]: 293
  Athanase: 293, 528
  Euphrosine (Mme. J. B. Bonnette): 435

Denis (cont'd),
François: 528
Jacque Babet: 329
Jean Baptiste: 247, 293
Marguerite (Mme. Manuel Derbanne): 326, 386
Maria: 329
Marie Elmina (Mme. Joseph Vercher): 528
Nanette (Mme. Jean Joseph Rachal): 247, 333
Philippe: 453
Deniston (var. Denniston),
Alexandre: 422, 566, 585, 640
David: 422, 545, 595
Denuertos?, Marie Adeline (Mme. Adrien Hugue Noffré): 122
de Odiardi (var. Ordiardi),
Chrisanto: 387
Jean Baptiste: 387
Derbanne (var. Dervan),
_____: 170
Derzelin: 386
Emanuel *fils* Pierre: 326, 386, 428
Emanuel *fils* Gaspard II: 188
Emerante (Mrs. M. T. Handy): 546 (bis), 660, 668
François: 22, 138-39, 146, 151
Gaspard II: 55, 68, 133, 144, 188
Jacques Dufrois: A-679
Jean Baptiste: 68, 161
Jean Baptiste *fils* J.B.[Gaspard II] 133, 336, 423?
Jean Baptiste *fils* J.B. Gaspard: 145, 423, 488, 491
Jean Baptiste Gaspard: 22, 24, 83 151, 337, 539, A-679
Joseph: 46, 94, 185, 206, 507
Louis: 24, 40, 43, 83, 94, 151, 159, 186, 222, 293, 305, 347, 460
Louis Gaspard: 83, 539, 602
Louis Solastie: 46, 200, 325
Marcelite (Mme. Raimond Vascocu): 144
Marguerite (Mme. Joseph Evariste Rachal): 333
Marie (Mme. Pierre Elie): 317, 649
Marie Argine (Mme. J. B. Grappe): 337
Marie Aspasie (Mme. Valery Anty): 280

Derbanne (cont'd)
Marie Caroline (Mme. Alexandre Pinson): 326
Marie Cyprienne (Mme. J. B. Anty Sr.): 64, 170
Marie Delphine (Mrs. William Middleton): 491
Marie des Neiges (Mme. Antoine Le Noir): 192, 273, 321, 397, 437
Marie Denis (Mme. Cezar Thomassie): 24
Marie Doralise, f.w.c. (Mme. Pierre Valsain Dupré): 395
Marie Elisa (Mme. Charles Dorsino De Blanc II): 555
Marie Louise (Mme. François Lavespère): 42, 82
Marie Roseline "Rosette" (Mme. J. B. Julien Rachal): 221, 362, 601
Marie Selema (Mme. Pierre La Renaudière): 325
Marie Suset (Mme. François Besson): 68
Ozmin Pierre: 418
Pierre I: 186
Pierre II: 333, 418, 511
Pierre Simphorien: 333, 511
Placide: 55, 188
Rose (Mme. Pierre Gourinat): 443
Solastie: 555 *[see also Louis Solastie]*
Ursin: 488
Derenny, Nolla (Mrs. John Colegan): 275
Dermonia?, Macedonio: 473
Deroque,
Joseph: 214
Nicolas: 214
Derouanne,
Lise (Mme. Antoine Le Noir): 300
Michel: 300
Deronce, Octave Henry: 174-75, 179, 196, 211, 374-75, 468, 586
De Rousseau,
Marie Azelie (Mme. Pierre Rabalais): 268
Pierre: 268
De Russy,
Elisa: 269
J. William A.: 345, 518, 520

De Russy (cont'd),
John Adolphe, 422
Lewis Gustave I: 241, 269, 296, 306, 518, 520, 529
Lewis Gustave II: 529, 589
Marie Emelie (Mme. Jean François Cortes): 241, 269
Thomas Edward: 529
W. H.?: 598
William: 529
Deschervaux (Deschenaux?), Joseph Crevier: 138-39, 280, 301
De Soto (var. Desoto, Soto) *[see also Soto]*
José Antonio Marcel: 49, 256, 452
Marcel II *[may be Remy Marcel]*: 256, 258, 261-62
Marianne (Mme. Paul Bouet La Fitte) 5, 79, 121, 237, 378
Marie des Neiges (Mme. François Rambin): 257
Marie Emanuelle (Mme. Athanase Poissot): 380
Remy Marcel: 49
Simon: 452
Despallier, B.: 423
Deterville, Theodore: 186, 197, 228, 404
de Torres *[see Torres]*
Dezong?, Ernestine (Mrs. James H? Haughteling): 364
Detuil *[see Bébé]*
Dewal?, Lougier: 590
Dial, Roda (Mrs. Patrick Wisby): 310
Diaz (var. Dias),
Francisco: 223
Julian: 223
Maria Rafael *[see Maria Rafael]*
Maria Sabina: 536
Maria (Dña. Francisco Caldenes): 76
Diser, Elisabeth (Mme. J. B. Poirier): 252
Dolet,
Marie Cephalide (Mme. Firmin Perot): 285
Marie Denise (Mme. J. B. Adlé): 139, 546
Pierre: 285
Dolores,
Ignatia: 428
Marie (Mme. Vincent Canbarreux): 428
Dolichamp (var. Dolychamp),
_____: 229
Antoine: 169, 229
Domingo, Joseph Alphonse: 116
Donnaghan, Mary (Mrs. Sylvester Berry), 284
Donovan,
Amos: 471
William: 471
Dorlon, Joseph: 352
Dortolan (Doctolon, Dortolon, d'Ortoland, d'Ortolant, Ortolan),
Damase, f.w.c. (Mme. Victor Le Brun Dagobert): 478
David: 107, 317
François Eugene, f.m.c.: 391, 563
Hortense (Mme. François Baudoin): 125
Jean: 107, 125
Remon: 391, 478
Doyle, Anastazia (mrs. James Furlong): 132
Dranguet,
Adelaïde Basilisse (Mrs. Joshua Beal Jessup): 499
Benjamin: 17, 49, 193, 197, 336, 356, 422, 499, 641
Celeste Cornelia: 641
Euphrosine Azemie (Mrs. David Deniston): 422
Marie Helmina (Mme. Jean Philipe Breda): 356
Drohon (Ohuont?), François: 447
Dromgoole, Will. A.: 40
Du _____, Louis: 97
Du Bois (var. Dubois, Duvois),
Antoine: 286
François: 18, 173, 192, 233?
Gabriel Jean: 31
Henriette (Mme. Pierre Gagnon): 173
Jean Baptiste I: 35, 195
Jean Baptiste II: 35, 54
Jean Pierre Marie: 21, 56, 87, 136
Joseph: 233
Marie Adelaide (Mrs. Eusevio Davis): 523
Marie Aspasye (Mme. Louis Arcoit): 18
Marie Aurore Azelie (Dña. Juan José y Barbo): 286

Du Bois (cont'd),
   Nicolas, 31
   Pierre: 65
   Valentin: 35, 53, 194, 195, 304
   Zédoinne: 523
Dubornée, Felicité (Mme. François Saucier): 72
Dubreuil,
   Jean Baptiste Oscar, f.m.c.: 496, 531
   Louis: 531
Ducotel?, C?: 369
Ducournau,
   J. Baptiste: 663
   Jean Adolphe: 631, 638, 650, 663
Ducreux, Celestine (Mme. Pierre Roy): 638
Ducrois, Sophie (Mme. Pierre Jean Abel Sers): 169
Dugas,
   Aurellia: 620
   Clara (Mme. Theophile Bossier): 628
   Pierre: 628
Dumarest, Jean Joseph: 281-82
Duncan,
   Alexandre: 540
   George W.: 540
Dunn,
   John R.: 178, 291
   M. C.: 547, 567, 643, 650
Dunois?, Augustin: 30?, 32
Dupart (var. Duparte),
   Arthemise, f.w.c. (Mme. François Metoyer I): 508
   Charles: 541
   Elisa, f.w.c. (Mme. Clement Llorens): 603
   Emile, f.w.c.: 156, 196, 508, 541, 603
   Guillaume: 148
   Guillaume Gille: 148
Dupont, Marie (Mme. Pierre Delaunay, Sr.): 233
Dup[illegible], O[illegible] 170
Dupré (var. Duprez),
   Antoine Valmont: 252
   Athanase: 35
   Athanaze Dufroy: 252
   Dufroy *[see Athanase Dufroy & Lufroy]*
Dupré (cont'd)
   Edouard, 396
   Elise *[see Marie Françoise Elise]*
   Emanuel: 174, 316, 395, 406, 481, 630, 636
   Emilie (Mme. Franklin Philogene Adlé): 677
   Joseph: 593
   Joseph Leon: 252
   Lufroy *fils* Pierre: 252
   Manuel Prevot: 3, 4, 9, 21, 23
   Marie Aurore (Mme. Joseph François Lattier): 23
   Marie Aurore (Mme. André Bey): 593
   Marie des Neiges Ezilda, f.w.c. (Mme. Belisaire Llorens): 395
   Marie Eloise (Mme. Jean Louis Delouche): 463, 594
   Marie Françoise: 8
   Marie Françoise Elise: 252
   Marie Marcelite (Mme. J. B. Derbanne): 488, 491
   Marie Zeline (Mme. Valentine Du Bois): 35
   Marie Zite? (Mme. Chaler): 210
   Numa *[see Sylvestre Numa]*
   Osite (Mme. Julien Delouche): 402
   Pierre: 23, 252
   Pierre Valsain: 395
   Sylvestre Numa: 252
   Valmont *[see Antoine Valmont]*
Dupuis (Dupré), Magdalenne (Mme. Charles Pierre Melançon): 14, 81
Dupuis?, François: 94
Durand, Raymond: 133
Du Rossé, Marie Asely (Dña. Ramon Antonio La Sada; Mme. Louis Saucier): 72
Durst,
   Jacob, 510
   Mary Victoire (Mrs. Antoine Woolf, Mme. Theophile E. Tauzin): 510
Duthil
   Edmond: 281
   Jacques: 281
Duvin? *[see Darvon?]*

Ector,
James: 456
Lydia: 451
Edens,
Alfred K.: 283
John: 283
Edwards, R.: 599
Elde,
Francisco: 70
Ignacio: 70
Elie (var. Eli, Ely, Hely, Bernard *dit* Elie),
Agapite: 317, 393, 513
Athanase "Athanasite": 317, 580, 584, 655
Celestin: 107, 192, 393, 580 *[see also Manuel Celestin]*
Landry: 107, 110
Manuel Celestin: 401
Marguerite (Mme. David Ortolan): 107
Marie Elise Bernard (Mme. Sylvestre Poissot; Mme. Louis Ouallet II): 317, 650
Pierre: 18, 317, 649
Ellis,
John: 341
John L: 340-41
Endemini, Chatherine (Mme. Antoine Messi): 470
Epron *dit* Reñois (var. Renoy, Frenois),
Elisa (Mme. J. B. Plaisance: 457
Marie (Mme. André Sansom): 373
René François: 59, 82-83, 112, 122-124, 457, 632
Victor: 632
Equis (var. Huaisse),
Maria (Dña. Manuel Cordova): 610
Maria Apolinaria (Dña. Manuel Procella): 537
Maria Estephania (Dña. Joseph Flores): 323?, 343, 384, 590
Espinosa, Rosa (Dña. Bernardo Torres): 37
Essourd *[see Hissoura]*
Estrada,
Catalina (Dña. Francisco Carmona): 1
Julio: 37
Everard, Marie Thérèse (Mme. Antoine Chopin): 532
Eudos(?), H.: 277
Fabre, Jean: 247, 265, 389
Fagot, Samuel: 55
Fallon,
J.: 533
James: 533, 556, 564
Fual, Elisabeth (Mme. Nicolas Keiffer): 548
Fauvelle, Auguste: 259-60, 452-53, 538
Favrot,
Augustin: 232
Marie Adelaïde (Mme. Charles Le Moine): 232
Fearing,
Frederic E.: 518
Martin: 518, 520
Feble? F?: 292
Feguen,
Mathieu: 599
Thomas: 599
Ferel,
Joseph Guadaloupe: 98
Maria Conception (Dña. Athanasio Barela): 98
Ferguson (var. Forguesson),
Mary (Mrs. Benjamin Bullitt I): 598
William: 275, 340-41
Fernandez,
Maria: 537
Maria Antonia (Dña. Encarnacion Procella): 537
Ferrier,
Celeste (Mme. Derzelin Derbanne): 386
Jean Baptiste: 136, 386
[see also Lalande Ferrier.]
Fiorenne?: 502
Figari (Figuera), L: 486, 551, 586
Flamigan, Alice (Mrs. John Otis): 657
Flanner, T. J.: 585, 641, 675
Fleming (var. Flemming),
____: 160
Bartholomew: 237, 276, 566
Constance: 237
Edward B.: 498, 530, 566
Francis: 237-38, 250, 378
Julia (Mme. Remy Casimir Perot): 276, 390
Fleury,
Paul Aimé: 444
William: 330, 444

Flores,
Andrea (Dña. Francisco Cardenes): 226
Cesaire: 412-14, 562, 609a
Ciriaque: 562
Dioniso: 592
F?: 226
Hilaire: 590, 609
Jesus: 399
José: 90
Joseph: 323, 343?, 384, 590
Joseph II: 343
Juanna (Dña. Desiderio Salcedo): 665
Maria Alfonsa (Dña. Juan José y Barbo II): 558
Maria Antonia (Dña. José Damian Arocha): 91, 119
Maria Antonia (Mme. Louis La Fitte): 381, 453
Maria Antonia, 25
Maria Isavel (Dña. Valentin de Leon): 37
Maria Josefa: 90
Maria Josefa (Dña. Joseph Jarnac): 323
Maria Josepha [de] la Vega (Dña. Juan Maria Lasarino): 25, 495
Maria Telesphor (Mme. Jean Chrisostomé Vascocu): 384
Maria Trinidad (Dña. Julian Grande): 2, 344, 609a
Onofre: 590
Pedro Chrisostomé: 117, 342-44, 380, 399, 562, 590, 609a
Vital: 115-17, 399, 558
Fontana, Michel: 357
Fontenot (var. Fonteneaux, Fonteneau, Fontenau, Fonteno),
Benjamin G.: 393, 498
Celemine *[see Marie Denis Celemine]*
Cesaire I: 41, 54-55, 79, 103, 113, 133-34, 144, 189, 217, 332, 378, 653
Cesaire II: 217, 237, 271?, 273, 300, 355, [illegible]
François Jean Baptiste: 189, 355
Gervais: 546
Jean Baptiste: 5, 41, 67, 73, 133, 188
L^{e}.: 41
Louis: 41, 403
Fontenot (cont'd),
Louis, 546
Marie Modeste (Mme. Jean Baptiste Trichel): 133
Marie Deneige Celemine (Mme. Hypolite Bordelon): 111, 566, 653
Marie Manette Felis (Mme. François Perot; Mme. Louis Clement Victor Mary): 41, 250, 403, 546 (bis); 619, 660
Marie Thérèze Constance (Mrs. Barthelemew Fleming): 237, 276, 566
Forcel, François: 552
Forguesson *[see Ferguson]*
Forstall, Edouard: 308
Fort,
Andres: 44, 631
Jacques: 44
Louis: 44
Marie Olandine (Mme. Timothé La Coste): 631
Marie Rosalie, f.w.c. (Mme. Joseph Perot): 271
Fournier,
Jean Baptiste: 351
Louise Victoire Stephanie (Mme. Pierre Pelli): 312, 351
Françoise, f.w.c.: 540
Françoise, slave: 10
Français, Nicolas, Rev.: 330, 335, 346
Frederic (var. Federic, Frederick, Phredieu [not to be confused with Fredieu/Phredieu]),
Armeline (Mme. Isaac Perot): 571
François: 22, 58-59, 64, 82-83, 86, 106, 122-23, 137, 177, 301, 464, 480, 571, 674
François Hubert: 461, 492, 674
J. Bte.: 539
Jean: 86
Joseph Roman: 492, 604, 621, 674
Marie Azelie (Mme. Etienne Brevelle Cheletre): 301
Marie Barbe (Mme. François Ro-nin): 7, 182, 367
Marie Catherine (Mme. J. B. Armand): 57, 108, 122, 159, 170, 282, 534, 539
Marie Euphrosine MAgdelene (Mme. J. B. Morentine): 287, 447, 542

Frederic (cont'd):
Marie Heloise (Mme. Jean Louis Chrisostomé Perot): 464
Marie Lolitte (Mme. Victor Poissot): 480
Marie Pelagie (Mme. J. B. Barthelemy Lattier): 8, 58, 362
Marie Rosalie (Mme. Pierre Quierry): 225, 309, 322
P.: 480
P. E.: 469, 492
Pelagie (Mme. Barthelemy Lestage): 221
Fredieu (var. Phredieu),
Antoine: 5, 191, 428, 571
Azelie *[see Barbe Azelie]*
Augustin: 5, 19, 191, 507
Barbe Azelie (Mme. Pierre Ternier, Jr.): 431
François: 82-83
Honoré: 5, 19, 28, 38, 45-46, 60, 75, 121, 205, 207, 239, 336-37, 377, 402, 415, 428, 431, 507, 530, 588, 596, 637
Jean Baptiste Isaac: 5, 54
Marie Aselie (Mme. Siboire Perot): 596
Marie Celina (Mme. Maximin Vercher): 415
Marie Olympe (Mme. Joseph Perot I): 420, 571
Freeman,
Jackson: 394, 589
John: 394
Fuentes,
Guadelupe (Dña. Juan de Luna): 202, 223
Ramond: 202, 223
Furlong,
James: 132
Nicholas: 124, 132, 407, 513, 612

Gaetz, Elize (Mrs. Jean George Hubner), 446
Gagné (var. Gagnier, Gaigné),
Angele (Mme. Louis Oualette): 612, 649
Louis Basil: 54
Manete (Mme. Michel Barberousse): 239
Marie Françoise: 28
Gagné (cont'd),
Marie Hyacinthe (Mme. J. B. Collet; Mrs. James Wallace, I): 2, 256, 298-99, 343
Marie Josephe Henriette (Mme. Toussaint Passaneau/Pinsonneau): 266
Marie Louise (Mme. Antoine Christian Hesser): 54, 562
Marie Rosalie "Rose" (Mme. Pierre Ternier): 28, 105, 431
Pelagie (Mme. J. B. Dominique Davion); 77, 110, 132, 176, 612, 655
Ursulle Felicité (Mme. Pierre Bouët La Fitte): 257, 297, 610
Gagnon,
Pierre I: 173, 192
Pierre II: 59, 160, 173, 176
Pierre N.: 124
Gaiennie (var. Gaiennie),
Amanda: 546
François: 490, 565
J? Emma (Mrs. T. J. Hickman): 490
Vallery: 440, 454, 490, 521, 527 546, 565, 659, 671
Gallien,
_____: 475
Adolphe: 622
Carles: 622
Eloise Neuville (Mme. Eleuther Brosset): 476
J. B. Neuville: 418, 424, 429, 476, 622
Louis: 424, 429, 440, 528
Louis Emmanuel: 397, 424, 429, 460, 506, 622, 625
Louis Neuville: 424-25, 476
Marie Adeline (Mme. Joseph Lattier II; Mme. Jerome Thomassie): 9, 208, 319, 429, 622
Marie Auresile (Mme. Beloni Vercher): 209, 415, 635
Marie Cephalide (Mme. J. B. Narcisse Quierry): 309
Marie Euranie (Mme. Firmin Joseph Lattier): 625
Marie Euphemie (Mme. J. B. Neuville Gallien): 424
Marie Jeanne Euphrosine (Mme. Jacques Vercher): 123, 162, 397, 418, 506, 528

Gallien (cont'd),
Marie Henriette (Mme. Marcelin Vercher): 506
Marie Julie (Mme. Remy McTire): 425
Marie Orezille *[see Marie Auresile]*
Melissaire Marie (Mme. Daunoye Vercher): 184
Neuville *[see Louis Neuville]*
Nicolas: 8, 9, 208, 347
Ophelia (Mme. Maximin Vercher): 635
William: 350
Galluchat, Catherine (Mme. J. B. Fournier): 351
Gar__, Gertrudes de los Dolores (Dña. Pedro Bela): 235
Garcia (var. Garcie),
Carlo: 627
Francisco: 414
Joseph: 414
Luzgarde (Dña. Alexandro Guerra): 572
Maria Arcoria (Dña. Juan José Ybarbo I): 558
Seraphine: 665
Tomas: 226
Gardiner, Thomas, Dr.: 276
Gargole, Maria Madlena (Mme. Antonio Perini): 501
Garguon, Arnéde: 128
Garnac, Margil: 609
Garnac *[see also Jarnac]*
Garner, Mary (Mrs. Robert Vaughn): 614
Garrau *[see Guarrand]*
Gaudrio, Marie Jeanne (Mme. Charles Benigne Bertrand): 527
Gaugh,
Thomas: 327
William: 327
Gautier (var. Gauthier, Gauttier, Geothier, Gottier),
_____: 485
J. P.: 476
Joseph: 447
Leonard: 56
Marie (Mme. J. B. Dejean): 448
Marie Palmier Celeste (Mme. Bernard Mericq): 56
Pierre: 447
René: 56
Gayoso,
Ferdinando: 577
Gayoso (cont'd),
L.: 577
Margueritte (Mrs. M. M. Robinson): 577
Genty,
Emelie (Mme. J. B. Olivier Rouquier): 550
Louis: 218, 498, 550
Geoffrion (var. Geogriant; Geoffrois, Geuffant),
Hélène (Mme. Gilbert La Cour): 201, 370, 439, 455
Jean: 266
Louis: 107, 110, 176, 513
Zélene (Mrs. T. J. Quisenberry), 513
Guiffar?, Jean: 300
Geothier *[see Gautier]*
Germaine, _____: 19
Gevarra, Felipo: 248
Giannani (?), Angelo: 501
Gibson *[see Kipson]*
Gilbert, Frances (Mrs. Peter Boyce): 578
Gillard,
Edouard Joseph: 230, 371, 404
Gilbert: 455
Jean Baptiste: 201, 230, 243, 349, 450
Jean Baptiste Auger: 230
Jean Baptiste Azenor: 451
J. B. M?: 371
Jean Marie: 243
Joseph: 201, 230, 243, 371, 404, 439, 450, 455
Josephine (Mme. Jean Marie Bret La Cour I): 201, 370
Marguerite Emelie (Mme. Jean Marie Gillard): 243
Marguerite Irma (Mme. Sylvere Baillio; Mme. J. B. Jerome De Blanc): 371
Marie Louise (Mme. Leandre La Cour): 404, 439, 451
Gillard, Numa: 451
Theodozia (Mme. Nicolas "Colin" De Blanc): 450
Gilmer,
Marvison B.: 657
Thomas M.: 657
Giminez *[see Ximenes]*

Ginger (var. Guinger),
Adam: 250
Christeno: 250
Jean Agues: 180, 250
Marie Helmina (Mme. Lezin Eugene Tauzin): 180
Glapion, Lisette, f.w.c.: 6, 47
Glass,
Mary (Mrs. James Wallace II): 298
William: 298
Glaudon, François Xavier de: 130
Gomez (var. Gommez),
Geonaeve [Genoveva] (Dña. Michel Medillen): 295
Maria Candida (Dña. Antonio Mancha): 314
Maria Manuela (Dña. Dolores Martinez): 89
Gongora (var. Gongre), Ignacia: 263
Gonin (var. Gonnin, Gonain),
François Xavier: 7, 182, 346, 367
Geneviève (Mme. Emanuel Le Vasseur): 99, 324
J. B.: 506
Marie Aurore (Mme. J. B. Bossier): 494, 674
Marie Modeste (Mme. Cezar Soulange Bossier; Mme. Joseph Soldini): 7, 367, 628
Sophie (Mme. Firmin Soto): 182
Thomase (Mme. Epron): 59?
Gonzales (var. Gonsalez, Gonzalez),
Andres: 537
Ignacio: 224
Juan Bautista: 219
Juan Bautista Francisco: 219
José Serafin: 65
Josepha (Dña. Domingo Ximenes): 556
Maria Olaya (Dña. Domingo Villareal): 535
Martin: 224
Gonzalez de Hermosillo, Rafael: 34
Gottier *[see Gautier]*
Goulain, J.: 489
Goulin, Fs.: 527
Gourinat (var. Gourinate),
Isaac: 443
Pierre: 443
Goutieres *[see Gutierrez]*
Gracia, Nicolas: 4, 23, 40, 136, 326, 373
Gradenigo, Brigitte (Mme. Louis Fontenot): 546
Graham, Thomas: 35, 53
Grandchamp (var. Grandchampt),
Jean Baptiste: 265, 389, 411
Raymond Villadary, 265
Grande,
Julian: 2, 258, 344, 609a
Maria Basilia (Mrs. Pierre Wallace; Mme. Pierre Robleau): 2, 258, 379, 592
Maria Vivianne (Mme. Jean Flores La Fitte): 344
Marie Antoinette (Mme. Cesaire Flores): 609a
Granderote, Marie Louise: 392
Grant,
Stephen I: 461
Stephen II: 461
Grappe,
Benjamin: 458
Felicité. f.w.c.: 113, 164
François I: 55
François, f.m.c.: 563
Gabriel: 563
Jacques: 563
Jean Baptiste I: 55
Jean Baptiste *fils* Jean Pierre: 337, 458
Jean Pierre: 55, 332, 337, 458
Magdeleine, f.w.c.: 10, 73, 157, 177, 249, 358
Marie Claire, f.w.c. (Mme. Louis Silvie): 113
Marie Jeanne, f.w.c. (Mme. Joseph de la Baume): 177
Marie Josephe, f.w.c.: 365
Marie Melisa (Mme. Paul Firmin Rachal): 332
Marie Pelagie (Mme. Louis Fonteneau); 41, 403
Marie Rose Sophronie (Mme. Placide Derbanne): 55
Onesime: 55
Pelagie, f.w.c.: 73, 149, 238, 271, 320
Suzette, f.w.c.: 391, 478
Gravier (var. Gravié),
Jean: 228
Jean Eustache: 228
Green, Mary (Mrs. Jonathan Jessup) 499
Greneaux (var. Grenaux),
Charles Emanuel: 135, 169, 181, 186, 191, 218, 240 (cont'd)

Greneaux (cont'd)
Charles Emanuel (cont'd) 264, 270, 285, 292, 327, 335-36, 353, 359, 367, 372, 385, 464, 482, 503, 505, 530, 565, 588-89, 594-95, 628, 638, 639, 650
Emanuel: 264
Emerantinne (Mrs. Robert Morrow): 639
Françoise Victoire (Mrs. John Johnson): 169, 190, 417
Marie Louise (Mme. Antoine Adlé): 385
Grillet (var. Grilliet),
Antoine: 60, 78, 353, 438
Cleri: 60, 676
J?: 67
Marie Barbe (Mme. Bertrand Plaisance): 19, 38, 99, 163, 207, 227
Marie Françoise (Mme. Louis Barthelemy Rachal); 42, 45, 71, 229, 337, 521
Marie Margarite (Mme. Bernard Hissoura, Sr.): 60, 78, 353
Theodore: 67-68, 99
Zeline (Mme. Spire Bordelon): 102
Gronley (Gronlus), Elisabeth (Mme. Pierre Buvens): 613, 626
Grovenor, A. S.: 659
Guarrand (Garrau), Marianne (Mme. François Monde): 228
Guerra,
_____: 536
Alexandre: 572
Venturo: 560, 572-573
Guerrero,
Maria Tiburcia (Dña. Juan José Martinez): 493
Patricio: 493
Guibert, Marie (Mme. François Baulos): 190
Guidon, Anne (Mme. Raymond Villadary Grandchampt): 265
Guinger *[see Ginger]*
[illegible]
Gulaen, Mary (Mrs. James Reyburn): 547
Gunny (var. Ganie)
George William: 178
Suzanne: 178
Wilson: 178
Guarrand, Marianne (Mme. François Monde): 135
Gutierrez (var. Gutiere, Gutieres, Goutieres),
Adout: 223
Antonio: 295
Augustin: 221
Bernada: 295
Juanna (Dña. Ramond Fuentes & Francisco Diaz); 202, 223
Manuel: 295, 559
Manuel II: 295
Manuela: 295
Petra: 295
Sévèr: 295

H_____, S.W.: 520
Haller, H. O.: 595
Hamilton,
Andrew: 411
Lucinda (Mrs. James P. Mears): 388
Handy, M. T.: 484, 585, 619, 668
Hanselman (var. Hanselmans, Hanzelman),
Catherine (Mrs. Conrad H.): 507
Charles: 449
Conrad: 507
Elmina (Mme. Joseph Marcolli): 449
Marie Louise (Mme. Joseph Derbanne; Mme. Honoré Fredieu): 186, 507
Hardy, John: 312, 638
Harmon (Armand), Marie Nancy, f.w.c.: (Mrs. John Davis): 88
Harrison,
James P.: 643
John: 561
Marguerite Ann (Mrs. William L. Tuomey): 643
William: 561
Hart, Simeon M.: 675
Hartley, Joseph H.: 96
Hartman,
Anna: 568
Augustin: 340
[illegible] M.: 568
John: 340, 509
John D.: 568
Peter: 509
Haughteling (var. Hauteling),
James H?: 364
James Lawrence: 364

Haurut,
François: 521
Martin Charles: 345 (bis), 356, 521
Hazleton,
Jno? H.: 502
Lucas: 11
Samuel: 11
Heard, Daniel M.: 291
Hector *[see Ector]*
Hely *[see Elie]*
Henderson, Sarah (Mrs. William Cowan): 306, 327
Henesi, Catherine (Mrs. Thomas Feguen): 599
Hengar, Marie (Mme. Arnould La Fargue): 466
Hennessy *[see Henesi]*
Henry, J.: 61, 673
Henyazan?, Marie (Mme. Pierre Huppé): 142
Hernandez (var. Hernand, Hernan),
Emanuel: 161, 456
Felipa (Dña. Domingo Quintero): 26
Jerome: 161-62
Maria Antonia (Dña. José Antonio Barron): 3
Maria Rita (Dña. Patricio Guerrero): 493
Pedro: 90
Silvestre: 143, 162
Herrera
Juan: 37
Maria Antonia (Dña. José Antonio y Barbo): 426
Maria Josefa (Dña. Faustino de Luna): 34
Herriman, Durent G.: 481, 483
Hertzog,
Amire R.: 142
Charles W.: 659
Clarisse (Mme. Valsim Lambre): 131
G. F?: 183
Henry: 505, 577, 640, 643-44, 650
Henry Mathieu: 66
Jean François: 21, 29, 59, 66, 82, 87, 93, 112, 129, 131, 142, 253, 302, 328, 348, 363, 650
Marie Desirée (Mme. J. B. Ovide Buard): 363
Marie Jeanne Phannie (Mme. François Placide Dacize Bossier): 253
Marie Jeanne Suzette (Mme. Louis Alexandre Buard): 328
Hertzog (cont'd),
Richard William: 66, 71, 131, 142
Hesser (var. Esser, Essert, Essedr),
Andres Isaac: 538
Antoine Christian: 54, 562
Christian: 54, 140, 150, 239, 380-81, 538, 647
François Mero: 647
Frederick Felix: 381
Marie Celina (Mme. Louis Dunoye Bossier): 150
Marie Josephe Adelaÿde (Mme. François Chabus, Jr.; Mme. Edouard Murphy, Jr.): 140, 292
Marie Josephe Celine (Mme. Joseph Victor Barberousse): 239
Marie Josephe Euphemie (Mme. Sylvestre Poissot): 380
Marie Louise Inocente (Mme. Cyriaque Flores): 562
Hewett (var. Hawyett),
John: 533
Margaret (Mrs. J. Fallon; Mrs. Patrick Shelly): 533
Hickman,
Peter Terry: 236, 369, 490
Thomas J.: 369, 490
William: 236, 369, 490
William Preston: 236, 369
Himel (var. Himil),
Antoine: 44
Eleonore (Mme. Alexandre Soulange Bossier): 7, 289, 346, 460
Marie Françoise: 44
Marie Locodite Buard (Mme. André Fort): 44, 631
Himenes *[see Ximenes]*
Hissoura *dit* Pantaleon (var. Essourd, Hissourd, Isourd, Isurd, and Isurde),
_____: 78, 84, 85, 88, 89
Adonis Isidore: 353, 415
Bernard I: 60, 78, 353
Bernard II: 60
Eusebe: 78, 84 - 85, 470, 588
Joseph: 665
Marie Aglaë (Mme. Jerome Messi): 470
Marie Chrisante (Mme. Isaac Plaisance): 588

Hoding?, Thom.: 306
Hopkins,
D.: 519
D. R.: 269, 372
Horen (var. Hotien, Hoker),
Catherine (Mrs. Matieu Feguen): 599
Thomas: 599
Hosea, Antoinette (Mme. Antoine Marie Luvini): 336
Houston? *[see Huten]*
Hoy, Guillaume: 522
Hubner,
Alfred Jean George: 445, 449, 465, 619
Jean George: 446
Hugonin, Marguerite (Mme. François Haurut): 521
Huppé,
J. A.: 87
Jean Baptiste: 142
Pierre: 142
Hurseaux, Marie Louise (Mme. J. B. Leroux): 454
Huten [Hutton? Houston? Newton?], Fevy [Phoebe], (Mrs. William Walker I): 658
Hyams,
Samuel: 345 (bis)
Samuel Myers: 345 (bis); 547, 650
Hymenes *[see Ximenes]*

Ibarbo *[see y Barbo]*
Isham, Mary: 568
Isurd *[see Hissoura]*

Jacques, Marie Orezille Babet Denis (Dña. José Marie Robles): 329
Janin (var. Jannin),
Joseph Toussaint, Dr.: 66, 93, 109, 168, 253, 363
Julien: 93
Jans?, D. F.: 495
Jarnac (var. Guisarnat, Zarnac, Sarnac)
François G.: 323
Gregorio: 220
Joseph: 323
Louis: 16, 220
Marie del Pilar (Dña. Antonio Solis): 16
[see also Garnac]
Jarreau (var. Jarau, Jarreaux),
Bernard: 236, 290, 305
Jarreau (cont'd),
Helena Perot (Mme. Ursin Derbanne): 488
Jean: 305, 361b, 488
Lucien: 305, 307, 310, 361a-b
Jarry, Jean François: 447
Jean Baptiste, free Negro: 400
Jean Baptiste Augustin, f.m.c.: 416
Jean Ris *[see Ris]*
Jessup,
Jonathan: 499
Joshua Beale: 499, 518, 637
Jobert, Marie Louise (Mme. Julien Jannin): 93
Johnson (var. Johonston, Jhonston),
Amanda *[see Victoire Emandée]*
François: 398
John: 169, 190, 418
Joseph: 398
Marianne Pamela (Mme. Abel Napoleon Sers): 169
Victoire Emandée (Mme. Pierre Baulos: Mrs. Ira Carter Ash): 190; 418
W. R.: 134
Jones,
Henry: 284
Mary Ann (Mrs. Thomas Jefferson Dendy): 613
Priscilla (Mrs. Henry Moses): 368
Thomas P.: 345, 354, 643
Juolly?, Mary (Mrs. Joel Walker): 96

Kaufman, J? S?: 345 (bis)
Kelly, James: 613, 618, 633, 672-73
Kempermens? (Kenysemers?), Marie Elisabeth (Mrs. Gerard Backen): 419
Kennedy, R.: 599
Kenoe, Catherine (Mrs. Nicholas Furlong): 132
Kiffer,
Nicholas I: 548
Nicholas II: 548, 601
Kile,
George W.: 673
Stephen W.: 673
Kimball,
A. C., 206
Asa: 345
Peter French: 345
Kerry *[see Quierry]*

Kipson, Mary (Mrs. John Freeman): 394
Kirby *[see Curby]*
Kons *[see Conts]*
Knight,
Jacob: 475-76, 488-89
William: 489
Knot, Margherite (Mrs. Silas Shelburne): 642

La Baume *[see de la Baume]*
La Berry (var. La Baire, La Bery, Labery, Lavery),
Magdeleine (Mme. Pierre Nolasco de Porcuna): 161, 277
Marie (Mme. Louis Rachal): 31, 247
Marie Françoise (Mme. Barthelemy Rachal): 4
Marie Louise Agathe (Mme. Françoise Peraut): 41, 188, 378
Labershe, George: 136
La Borde, Francise (Mme. Dominique L'Herrison): 438
La Caze (var. Lacasa, La Case, Lacase, Lacasse, Lacassas),
Antoine: 557
Benjamin: 632
Caroline (Mme. Pierre Du Rousseau): 268
Celeste (Mme. Augustin Favrot): 232
Celestin, f.m.c.: 294
David: 280
Etienne: 124, 152-53, 280
Etienne II: 153-55
Felicité (Mme. J. B. Le Moine I): 124, 153,194, 232, 304
Felicité (Mme. J. B. Le Moine II): 124
Jacques: 281
Marie Henriette (Mme. Edmond Duthil): 281
Michel, f.m.c., 203
Rosalie, f.w.c.: 203, 294
Lacobee *[see Loucouvichi]*
La Coste (var. Lacoste),
Emée (Mme. Theophile E. Tauzin): 637
J. (T?): 617, 637
Laurent: 447, 631, 637
Timothée: 631
La Cour (var. Lacour, La Court, Le Cour),
A.: 404
Armand: 448
Aurelia Petronie (Mme. Gilbert La Cour II); 439
La Cour (cont'd)
Azelie Cecile (Mme. Gilbert Gillard); 455
Azenor Theodule: 404
Bret *[see Jean Marie Bret]*
Cecille (Mme. J. B. Gillard): 230, 243, 450
Colin: 455
Colin *[see also Nicolas]*
Françoise (Mme. Jean Marie Bret La Cour II): 201
Gaspard I: 40, 58, 151, 212, 225, 361b
Gaspard II "Gasparite": 318-19, 361b, 488-89
Gilbert I: 201, 230, 370, 439, 455
Gilbert II: 439, 455
Jean Marie Bret I: 201, 370-71, 439, 450
Jean Marie Bret II: 201, 230, 243, 370-71
Leander I: 201, 278, 404, 439, 451
Leander II: 451, 455
Magdeleine Euphemie (Mme. Nicolas La Cour): 370
Marguerite "Fanny" (Mme. François Jules? Joseph? De Blanc): 230, 371, 450
Marie Emely (Mme. J. B. Lattier, Jr.): 58
Marie Lise (Mme. Manuel Rachal): 40, 225, 318, 440, 489
Nicolas: 370
Nicolas *[see also Colin]*
Petronille (Mme. Joseph Gillard II): 243, 371, 455
Pierre: 418
Theodule *[see Azenor Theodule]*
Tranquilline (Mme. François Derbanne): 151
La Fantasy, Marguerite (Mme. François Metoyer I): 48
Lafargue,
Arnould: 466
Pierre Adolphe: 466
La Fitte (Laffite, Laffite, Laffitte, Laphite),
Celeste (Mme. Firmin Poissot; Mrs. Francis Fleming): 121, 237, 378
(cont'd)

La Fitte (cont'd),
Celimene (Mme. Antoine St. Vigne): 453
Celine (Mme. Étienne Davion): 110, 612
Césaire: 115-17, 259-60, 342-44, 592
Clement: 115, 297, 299, 610
Emmanuel: 79, 343-44, 381, 412-13, 436, 561, 610
Felicité (Mme. Cézaire Fonteneau, Sr.): 217
François Joseph: 257
Jean Flores: 344
Joseph: 115, 259-60, 592
Louis: 381, 453
Marie Celemine (Mme. Charles Rambin): 259
Marie Denise (Mme. Louis Basil Gagné): 54
Marie Joseph (Mme. Joseph Loucouvichi, II), 412
Marie Louise (Dña. Raphaël de la Garza): 342
Marie Louise (Mme. Césaire Prudhomme): 413
Marie Louise Lise (Mme. J. B. Isaac Fredieu): 5
Marie Madeleine (Dña. Pedro Crisostomé Flores): 562, 609a
Marie Pompose (Mme. J. B. Fonteneau): 189
Paul "Cadet" Bouët: 5, 79, 110, 121, 237, 378
Pierre: 592
Pierre B.: 65, 100, 256-68, 297-99, 342, 379, 610
Remy: 260
Sévère: 297
La Flore (var. Laflor, Floer),
José: 76
Manuel: 88
Lafon, J. B.: 56, 507, 546
La Lande (var. Lallande),
[see also Lalande Ferrier]
Jean: 77, 655
Suzette (Mrs. Pierre Wallace): 584
Lalande Ferrier, Louise Desirée (Mme. François Gainnié): 369, 490, 565
Lamarle (var. Lamarelere), Eugenie (Mme. Alexis Gustave Lemée): 644, 671
La Mathe (var. Lamatte, Lamatt, Lamote),
Celeste: 407
Louis I: 52, 73, 126, 216, 407, 410, 634
La Mathe (cont'd)
Louis, II: 73, 216, 238, 358, 407, 634
Marguerite Celestine (Mme. Jacob Elisée Roques): 407, 634
Marie Florentine: 407
Lambre,
Aurore (Mme. François Benjamin Metoyer): 12, 87, 288, 302, 565, 659, 671
Catherine (Mme. Emmanuel Prudhomme): 288
Catherine Pelagie (Mme. François Paul Bossier): 151, 218, 253
Cephalide (Mme. J. B. Le Comte): 618
J. J.: 675
J. P?: 618
Jean Baptiste Valsin: 328, 363
Jean Jacques: 21, 131, 176, 272, 390
Julia (Mme. Remy Casimir Perot): 390
Laïza (Mme. Lestan Prudhomme): 129
Marie (Mme. Antoine Prudhomme): 66, 93, 109, 129, 142, 168, 659
Marie Asely (Mme. Charles Noyrit): 12, 500
Marie Aspasie (Mrs. Simeon H. Hart): 675
Marie Aurore *[see Aurore]*
Marie Delphine (Mme. Claude Antoine Choppin): 87
Marie Emerante (Mme. Neuville Prudhomme): 109, 331
Remy: 12, 21, 87, 109, 127, 129, 131
Suzette (Mme. J. B. Cloutier): 127, 546
V. *[Veuve?]*: 87, 142, 253, 302, 565, 618
Valsin: 131, 302
Lamour, Suzanne Lucas: 621
Landreau (var. Landreaux),
François: 505, 629
H., *fils*: 66
Jean Baptiste: 74, 89
Joseph Ambroise: 629
Lange,
Dominique I: 267
Dominique II: 267

Langlois,
______, (Mme. François Terence Chaler): 210
Auguste: 22, 74, 83, 139, 282, 350
Elmina (Mme. Norbert Lestage): 492
Felix: 184, 281-82
Lestan: 108, 128, 289, 301, 492
Ludger: 139, 184, 350, 425, 589
Marie Louise Carmelite (Mme. François Derbanne): 22, 151
Marie Thérèse (Mme. Pierre J. Aleman): 61
Lankford, Luivinia (Mrs. John Edens): 283
La Place,
Jean: 148, 218, 241, 345, 345 (bis), 390
Pierre: 241
La Plante (var. Laplante),
Louis: 166
Marcel: 166
Marie: 166
La Renaudière (var. Arnaudière, Larnodiere, Larnaudière),
J. B.: 325, 460, 494
Louis: 494, 605
Marie Magdeleine (Mme. François G. Jarnac): 214, 323
Pierre: 325, 494
Laroche, Clement: 252
Larouille *[dit of Simon. See Simon.]*
Lartigue, Jeanne (Mme. Henry Mathieu Hertzog): 66
Lasa (Soso? Lasarino?)
José: 672
Maria Justa (Dña. Desiderio Salcedo): 672
Lasada, Ramon Antonio: 72
Lasarino (var. Lazarino, Lazarin),
Joseph: 25, 130
Juan: 90-91
Juan Marie: 25-26, 84, 495
Lasoya *[see Losoya]*
Lasuache?, Hélène (Mme. George Labershe): 136
Lattier (var. Lattar, Latier),
F.: 489, 507, 517, 525, 539
Felonise (Mme. Derzelin Gallien): 137
Firmin: 325, 429, 582, 602
Firmin Joseph: 625
François I: 23, 64, 137, 163, 207, 210, 212, 349, 579, 582, 602
Lattier (cont'd),
François II: 163, 210, 301, 310, 337, 349, 463, 469
J.: 534
J. B.: 166
Jean Baptiste I: 9, 58, 137
Jean Baptiste II: 9, 22, 58, 64, 208
Joseph I: 23, 290
Joseph *fils* J. B.: 9, 58, 208, 319, 429, 625
Joseph: 64, 236
Joseph François: 8, 9, 23-24, 45
Marie Azelie (Mme. Louis Gallien): 429
Marie Catherine (Mme. Louis Thomassie, I): 4, 8, 24, 208
Marie Clara (Mme. Louis Raymond Rachal): 319
Marie Eloise (Mme. Neuville Gallien): 424-25, 476
Marie Françoise (Mme. Noel Gallien): 429
Marie Louise (Mme. J. B. Ignace Anty, II): 64, 210, 377, 569, 579
Marie Zeline (Mme. Isaac Plaisance): 207
Michel: 290, 517
Sévère: 169, 184, 208, 212, 246, 319, 377, 429
T.: 569
Laurens *[see Llorens]*
Laurents,
Alfred: 616, 638, 664
Benoist: 349, 532, 664
Lauve, Arnaud: 19, 38, 60, 87, 140, 163, 186, 584
La Vega, Maria Josefa *[See Maria Josefa [de] la Vega Flores.]*
Lavespère,
Clement Oduhigg: 554
François: 22, 42, 82, 86
H. B.: 554
Hilaire: 42, 229, 554
Marie Felicité (Mme. François Frederic): 301, 464, 480, 571, 674
Marie Helaine (Mme. Julien Rachal): 86
Melanie (Mme. Julien Rachal II): 274, 448
Pierre Geodfroy: 82

Lavie, Margueritte (Mme. Pierre Caubarreaux): 428
La Violette (var. Laviolette),
Julie (Mme. Pierre Cholette, Mme. Joseph Moreau, I): 435, 605
Pierre: 238
Layssard (var. Lesard, Lessart),
Adeline (Mrs. John Cannon): 581
Felonize (Mme. Auguste Baillio): 236
Lazarino *[See Lasarino.]*
Le Brun,
Aimé Adelaïde (Mme. François E. Tremaux): 617
Marie Jeanne (Mme. Charles Le Moine II): 46, 136, 200
[See also Dagobert]
Le Clerc, Marie (Mme. Pierre Derbanne I): 186
Le Comte (var. Le Compte),
Ambroise I: 496
Ambroise (I or II?): 187, 204
Ambroise II: 120, 206, 218-19, 253, 264, 288, 292, 302, 328, 385, 445, 510, 618, 637, 650
Desirée: 650
Jacques: 240
Jean Baptiste: 8, 9, 40, 58, 64, 87, 120, 142, 618
Magdeleine, f.w.c.: 375
Marie Alphonsine, f.w.c. (Mme. Antoine Nerestan Rachal): 496
Marie Cephalide Laura (Mme. Henry Hertzog): 650
Marie Françoise, f.w.c.: 43, 496
Marie Louise, f.w.c.: 152
Marie Marguerite, f.w.c. (Mme. Cyriaque Monet): 375
Marie Marguerite, f.w.c. (Mme. Dominique Metoyer): 43, 80, 157, 164, 174, 249, 251, 406, 481
Marie Perine, f.w.c. (Mme. Pierre Metoyer II): 74, 123, 244
Marie Thérèse, f.w.c. (Mme. Louis Metoyer): 74
Tranquilline: 227, 240, 246, 437, 449, 457
Lecoubiche *[See Loucouvichi.]*
Le Court de Presle (var. Lecourt, Le Cour, La Cour, Lacour, de Prelle),
Antoine: 316
Athanase Barthelemy: 421
Barthelemy: 128, 154, 167, 316, 404, 421, 634
Le Court (cont'd)
Cecile (Mme. Athanase Dupré): 35
Cezaire: 152-54
Eloy *[See Jacques Eloy]*
Jacques Eloy: 316, 549
Jacques Zepherin, f.m.c.: 316
Jacques Valcour?, 143
Louis Barthelemy, f.m.c.: 405
Marie Antoinée (Mme. Nicolas Gallien): 8, 9, 208, 347
Marie Françoise (Mme. Pierre Dupré): 22, 252
Marie Louise (Mme. Pierre Cezaire Brosset): 437, 475
Marie Pelagie, f.w.c. (Mme. Joseph A. Metoyer): 51, 123, 196, 459, 483, 553
Neuville: 167
Seberine, f.w.c. (Mme. Joseph Rachal): 544
Tranquelline: 128
Valery: 80, 544
Zeline, f.w.c. (Mme. Louis Casimir Rachal): 633
Lee,
Elisabeth (Mme. Sévère La Fitte): 297
Francis, Lt.: 241, 269, 279
Isaac: 297, 299
Nancy (Mrs. Maximilien Wallace): 299
P. O.: 345 (bis)
Lefebre,
Augustin: 340, 509
B. V.: 509
Marie Louise (Mrs. James Calahan, Mme. J. B. Alexandre Vascocu): 408, 509
Le Forte, Marie Sophie (Mme. Benoist Laurents): 664
Legrand, Anastasie Beatrice (Mme. Jean Paul Pinson): 326
Le Maitre (Le Metre), Marianne (Mme. Guillaume Hoy): 522
Lemée,
_____: 351
Adolphe: 577
Alexis Gustave: 644, 671
Marie Antoinette Ida (Mme. Pierre Alcide Buard): 644
Eugenie: 312, 671
Marie Louise Eugenie (Mme. Felicien Benjamin Metoyer): 671

Lemel,
_____: 583
Marie Atanasie, f.w.c. (Mme. Pierre Rachal II): 583
Le Moine (var. Lemoine, Le Moyne)
Ambroise: 304
Antoine I: 53, 194-95, 304?
Antoine II: 35, 53, 304?
Caroline (Mme. Etienne La Caze): 153
Charles, II: 46, 136, 200
Charles *fils* Antoine: 194-95
Charles *fils* J. B.: 232
Elenne (Mme. Solastie Derbanne): *[See Marie Hélène.]*
Felicité (Mme. Charles Le Moine): 194
Heloïse (Mme. Valentin Du Bois): 195
Jean Baptiste, I: 82, 124, 153, 194, 232, 304
Jean Baptiste, II: 124, 304
Jean Baptiste *fils* Antoine I: 304
Marie (Mme. Jean Massippe): 59, 71, 255
Marie Cephalide (Mme. J. B. Le Moine): 304
Marie Frosine (Mme. Pierre Godfrois Lavespère): 82
Marie Hélène (Mme. Louis Solastie Derbanne; Mrs. Isaac Birtt): 46, 200, 325, 555
Marie Louise (Mme. Antoine Rachal): 40, 143
Pelagie (Mme. Jean Baptiste Ferrier); Mme. George Labershe): 136
Lennard (var. Lenard),
_____, Justice of the Peace: 511
J. B.: 614
Thomas M.: 356
Le Noir (var. Lenoir),
Antoine I: 300
Antoine II: 192, 273, 300, 321, 397, 437
Celina (Mme. Ablin Brosset): 437
Jean Baptiste: 397
Marie Célimène (Mme. Ursin Sorrell): 321
Marie Cephalide (Mme. Julien Besson): 273
Leonard, B.: 11, 17, 279
Leroux,
Jean Baptiste: 454
Joseph: 454, 466
Le Roy, Nicolas Charles: 232, 316, 325, 346 (bis), 486-87, 497, 500
Lestage,
Jean Baptiste: 7, 492
Jean Baptiste Barthelemy: 7, 221, 362
Joseph: 57, 362
Marie Aimée (Dña. Agustin Gutieres; Mme. Onesime Rachal): 221
Norbert: 492, 502, 534
Leten, Isabelle (Elisabeth Latham?) (Mme. Cesaire La Fitte): 115, 117, 259-60, 342, 344, 592
Le Vasseur (var. Levasseur, Vesseur),
Emanuel: 99, 324, 589
François I: 415
Geneviève Alineide? (Mme. J. B. Faustin Plaisance): 99
Jean François: 193, 446
Ludger: 99, 589
Marie Celina (Mme. Alfred Jean George Hubner): 446
Marie Constance (Mme. Marcelin Tauzin): 193
Marie Judith: A-679
Marie Modeste (Mme. Henry Theodore Chabot): 324
L'Evêque, Francinne Anne (Mme. Victor Marion de Montilly): 617
Levy?, Louis Pierre: A-679
Levy, Miriam (Mrs. Samuel Hyams): 345 (bis)
Lewis,
Charles: 306
Charles George: 134, 185, 239, 264, 306, 327
[See also Louis.]
Leyba (Leyva), Maria Guadalupe (Dña. Antonio Castro): 62
Leyton *[See Leten.]*
L'Herisson,
Dominique: 438
Jean Victor: 438, 453
V. T.: 485
Lidé, Isabelle (Mme. Jean Baptiste Rougeot): 277
Lintheart?, Samuel F.: 275

Littleton, Marie (Mrs. William Plunket): 146
Litton *[See Leten]*
Llorens (var. Lorens, Lorenze, Laurens, Llores),
Arsene, f.w.c.: 515
Belisaire, f.m.c.: 395
Clement, f.m.c.: 603
Emanuel, f.m.c.: 6, 47-48, 51, 74, 80, 91, 141, 156, 164-65, 171, 198, 211, 215, 249, 267, 406, 459, 497, 623
Lodoiska, f.w.c. (Mme. Joseph Metoyer): 459
Seraphin, f.m.c.: 51, 198, 242, 395, 460, 515, 553, 602
Seraphine, f.w.c. (Mme. Auguste Dorestan Metoyer): 515
Suzanne, f.w.c. (Mme. Emile Belisaire Chevalier): 515, 623
Local, Emelye? Victoire (Mme. René Gottier): 56
Lodge?, Margaret (Mrs. John Ellis): 341
Long,
Honora (Mrs. Patrick O. Tuomey): 643
James: 39
William: 160
Longino,
John Thomas: 354
Thérèse Anne (Mme. François Rouquier, II): 354
Longoria,
Caledonio: 70
Ignacio: 30, 352, 495
Jean: 426
Maria Nicolasa (Dña. Francisco S^{n}. _____a; Dña. Joseph Miguel Delgado; Dña: Francisco y Barbo): 30, 352
Lonnes, Celeste (Dña. Juan Bargas): 570
Lopez,
Ignacio: 88
José I (Ossé): 262
José II (Ossé Vio): 262
Santiago: 88
Losoya, Domingo: 16, 30
Loucouvichi (var. Loucoubiche, Loucouviche, Lacobee),
Gabine: 436
Joseph I: 50, 412
Loucouvichi (cont'd)
Joseph II: 412
Marie (Mme. Jean Andres Valentin): 50
Louis, Apley (Mrs. John Thomas Longino): 354
Luvini,
Antoine Marie: 336
Jules Cezar Napoleon: 293, 336, 498, 505, 566, 585, 668
Luyster,
Abraham R.: 656
William: 656

M_____, José: 14
Macfierson, Maria (Mrs. John Harrison): 561
Magdonnel,
Louise (Mme. Guillaume Hoy II); 522
Luc?: 522
[See also McDonald.]
Mahle, John H.: 275
Mailloud, _____: 36
M_____N?, Catherine: 533
Maillioux (var. Mailloud, Malloud, Mayeu, Mayeux, Mayou),
Jeanne Françoise (Mme. François Paul): 183
Françoise, f.w.c. (Mme. Firmin C. Christophe): 339, 352
Lauran II: 27
Marie Louise (Mrs. George Mc Tier): 209, 217, 350, 394, 425, 503, 589
Marie Thérèse (Mme. Michel Rambin): 27, 36, 65, 114, 117, 259-60
Malbert,
Marie des Neiges (Mme. Nicolas Beaudouin): 125
Marie Françoise (Mme. Jacques Fort): 44
Maliqe,
Heloise (Mme. Victor Epron dit Renois): 632
Josette (Mme. Antoine Du Bois): 286
Marie Antoinette (Mme. Zédoinne Du Bois): 523
Marie Eulalie (Mrs. John Sibley): 279, 345, 547

Malige (cont'd),
Marie Jeanne (Anne) Manet (Mme. François Chabus): 11, 140
Noel: 632
Malloud *[See Maillioux.]*
Mallough?, Marie Marguerite: 116
Mancha,
Antonio, 314
Maria Beneta: 314
Manna, Peniy (Mrs. Johon Birtt): 502
Mansolo (var. Mansola),
Juan Bautista: 484
Juana Francisca (Dña. Felix Del Rio): 609
Mansolo, Maria Anastasia (Dña. Joseph y Barbo): 32, 352
Many, Jas. B.: 296, 462
Marcoli (var. Marcolli, Maricolli),
Bernardo: 607
Jean: 585
Joseph: 449, 469
Laurent: 449, 585
Marey (var. Mary),
[See also Marey.]
Clément Casimir: 403
Louis Clément Victor: 403, 503, 619
Marguerite Denize, f.w.c.: 203
Marie Angelie, f.w.c.: 662
Marie Delphine Laisa, f.w.c.: 203
Marie Françoise, f.w.c.: 416
Marie Jean-Louis, f.w.c.: 662
Marie Jeanne (Coindet) f.w.c.: 141
Marie Jeanne (Trichel) f.w.c.: 126
Marie Jeanne (?) f.w.c.: 272, 396
Marie Jeanne *[See De Mézières.]*
Marie Louise Thérèze (Brevel), f.w.c.: 289, 346 (bis)
Marie Manon, f.w.c. (Mme. J. B. Augustin): 416
Marie Marguerite (Le Comte): 496
Marie N______ (Lemel): 583
Marie Pompose (Prudhomme): 486
Marie Rozalie, f.w.c. (Mme. St. Cyr Metoyer): 396
Marie Suzette (Maurin), f.w.c.: 198
Marie Ursulle Louise/Luson (Le Court): f.w.c.: 80, 128, 154, 167, 316
Marion de Montilly,
Celina (Mme. Louis Schmitt; Mme. Joseph L. Tremaux): 617
E.: 617
Victor: 617
Mariotte (var. Mariote), f.p.c.,
Jean Baptiste Saint Ville: 251
Marie Adelaÿde: 174, 213, 251, 267, 406, 633
Marie Adelaÿde II (Mme. J. B. Cecil): 213
Marie Philomene (Mme. Dominique Lange II): 267
Marmela *[See de Marmela.]*
Marrs,
Caledonia C. (Mrs. James M. B. Tucker): 654
John: 654
Marshal, Ann (Mrs. George Kile): 673
Martin,
_____ D.: 518
Abigail "Abby" (Mrs. Martin Fearing): 518, 520
Harriette (Mrs. Noah H. Allen): 520
Martine, Louis Frederic: 324, 663-664
Martineau, Joseph: 326, 386, 456
Martinez (var. Martines),
Candelaria: 609
Dolores: 89
Esmeregildo): 587
Juan José: 366, 493
Juan Maria: 560, 570, 572
Juliana (Dña. Vicente y Barbo): 587
Manuel: 366
Maria Rafaela (Dña. José Andres Ayala: 89 *[See also Rafaela.]*
Maria Tomasa (Dña. José Leander Sanchez): 234
Rafaela: 616 *[See also Maria Rafaela.]*
Marunos, Manuel: 76
Marzille, Françoise (Mme. Jacques Duthil): 281
Massip (var. Massippi, Masilde),
Dorothée (Mme. Étienne La Caze); 124, 153, 280
Fanny (Mme. Jacques La Caze): 281
François: 106, 346
Jean: 59, 71, 106, 255
Marie Louise (Mme. Jean Renaud Aguesse I): 185, 315, 335
Marie Louise (Mme. Baltazard Brevel): 255, 557

Massip (cont'd),
Marie Rosaline "Rose" (Mme. René François Epron *dit* Renoy): 59, 455, 632
Pierre: 59, 71, 280
Maurin,
[See Morin.]
Mauro (Moro): Aimé: 412-414
Mauro *[See also Mora, Moreau.]*
Maury, L.: 619
Mayou *[See Maillioux.]*
McClean *[See McLean.]*
McConault, William: 206
McConnell, T.: 529
McDonald (var. McDonato, McDannel),
J. W.: 567
Luca: 262
Marie Milagie (Dña. José Lopez II): 262
Peter: 266, 346
T_____: 346
[See also Magdonnell.]
McGown,
James: 564
Mary (Mrs. Henry White): 564
McGraw, James: 597
McKey, James: 366
McLaskee, Heleine (Mrs. James Moore): 456
McClean (var. McLean),
Lothland: 615
Neill: 615
Sara (Mrs. Lothland McClean): 615
McPherson *[See Macfierson.]*
McTire (var. McTyer, McTyre, Mactaire, McTaer, McTier),
Elisa (Mrs. Jackson Freeman): 394
Eugenie (Mme. Hypolite Bordelon II): 503
George: 36, 209, 217, 350, 394, 425, 503, 589
Jean Baptiste: 209
Marie Eugenie (Mrs. William Russell; Mme. Cezaire Fonteneau II): 217
Marie Louise (Mme. Ludger Langlois, Mme. Ludger Levasseur): 350, 589
Remy: 425
Mears,
James H.: 329
James P.: 388
John H.: 388
Mechamps *[See Michamps.]*
Medillen,
Isabelle (Dña. Manuel Gutieres); 295, 559
Michel: 295
Medina,
Juan José: 3, 37
Masalina (Dña. José Maria Murquiz): 91
Melançon (var. Mananson, Menanson),
Charles I: 15, 81, 494
Charles II: 648
Charles Pierre: 15, 81
Michel: 81
Michel U.: 648
Melder *[See Van Melder.]*
Melone/Mellone *[See Molone.]*
Menchaca, Antonio: 98, 512
Mercier, Josette (Mme. Emanuel Le Vasseur): 589
Mericq, Bernard: 56
Mery, Aristide: 542
Mery *[See also Marey.]*
Messi,
Antoine: 470
Jerome: 470
Messy, Henrietty, f.w.ç.: 211
Metcalf, Ann (Mrs. John Hewitt): 533
Metoyer,
_____: 204, 288, 302
Ambroise Azenor, f.m.c.: 581, 583, 608
Ambroise Chastan Dominique, f.m.c.: 481, 544
Athanase "Tanasite" Vienne, f.m.c.: 203, 213, 244, 251, 544
Auguste, f.m.c.: 10, 48, 51, 80, 172, 486-87
Auguste Dorestan, f.m.c.: 515, 530, 553, 586
Augustin Prudans, f.m.c.: 427, 486-87, 551, 586, 608, 646
Aurore: 669 *[See also F. Aurore.]*
Benjamin: 670 *[See also François Benjamin.]*
Celina, f.w.c.: Mme. Maximin Metoyer): 483
Dominique: 43, 80, 157, 164, 174, 249, 251, 316, 406, 481
[See also J. B. Dominique.]

Metoyer (cont'd)
Elina, f.w.c. (Mme. Théophile Louis Metoyer): 553
F. Aurore (Mme. Eugene Valery De Blieux): 669
F. Azenor: 636
Felicien Benjamin: 671
Felicité Florentine, f.w.c. (Mme. Antoine Théodule Monette): 636
Florival *[See François Florival.]*
François: 369, 659, 663-64
François I, f.m.c.: 48, 118, 508
François II, f.m.c.: 118, 409, 508
François Benjamin: 12, 21, 45, 48, 56, 66, 87, 129, 131, 288, 302, 311, 348, 369, 490, 565, 659, 671
François Florival, f.m.c.: 459, 486, 552, 586, 608, 623, 634
François Gassion, f.m.c.: 164, 167, 215, 334, 603, 645
Heloïse: 546, 565
Hypolite, f.m.c.: 586
J. L., f.m.c.: 515
J. B., f.m.c.: 156, 165, 172, 196, 624
Jean Baptiste *fils* Augustin, f.m.c.: 6, 10, 47-48, 80, 141, 164, 215, 339, 374-75, 395, 427, 468, 479, 486-87, 552, 586, 611, 624, 634, 645-46
Jean Baptiste *fils* Louis, f.m.c.: 6, 10, 74, 80, 242, 334, 339, 374, 395
Jean Baptiste Dominique, f.m.c.: 51, 74, 242, 244, 249, 336, 576, 630
Jean Baptiste Dominique *[younger brother]*, f.m.c.: 157, 242
Jean Baptiste Leandre, f.m.c.: 339
Joseph, f.m.c.: 396, 459?, 509
Joseph I *[See Joseph Antoine.]*
Joŝeph II, f.m.c.: 167, 174, 196, 211, 215, 338, 396, 406, 421, 427, 459?
Joseph Antoine, f.m.c.: 51, 123, 196, 483, 553
Joseph Augustin, f.m.c.: 141, 165, 171, 175, 203, 213, 251, 338, 409, 427, 481, 531, 549, 611, 636, 645
Joseph François, f.m.c.: 508

Metoyer (cont'd),
Joseph Ozeme Dominique, f.m.c.: 249, 251, 544, 630
Joseph Valcour, f.m.c.: 468, 515
Leandre *[See J. B. Leandre.]*
Louis, f.m.c.: 74, 118
Louis Dominique, f.m.c.: 636
Louis Florentin, f.m.c.: 164
Marie Aglaë, f.w.c. (Mme. Louis Porter; Mme. Emile Colson): 242, 338
Marie Anaïse, f.w.c. (Mme. C. N. Rocques, II): 479
Marie Angelique, f.w.c.: (Mme. Louis Dorsineau Fort): 271
Marie Anne Cephalide (Mme. F. Xavier Archinard): 302
Marie Aspasy, f.w.c. (Mme. Seraphin Llorens): 51, 395, 515, 603
Marie Barbe Meluissine, f.w.c.: (Mme. Bernard Dauphine; Mme. C. N. Rocques I): 487, 646
Marie Celine, f.w.c. (Mme. Eloy Le Court): 316
Marie Cephalide, f.w.c. (Mme. J. B. Saintville Mariotte): 251
Marie Deneige, f.w.c. (Mme. Pierre Metoyer, III): 123, 608, 645
Marie Emelie, f.w.c. (Mme. Athanase Vienne Metoyer): 244
Marie (Jeanne) Adelaide "Adelle" f.w.c. (Mme. Jerome Sarpy): 48, 468, 497, 608
Marie Julia, f.w.c. (Mme. F. C. Christophe II): 552
Marie Louise, f.w.c. (Mme. J. B. Florentin Conant): 427, 551, 611
Marie Louise, f.w.c. (Mme. Louis Barthelemy Le Court): 406
Marie Louise, f.w.c. (Mme. François Mulon): 409
Marie Marguerite, f.w.c. (Mme. Emanuel Dupré): 174
Marie Ositte, f.w.c. (Mme. Neuville Le Court): 167
Marie Perine, f.w.c. (Mme. Pierre Nerestan Rachal): 43, 544, 583, 630

Metoyer (cont'd),
Marie Pompose, f.w.c. (Mme. C. N. Rocques, I): 6, 374, 479, 497, 586, 634, 646
Marie Rose, f.w.c.: (Mme. J. B. Baltazar): 156, 165, 171, 196, 334, 389, 396, 551
Marie Silvie (Silby), f.w.c. (Mme. Valery Le Court): 80, 544
Marie Susanne, f.w.c. (Mme. J. B. Espallier Rachal): 389, 531, 633
Marie Susanne, f.w.c.: 172, 211
Marie Susette, f.w.c. (Mme. J. B. Louis Metoyer): 74
Marie Suzette, f.w.c. (Mme. Elisé Rocques): 47, 198, 375
Marie Thérèze, f.w.c. (Mme. Augustin Cloutier): 10
Marie Thérèze Elisabeth (Mme. Louis Narcisse Prudhomme): 168, 181, 204, 308, 376, 500
Maxille, f.m.c.: 6, 43, 47, 80, 211, 468, 479, 483
Maximin, f.m.c.: 483
Narcisse, f.m.c.: 157
Nerestan Pierre, f.m.c.: 374, 487, 497, 515, 586, 634
Nicolas Augustin, f.m.c.: 6, 47-48, 118, 165, 171, 198, 215, 334, 603, 645-46
Octave, 644
Octavie (Mme. Adolphe Prudhomme) 659
Ozeme *[See Joseph Ozeme Dominique.]*
Perine (Le Comte), f.w.c.: 175
Perine, f.w.c. (Mme. Pierre Mission Rachal: 576
Perine, f.w.c. (Mme. François Gassion Metoyer): 645
Pierre II, f.m.c.: 6, 43, 47-48, 74, 122, 167, 244, 374, 515
Pierre III, f.m.c.: 122, 165, 171, 175, 203, 242, 244, 392, 421, 553, 608, 645
Pierre Victorin: 87, 127, 129, 168, [illegible], [illegible], [illegible]
St. Cyr "Sincir", f.m.c.: 213, 396, 531, 549
Susanne Lise (Mme. Pierre Phanor Prudhomme): 288
Tanasite *[See Athanase Vienne Metoyer.]*

Metoyer (cont'd),
Théophile Louis, f.m.c.: 553
T^{nte} (Athanasite?), f.m.c.: 630
Valcour *[See Joseph Valcour.]*
Valsin, f.m.c.: 576, 633
Vienne, f.m.c.: 630
Michamps (var. Mechamps),
Adèle (Mme. Antoine Balzaretti): 620
Aurore (Mme. Jean Marcoli): 385
Eugene I: 94
Jean Eugene: 64, 83, 86, 94, 585, 620, 651
Louis Eugene: 651
Michel *dit* Zoriche *[See Zoriche.]*
Micheli,
Vicente I: 512
Vicente II: 512, 560, 570, 572
Middleton,
Isaac S (J?): 491
William: 491
Milan, Clarisse (Mme. Pierre Dugas): 628
Miller,
Helmina (Mme. Jean Agues Ginger): 180, 250
Jean Pommier: 301
Mills, Thankful (Mrs. Charles Slocum): 17
Minta, Jayme: 373
Minta *[See also Ninta.]*
Miró, Joseph: 472-73, 493, 535
Mobley, Madison: 676
Moise,
Cecila (Mrs. Theodore J. Moise): 614
Theodore J.: 614
Molane, Stephania (Dña. Antonio Gutieres): 295
Molony (var. Molone, Melone, Mellone, Mallony),
Joseph Jeremy: 597
Margaret (Mrs. Joseph Smith): 597
John: 533
Monde,
Catherine Prudence (Mme. Aimé Caron; Mme. Jean Eustache Gravier): 135, 228
Françoise: 135, 228
Mondez, Joseph Maria: 89

Monet (var. Monette),
Antoine Theodule, f.m.c.: 636
Baltasar *[See Baltazar, J. B.]*
Baptiste, f.m.c.: 375
Cyriaque, f.m.c.: 375
Dorothée (Mme. J. B. Baltazar I), f.w.c.: 375, 541
Louis, f.m.c.: 152-5, 636
Marie Elina, f.w.c.: 375
Marie Lise, f.w.c.: 375
Monguey, Josepha (Dña. Victoriano Ombrero): 609
Monroe, George: 214, 323
Montier,
Bernard: 485
Frederic: 485, 509
Moore, James: 456
Mora (var. More),
[See also Mauro, Moreau.]
Gertrude (Dña. Vital Flores): 358 399
José: 607
Juan: 1, 2, 25 - 27, 62
Maria (Dña. Juan y Barbo): 286
Mauricia (Dña. Joseph Loucouvichi): 50, 412
Morantine (var. Morantin),
_____: 79
Jean Baptiste: 200, 287, 447, 476 542
Jean Benjamin: 542
Marie Adelize (Mme. Joseph Gautier): 447
Marie Basilice (Mme. Michel Anty): 287
Moreau (var. Maesro, Moro, Mauro):
[See also Mauro, Mora.]
An.: 514, 517, 524-26, 610
Alexandre: A-681
Joseph I: 605
Joseph II: 605
Marie Josephine (Mme. François Baudry II): A-681
Pierre: A-681
Morelle, Phanie (Mrs. Alexandre Deniston): 422
Moreno,
Ives: 514, 526
Joseph: 526
Marie Artemise: 526
Morgan,
Jean Thomas: 421
Raphaelle: 430
Morgan (cont'd),
Thebeta (Mme. Benjamin Cavert): 96
Thomas Alexandre, Dr.: 225, 287, 305, 347, 349, 368, 377, 397, 430
Morin (var. Morine, Maurin, Maurine, Moriom),
Antonia Bella (Dña. Joseph Ramos I): 357
Conce[p]tion (Dña. Mariano Basques): 128, 433-34
Estevan: 138, 154, 322
Gertruda (Mme. Cezaire Le Cour): 154
José: 467
Louis, f.m.c.: 198, 339, 374-75, 468
Marie (Mme. François Valery): 138
Marie (Mme. Edward Bolein): 561
Pantaleon: 322
Morrow,
Robert: 639
William Penn: 550, 639
Morse,
Bryan: 360
George W.: 617, 657
Peabody Atkinson: 359-60, 382, 465, 545, 567, 577, 595, 617-618, 637, 657
Moses,
Henry: 368
McKendrick: 368
Moting?, J.: 673
Müller (var. Muler, Miller),
Anna Catherine (Mme. Eugene Michamps): 94, 585, 620, 651
Barbara (Mrs. Frederick Müller): 94
Frederick: 94
Mulon (var. Mullon),
François, f.m.c.: 409
Louis, f.m.c.: 409
Victoire, f.w.c.: 156, 541
Murphy,
Edouard II: 292, 437
Edouard Césaire: 292
Marie Eugenie (Mme. Louis Joseph Tauzin); 264
T? L. P.: 531
Murquiz (var. Murques),
Joaquin: 91

Murquiz (cont'd),
José Maria: 91

N______, A. G.: 38
Naffrey *[See Noffré.]*
Navarro Avila, Conception (Dña. Teodoro Quintero): 600
Negrevernis, Francisco: 357, 469, 573
Neisen, Jean Baptiste: 410
Nelson, Catherine (Mrs. Thomas Gaugh): 327
Nelson? *[See Nolsem.]*
Newton, Aney (Mrs. Thomas Blanchard): 296, 641
Nicolas, Ane H. (Mrs. W. Robinson): 577
Ninta, Jacques: 373
Ninta *[See also Minta.]*
Nivet, Francisca, f.w.c.: 51
Noffré (var. Naffrey, Nafret),
Adrien Hugue: 122
Marie Louise Adelaïde (Mme. J. B. Armand): 122, 461, 648
Noiret *[See Noyrit.]*
Nolasco de Porcuna,
Florentine (Mme. Sévèrin Rougeot): 277
Marie Agathe (Mme. Emanuel Hernandez): 161
Pierre: 161, 277
Nolsem, Marie (Dña. Francisco Garcie): 414
Nongrilper, Christine (Mrs. Amos Titus): 594
Normand, François Marie, Dr.: 145, 151, 208, 229, 274, 309, 347, 368-69
Norris (var. Norriss),
Joseph T.: 524-26, 591
Marie C. (Mrs. William Donovan): 471
Marie Pelagie Recia (Mme. Onoré Robleau): 525
Nathaniel: 471, 524-25, 591
Samuel T.: [illegible]
Noyrit (var. Noiret),
Charles: 12, 19, 60, 87, 127, 142, 229, 302, 390, 500
Marie Caroline (Mme. Louis Narcisse Prudhomme): 500
Graciano: 12

Oaks,
Josiah: 291
Obadiah: 291
Ochmichen, C. G.: 351, 359
Ocon:
José Antonio: 90
Paulo: 202
Pedro: 69, 90
O'Connor:
John: 97
Marie Severine (Mme. J. B. Vascocu): 97
Matthew: 564
O'Doherty, Patrick James: 670
Ohuont *[See Drohon.]*
Oliveros, Juana (Dña. Estevan Solis): 16
Olivier, Nanette (Mrs. Luc Magdonnell): 522
Ombrera (var. Ombrero),
Anisetta (Dña. Ignatio Sanchez): 627
Marie Anisette (Dña: José Alexo del Rio): 609
Victoriano: 609
Ortis,
Juan Bautista: 155
Nazario: 155
Ortolan *[See Dortolan.]*
Otis,
John: 657
Sarah Ann (Mrs. Abda H. Christian): 650
Oualette (var. Walette, Woilet),
Louis: 612, 649
Melisa: 612

Pachero, Maria Juana (Dña. Antonio Pru): A-680
Padilla (var. Padia),
Cayetano: 607
Felipe: 607
Maria (Dña. Joseph San Miguel): [illegible]
Maria (Dña. Leqnire Procella): 434
Maria de la Concepcion (Dña. Joseph Andres Acosta): 62
Paillette, Wm.: 218
Palvado,
Adelaide (Mme. Noël Malige): 632
Jean: 27

Palvado (cont'd),
Jeanne (Dña. Bazile Avarez): 432
Marie Angela (Mme. Jean Baptiste Azenor Rambin): 27
Marie Josephe (Mme. J. B. Plaisance): 227, 240, 393, 457, 546 (bis), 660
Pannell,
Alexander W.: 359
Henriette Mathilde: 359
Pantaleon *[See Hissoura dit Pantaleon.]*
Paria, Maria Lena (Dña. Manuel del Rio): 234
Parker,
Elisha: 365
Mary Ann (Mrs. Isaac Lee): 297, 299
Passaneau,
Marie Hyacinthe (Mme. Jean Pierre Cheletre II): 266
Toussain: 266
Patterson, John: 533
Patton, John C.: 519, 615
Pauche *[See Poché.]*
Paul,
Felix François Gracien: 183, 313
François: 183
Pavie,
C.: 296, 354
Eliza: 241
Marie Louise Hélène Euphrosine (Mme. Marie Athanase Poissot): 17, 121
Payne,
John F.: 509
William: 275
Peche, Simon H.: 499
Peetermans, Louis: 383, 419
Pelli,
Benoit: 351
Pierre: 350, 367, 449
Peña, Chrysostomé: 352
Penkerton?, Chas. H.: 499
Penn, William: 128
Pereau *[See Perot.]*
Pereyrot, Maria Adelina (Dña. Juan Bautista Mansolo): 484
Perez (var. Peres, Perres),
Lodoïska (Dña. Ferdinando Gayoso): 577
Marie Juliane (Mme. Clément Cortes): 473
Perez (cont'd)
Maria Visente (Mme. Charles Simon *dit* Larouille): 126, 130, 216, 410, 442
Simon: 678
Perini,
Antonio: 501
Severino: 501
Permonio *[See Carmona.]*
Perot (var. Peraut, Perault, Perrot),
Aimée (Mme. Emanuel Derbanne): 188
B.: 629
Breville: 305, 307, 402
C. Omer: 655
Casimir: 276, 285, 390 *[See also Remy Casimir.]*
Celeste, f.w.c. (Mme. Louis La Mathe I): 216, 407, 634
Celine (Mrs. Benjamin Bullitt): 598
Cezaire: 134
Chrisostomé: 108, 133, 163, 199, 222, 239 *[See also Jean Chrisostomé & Jean Louis Chrisostomé.]*
Cyriaque: 498, 513, 580, 653
Derzelin *[See Louis Derzelin.]*
Faustin *[See Jean Chrisostomé Faustin.]*
Firmin: 276, 285
François I: 41, 188, 378
François II: 23, 28, 31, 41, 107, 110, 250, 403, 546 (bis), 619, 660
Gabriel: 285, 480
Guilma: 546 (bis), 660
Isaac: 571
Jean Baptiste: 28, 173, 245, 322, 378, 391, 403, 458, 530, 596, 676
Jean Chrisostomé: 28, 67, 308, 464
Jean Chrisostomé II?: 245, 402, 597, 629
Jean Chrisostomé Faustin: 67, 102, 189, 191, 273, 355, 498, 653, 666
Jean Louis: 431, 612, 655, 670
Jean Louis Chrisostomé: 28, 182? 239, 464, 580

Perot (cont'd),
  Joseph I: 386? 420, 571
  Joseph II: 386?, 420
  Joseph, f.m.c.: 271
  L: 498, 505
  Louis: 41, 55, 104, 113, 332, 378, 403
  Louis Derzelin: 173, 176, 188, 283
  Madeleine, f.m.c. (Mme. Remon Dortolant): 391, 478
  Marie Amire (Mme. François Henry Trichel): 245
  Marie Azelie (Mme. Adam Ginger): 250
  Marie Azolie (Mme. Marcelin Tauzin): 666
  Marie Cephalide (Mme. J. B. Trichel II): 134
  Marie Celine (Mme. F. J. B. Fonteneau; Mme. Louis F. Neuville Vienne): 189, 355
  Marie Celina (Mme. Athanas Ely): 580
  Marie de l'Incarnacion (Mme. Julien Besson): 68
  Marie Deloize, f.w.c. (Mme. Noel de Mézières): 149
  Marie Emma (Mme. Onesime Plaisance): 619
  Marie Felicité (Mme. Jean Pierre Grappe): 332, 337, 458
  Marie Josephe (Mme. Placide Derbanne): 55
  Marie Josephe Suset (Mme. Gaspard Derbanne II): 55, 68, 133, 144, 188
  Marie Louise (Mrs. Alfred K. Edens): 283
  Marie Magdaline (Mme. Jean Louis Vascocu): 63, 97, 270, 384
  Marie Melisa: 629
  Marie Touton Modeste (Mme. Manuel Hilaire Bordelon): 67
  Melanie (Mme. Avit Davion): 176
  R.: 675
  Remy: 18, 28, 387, 394, 403
  Remy Casimir: 276, 390
  Siboir: 393, 530, 596
  Tonton, f.w.c. (Mme. Charles Simon II): 238
  Valery, f.w.c.: 320
  Zelia (Mme. Leonard Trichel): 498
Perry, J. S. M.: 456
Petrovic,
  Charles A.: 656
  H. M. (W.?): 519
  Peter: 354, 359, 519, 656
Picque, C. L.: 315
Piedvert (Pierverde), Marie Jeanne (Mme. J. B. Besson I): 75, 205, 273
Pigot, Marie Madeleine (Mme. Henry Chabot): 324
Pillet, Louis Pierre: 81
Pinçon (var. Pinson),
  Alexandre: 326, 386
  Jean Pierre: 326
Pinsonneau *[See Passaneau.]*
Piver, Louise Aimé (Mme. Remond Castanedo): 663-64
Placide? Plaude?,
  Noel: 199
  Vincent: 199
Plaisance,
  _____: 240
  Bertrand: 19, 38, 46, 99, 163, 186, 206-07, 227
  Celeste: 108
  Edouard?: 240, 464
  Faustin *[See Jean Baptiste Faustin.]*
  Isaac: 19, 60, 76, 78, 163, 206-207, 227, 293, 337, 424, 475, 530, 588
  Isidore Rock: 227, 293, 397, 467
  Jean Baptiste I: 227, 240, 393, 457, 546 (bis), 660
  Jean Baptiste II: 457, 677
  Jean Baptiste Faustin: 99, 227, 240, 393?, 619
  Julia (Mme. Guilma Perot): 546 (bis), 660
  Marcelitte (Mme. Agapite Elie): 393
  Marguerite Lise (Mme. Isidore Rock Plaisance): 227
  Marie Françoise Phannie (Mme. François Lattier): 163, 469
  Marie Louise Celine (Mme. Louis Jerome Rachal): 38
  Marie Lucie (Pompose?) Mme. J.B. Gaspard Derbanne): 133, 337, 423
  Marie Susanne (Mme. Honoré Fredieu): 19, 415, 431, 507, 596

Plaisance (cont'd),
Onesime: 619
Roquie: 662 *[See also Isidore Rock.]*
Plauché,
Jean Baptiste: 308, 331
Jean Joseph Alexandre: 308, 376
Plomage, Elisabeth (Mrs. James Smith): 597
Plunket,
Marguerite (Mme. Felix St. André): 146
William: 146
Poché (var. Pauché),
François: 475
Luc: 405, 425, 433-35, 475-76
Marie Eugenie (Mme. Charles Dorsino De Blanc I): 451, 555
Poirier (var. Poirrier, des Poirier),
Antoine: 591
Elisabeth (Mme. Lufroy Dupres): 252
François: 514, 517, 524
Jean Baptiste: 252, 514
Jeanne (Mrs. Nathaniel Norris): 471, 525
Joseph: 514
Louis: 524
Louise: 514
Marie (Mme. François Rachal): 526
Marie Chaterine: 514
Marie Elisabeth: 514
Marie Jeanne Olina: 514
Marie Laisa Selvina: 514
Marie Zelia: 514
Pierre Periac: 524
Urene (Mme. Victor Valentin): 591
Ursin: 517
Poissot,
_____: 502
Antoine: 563
Athanase: 380
Damas: 233
Delize (Mme. Pierre Delaunay, Jr.): 233 *[See also Denise.]*
Delphine: 276, 285, 390
Denise (Mme. Noel Placide?: Mme. J.B. Derbanne): 199, 423
Firmin: 17, 121, 237
Françoise (Mme. J. B. Brevel II): 255
Froisine (Mrs. Michel Sack; Dña. Manuel Gutierrez): 559
Marie Agnes, f.w.c. (Mme. Augustin Metoyer): 6, 47, 165, 172, 198, 215, 334, 645
Poissot (cont'd),
Marie Athanase (Sieur): 5, 17, 121
Marie Azoline (Mme. François Agaisse) 335
Marie Delphine (Mme. Cezaire? Perot) 134
Marie Delphine (Mme. Louis Genty): 550
Marie Denise (Mme. Manuel Phonde; Mme. Jules Barthelemy Bretel): 621
Marie Henriette (Mme. Amadée Rachal): 604
Marie Lise (Mme. Jacques Agaisse): 315
Marie Marcelite (Mme. Françoise Landreaux): 505, 629
Marie Marcelite (Mme. Jean Renaud Agaisse): 185
Marie Merante (Mme. Leon Totin, Mme. Louis Gaspard Derbanne): 83
Marie Victoire (Mme. Joseph Guillaume Bauvard de St. Amans): 529
Paul: 83, 185, 200, 233, 315, 317, 335, 423, 480, 621
Remy: 604
Sylvestre *fils* Athanase: 380
Sylvestre *fils* Paul: 317, 649
Victor: 480
Pommier (var. Pomié),
Marie Felicité (Mme. Pierre De louche): 349, 463
Pierre: 132
Pongez, Maria Josepha (Dña. Cayetano ramirez): 661
Ponthieu, Alexandre: 12
Porter,
Jacques, f.m.c.: 175
James F.: 31
Louis, f.m.c.: 242, 338
Posos, Albina (Dña. Francisco Ximenes): 665
Pougeot, Jean Marie (Mme. Louis St. Vigne): 453
Power,
Ellen (Mrs. Stephen W. Kile): 673
William: 673
Prado,
Juan: 574
Martin: 574
Pratt, Jean: 272, 355, 387, 390, 403
Predo?, Martina (Dña. Francisco Cardenes): 226

Procela (var. Procel, Procella),
    ___tos Santos (Todos Santos?): 79
    Encarnacion: 537
    Gertrude (Dña. Ignatio Cortinas): 311
    José Maria: 32
    Leonire: 434
    Luis: 49, 61-62, 65, 79
    Manuel: 537
    Maria: 560
    Maria (Dña. Vicente Micheli II): 512
    Maria (Dña. Thomas Basques): 434
    Maria (Dña. Charles Cordovant): 442
    Maria Ignacia (Dña. José Flores; Dña. Pedro Ocon): 90
    Maria Jetrudis (Dña. José Miguel y Barbo); 32
    Maria Louisa (Mme. Guillaume Bébé II): 560
    Marie Salome (Mme. Manuel La Fitte): 79, 412-13
    Pedro: 1, 2, 70, 79
    Phelipe: 537
Prou (var. Pru),
    Antonio: A-680
    Carmelita: 661
    Maria Guadalup (Dña. José Luis de la Bega): A-680
Proveau, Marcellite (Mme. Antoine Poirier): 591
Pru *[See Prou.]*
Prudhomme (var. Prud'homme),
    _____: 12, 21, 87, 142, 302, 354, 360, 659
    _____, *fils*: 288, 546 *[See also J.B.]*
    A.: 640
    Adolphe: 545, 550, 659
    Anne (Mme. Guillaume Dupart): 148
    Antoine: 66, 93, 109, 129, 131, 142, 148, 331, 659
    Arthemise (Mrs. Pierre Wallace, II): 379
    Carmelite (Mme. Pierre Periac Poirier): 524
    Cesaire: 379, 413
    Desirée *[See Marianne Desirée.]*
    Emmanuel: 288
    François: 54, 381
    Gabriel Ste Anne: 168, 181
    Henriette Amire (Mme. Richard Guillaume Hertzog): 66
    Jean: 168, 671
Prudhomme (cont'd)
    J. B.: 17, 42, 120, 168, 204, 207, 586-87, 500
    Jean Baptiste: 345 (bis)
    Jean Baptiste: 379, 413
    Jean Baptiste: 524
    Joseph Jean Baptiste: 298-99
    Lestan: 129, 142, 253, 331, 376, 500, 507, 550, 659, 669
    Louis Narcisse I: 135, 148, 168, 181, 204, 308, 331, 376, 500, 510 *[See also Narcisse.]*
    Louis Narcisse II: 500, 550
    Marie Magdeleine Bastien (Mme. Pierre Roblo): 115, 258, 525, 590
    Marianne Desirée (Mme. Jean François Hertzog): 131, 253, 328, 363, 650
    Marie: 87, 142
    Marie Aglae (Mme. Gabriel Ste. Anne Prudhomme): 168
    Marie Ant. (Mme. Joseph Toussaint Jannin): 93
    Marie Clara (Mme. Neuville Prudhomme): 331
    Marie Clarisse (Mme. Charles Emile Sompayrac): 376
    Marie des Neiges (Mme. J. B. Timothé Adlé): 263, 538
    Marie Emelie (Mrs. Samuel M. Hyams): 345 (bis)
    Marie Euphrosine (Mme. Emanuel Trichel): 160, 245, 387
    Marie Louise (Mme. François Rouquier): 354
    Marie Ophelie (Mme. Jean Joseph Alexandre Plauché): 308
    Marie Pompose (Mme. Pierre Dolet): 285
    Marie Sephalide Elisa (Mme. Paul Victor Sompayrac): 181
    Marie Susanne (Mme. Remy Lambre): 12, 21, 88, 109, 127, 129, 131
    Marie Thérèse (Mme. Joseph Valentine): 514, 517, 591
    Marie Thérèse Aspasie, f.w.c. (Mme. Florival Metoyer): 486
    Marie Virginia (Mme. Louis Alexandre Buard): 204, 328
    Narcisse II: 168, 181, 296, 302, 331, 360, 482 *[See also Louis Narcisse.]*

Prudhomme (cont'd)
Neuville: 105, 109, 142, 253, 331
P?: 218
Pierre Phanor: 168, 204, 287, 302, 308, 500, 610, 639, 671
Ste. Anne *[See Gabriel Ste. Anne.]*
Severin, f.m.c.: 486, 552
Suzette (Mme. J. B. Le Comte; Mme. J. B. Huppe): 142
Théophile: 507, 601
Puiraveau, Jean: 417, 493, 505

Quierry (var. Querry, Query, Thiery, Kerry),
Adele (Mme. Athanase Barthelemy Le Court): 421
Jean Baptiste: 421
Jean Baptiste Narcisse: 225, 290, 309
Marie (Dña. Pantaleon Morin): 322
Pierre: 225, 309, 322
Quinnally, James: 88
Quiñones,
Joseph: 20
Maria Juliana (Dña. Joseph Felix Barela): 20
Quintero,
Domingo: 26
Felipa (Dña. José Santos): 600
Teodoro: 26, 570, 600
Quisenberry,
Henry: 513
Nerey: 513
Thomas Jefferson: 513, 668

Rabalais,
Joseph: 268
Pierre: 268
Rachal,
_____: 649
Adele *[See Marie Louise Adele.]*
Adelaide, f.w.c. (Mme. J. B. Dominique Metoyer): 242, 244, 338, 576, 630
Adelle (Mme. Pierre Michel Zorichi, II): 466, 542
Adolphe: 593
Amedée: 57, 469, 534, 604
Antoine: 40, 143, 278
Antoine Barthelemy: 71, 162, 229, 265, 293, 333, 405, 488, 491, 521

Rachal (cont'd),
Antoine Nerestan, f.m.c.: 496
Asalie (Mme. Cyprien Rachal): 604
Barthelemy: 4, 31, 222
Barthelemy Ludger: 112
Barthelemy *[See also Antoine Barthelemy.]*
C.: 598
C. F?: 555
Clément: 42, 45, 105, 152, 158, 163, 222, 229, 349, 361b, 377, 477
Cleselia (Mrs. Jacob Knight): 489
Cyprien: 469, 604
Cyriaque *[See Louis Gassion Cyriaque.]*
Derzelin *[See Etienne Derzelin.]*
Dominique: 38, 105, 108, 159, 332, 402
Dorsino *[See François Dorsino.]*
Elisée: 318
Elisée Julien: 430, 448, 489
Eloy: 346
Emanuel: 19, 40-41, 225, 318, 440, 489
Emanuel Hilaire: 581
Etienne Derzelin: 182, 225, 254, 303, 309, 349, 469, 492
Euphrosine (Mme. J. B. Cheletre): 158, 246, 301
Euphrosine (Mme. Michel Derouanne): 300
F.: 629
Felicie Emelie (Mme. Emanuel Hilaire Rachal: 581
Firmin: 159
François Dorsino: 526, 574
François Fermin: 458
Hilaire: 45, 247
Isaac: 222, 255, 534?
J. O.: 621
Jean Baptiste: 31
Jean Baptiste Barthelemy: 45, 222, 254, 511
Jean Baptiste Barthelemy II?: 655
Jean Baptiste Clément: 152, 166, 254, 303, 475, 489, 532 *[See also Clément.]*
Jean Baptiste Espallier, f.m.c.: 389, 531, 633

Rachal (cont'd),
Jean Baptiste Julien: 221, 362, 601
Jean Baptiste (Louis): 43, 605?
Jean Baptiste Valière: 655
Jean Joseph: 247, 333
Jerome *[See Louis Jerome.]*
Jose[ph], 31, 461, 469
Joseph, f.m.c.: 544
Joseph *[See also Jean Joseph.]*
Joseph Evariste: 333
Julien I: 86
Julien II: 86, 274, 448
L.: 348
L. A.: 554, 579
Louis II: 31, 247
Louis *fils* Julien II: 274
Louis (?): 318
Louis Barthelemy I: 42, 45, 71, 229, 337, 521
Louis Barthelemy II: 57, 137, 222, 534, 579
Louis Casimir, f.m.c.: 633
Louis Gassion Cyriaque: 348, 388, 454
Louis Jerome: 38, 40, 42, 45, 105, 250, 273, 353
Louis Julien: 4, 143, 274, 318-19, 624
Louis Raimond: 319
Louis Solastie: 143, 454, 504, 527
Ludger: 163, 170, 221, 282, 362
Manette (Mme. Narcisse Rachal; Mrs. Samuel Reed): 231, 511
Marie Adelle *[See Adelle.]*
Marie Adelle (Mme. Gabriel Jean Du Bois): 31
Marie Agathe (Mme. Hilaire Lavespère; Mme. Antoine Dolichamp): 42, 229, 554
Marie Aglae (Mme. J. B. Anty): 579
Marie Aimé *[See Marie Emée Dorsino.]*
Marie Ausite (Mme. François Roubieu): 183, 578
[illegible]: 222
Marie Catherine (Mme. Louis Rachal): 274
Marie Cidalisse (Mme. Louis Thomassie II): 4
Marie Celina (Mme. Joseph Dupré): 593

Rachal (cont'd)
Marie Celina, f.w.c. (Mme. J. B. Oscar Dubreuil): 531
Marie Clementia (Mme. Elisée Rachal): 318
Marie Clementine (Mrs. Richard Woods): 440
Marie Emée Dorsino (Dña. Juan Prado): 574
Marie Emelie Narcisse (Mme. Siboire Perot): 511, 530, 596
Marie Florentine (Mme. Charles C. Bertrand): 527
Marie Françoise (Mme. Antoine Rachal): 278
Marie Françoise Arthemise (Mme. Pierre Massip): 71
Marie Henriette (Mme. Joseph Le Roux): 454
Marie Jacob (Mme. André St. André): 29, 145-46
Marie Josephine (Mme. Joseph Lestage): 362
Marie Laisa (Mme. Louis Narcisse Vanier): 278
Marie Lolette (Mme. Pierre Sebastien Compère): 348, 388
Marie Louise Adelle Monet: 574
Marie Louise Desirée (Mme. Pierre Simphorien Derbanne): 45, 511, 530
Marie Luce (Mme. Alexis Cloutier; Mme. Martin Charles Haurut): 521
Marie Maneta (Mme. Narcisse Rachal): 361a
Marie Marcelite (Mme. Yves Moreno): 526
Marie Melisa (Mme. Barthelemy Ludger Rachal): 112
Marie Nanon (Mme. Jerome Hernandez); 161-62
Marie Ophelia (Mme. Lorenzo de Soto); 601
[illegible]
Marie Roselia (Mme. Joseph Moreau): 605
Marie Susanne "Suzette" (Mme. Jean Chrisostomé Perot; Mme. Joachim Delouche); 245, 402, 598, 629
Marie Susette (Mme. Charles F. Benoist): 92, 532

Rachal (cont'd),
Marie Susette (Mme. Joseph Edouard Armand): 57, 534
Marie Suzette (Mrs. William Porteous Cannon): 581
Marie Zeline, f.w.c. (Mme. Lucien Coindet); 389
Melisine, f.w.c. (Mme. Vienne Metoyer): 630
Mission *[See Pierre Mission.]*
Narcisse: 231, 361, 530
[Narcisse] Antoine Seraphine: 361a
Narcisse Barthelemey: 40, 45, 138
Octave: 268
Onesime: 221
Osite *[See Marie Ausite.]*
P. O.: 632
Paul Firmin: 105, 332, 337
Pierre Mission, f.m.c.: 43, 544, 576, 583, 630
Pierre II, f.m.c.: 583
Prudent: 159, 182, 629
Seraphin: 420, 504, A-681
Silvestre: 40, 146, 231, 252, 277-78, 318, 348, 361a, 388
Silvestre Julien: 86
Théodore Clément: 648, 674
V. R.: 604
Victor: 333, 420
Victor Demas: 108, 170, 582, 602
Victor [Julien]: 287, 430, 440, 491, 532, 539, 554
Victorine (Mme. Firmin Lattier): 582, 602
Villére: 534, 539
Racio (Recio), Ignacio: 235, 607
Rafael, Maria (Dña. Anselmo Cortinas): 536
Ragan, G. A.: 185
Ragland, Fenelon? W.: 178
Rambin,
Adelaïde *[See Marie Françoise Adelaïde.]*
André Michel: 36, 256-68, 516, 522-23, 609, 647
Auguste: 523
Charles: 259, 379, 436, 558-59
Edouard Lestang: 117, 436
Felicité (Mme. Remy La Fitte): 260
François: 8, 114, 256-57, 261-63, 538, 561
Jean Baptiste Azenor: 27
Lestan *[See Edouard Lestang.]*
Rambin (cont'd)
Louis Neuville: 259-60
Marie Catherine (Mme. François Joseph La Fitte): 257
Marie Desirée (Mme. Denis Casenave): 114
Marie Emelia (Mme. François Mero Hesser): 647
Marie Euphrosine (Mme. Michel Chamard); 13, 49
Marie Françoise Adelaÿde (Mme. Christian Hesser); 54, 140, 150, 292, 380-81, 538, 647
Marie Pompose (Dña. Joseph Garcie): 414
Michel: 27, 36, 65, 114,117, 259-60, 414 *[See also André Michel.]*
Neuville: 610
Ramez, Maria Guadeloupe (Dña. Ignacio Gonzales: 224
Ramirez (var. Ramires),
Asumption: 661
Cayetano: 661
Jossé: 234
José de Jesus: 314
Maria Incarnacion (Dña. Nicolas Bela); 235
Ramones, Antonio: 347 (bis)
Ramos, Joseph: 357
Ransdell, John H.: 490
Rapicault, Louise (Mme. François Archinard): 302
Ratio, Ignatio: 357
Raubelo *[See Robleau.]*
Recío *[See Racio.]*
Read, Sarah (Mrs. M. Waters): 385
Reed (Rhea), Samuel: 231
Reeve?, G. W.: 354
Renaud *[See Agaisse, Reynaud.]*
Renderne?, Theodora (Dña. Antonio Cordero): 214
Renois *[See Epron.]*
Reyburn,
James: 547
William Patrick: 547, 577-78
Reynaud, J.: 265
Reynaud *[See also Agaisse.]*
Reynolds, Ignace/?Agnes (Mrs. Peter Burnett); 275
Raimond (Remond): Magdalena (Mme. André Vascocu); 78, 85

Richard, Henriette (Mme. François Trotreau): 504
Riguelli, Pascoalina (Mme. Laurent Marcoli); 449, 585
Ris (var. Jean Ris, Jnt. Ris, Jeanris, Jean-Risse),
Celeste Jean (Mme. Louis Vascocu): 191, 443
Eleanor Jean (Mme. François Du Bois): 18, 173, 192
Jean: 63, 84
Marie (Mme. Michel Denis Caseneuve): 36, 114, 516
Marie Aspasy: 63, 419
Marie Barbe: 101
Marie Marcelite: 84, 384, 658
Risher, Jno. W.: 394
Rival, Marie (Mme. J. Baptiste Ducournau): 663
Rivas, Juana Maria (Dña. Joseph Lasarino): 25
Rivers,
Leonard: 678
Louise Eliza (Mme. Antonio Perini): 501
William: 501
[See also Del Rio.]
Robertson?, G.: 12
Robin, Anne "Nanette" (Mme. Pierre Beaudouin): 15, 81, 347
Robinson (var. Robinston),
F?: 217
Joseph Toole I: 160, 372
Joseph Toole II: 160, 250, 321, 372, 387
M.: 577
M. M.: 577
Marie (Mrs. Joseph Toole Robinson I): 372
Mary (Mrs. Abraham R. Luyster): 656
Roblo (var. Robleau, Robles, Roubelor, Raubelo, Roublot),
Augustin: 525
Edouard Lestang: 150
François: 329
José Marie: 329
Marie (Dña Onofre Flores): 590
Marie Celine (Mme. J. La Fitte): 115
Marie Cephalide: 525
Marie Cephalide (Mme. Pierre La Fitte): 592
Onore: 525
Roblo (cont'd),
Pierre I (100, 115, 258, 525, 590
Pierre II: 258, 592
Pierre Ceser: 525
Rocheto, _____: 15
Rocques (var. Roques):
C., f.m.c.: 645
Charles Nerestan, I, f.m.c.: 6, 43, 74 118, 167, 172, 174, 198, 211, 267, 334, 339, 374-5, 395 479, 481, 486-87, 497, 541, 586, 634, 646
Charles Nerestan II, f.m.c.: 479, 497, 515, 608, 623, 634, 646
Elisée, f.m.c.: 43, 47, 48, 74, 198
Jacob Elisée, f.m.c.: 551, 634
Marie Elise, f.w.c. (Mme. Pierre Neres Metoyer): 374-75
Marie Silvanie, f.w.c. (Mme. Jerome Sarpy II): 497
Marie Thérèze, f.w.c. (Mme. François Florival Metoyer): 586
Pedro: 6, 47
Rodriguez (var. Rodrigue),
Antonio: 235
Dolores (Dña. Marcelino de la Garza): 95
Feliciana (Dña. Juan B. de Soto): 601
Joachin: 95
Manuel: 3
Maria Cruz (Dña. Juan Cortes): 535
Roi *[See Roy.]*
Rogueol, Jn.: 618
Roiff?, Catharine (Mrs. Thomas Horn): 599
Rond,
Joseph François: 75, 384, 651
Marie Louise: 651
Michel: 75
O?: 651
Roques *[See Rocques.]*
Rosalie, f.w.c. *[See La Caze.]*
Rosales (var. Rossales),
André: 295
Julian: 26
Maria Ignacia (Dña. Teodoro Quintero): 26, 569
Rose, Catherine (Mrs. William Knight): 489

Ross, Jeanne (Dña. J. B. Ortis): 155
Rossier, Maria Juana (Mme. Michel Rond): 75
Rossignol, Marie Louise (Mme. Antoine Biossat): 520
Rossuy?, V.: 360
Rost,
  Emile: 326
  P. N.: 94
Roubelot *[See Roblo.]*
Roubieu,
  Auguste: A-679
  François: 183, 281, 578
  Françoise Adelaÿde (Mme. Felix François Gracien Paul): 183
  J.: 669
  Lucinda (Mrs. Michel Boyce): 578
  Marie Euphemie (Mme. Jacques Dufrois Derbanne): A-679
  Oscar: 183, 220, 466
  Pauline: 670
Roublot *[See Roblo.]*
Rougeot,
  Jean Baptiste: 277
  Severin: 277
Rouquier,
  Elisa, f.w.c. (Mme. Celestin La Caze): 294
  François I: 354
  François II: 19, 37, 74, 313, 354, 550
  François Jacques, f.m.c.: 294
  Henriette (Mrs. John Charles Carr): 284, 313, 441, 640
  J. B. Olivier): 498, 505, 507, 530, 550, 666
  Jean Baptiste, f.m.c.: 294
  Jean François: 394
  L. J.: 628, 631, 639, 663-64
  Marie Josephine (Mme. Jean Cortes): 148, 241, 269, 441, 640
  Marie Aimé (Mrs. James Bludworth): 296, 398, 462
  Olivier: 431
  Suzette, f.w.c.: 294, 400
  V^{e} (*Veuve* = Widow): 142, 284
Rouzet, _____: 20
Rowzee?, _____: 30
Roy (var. Roi),
  Auguste: 638
  Etienne: 187, 346 (bis)
  Noel: 187
  Pierre: 638 *[See also Le Roy.]*
Royer,
  François: 178
  Marie Reine (Mrs. G. W. Gunny): 178
Rueg, Louis: 671
Ruelle, Lise: 288
Ruiz (var. Ruez, Ruis),
  _____ H.: 181
  Francisco: 1, 2
  Maria (Dña. Pedro Cordova): 263
  Maria: 426
  Maria Gertrude: 224
  Maria Loreta de Guadaloupe (Dña. Martin Gonzales); 224
  Maria Paula (Dña. Mariano Sanchez); 33
Rushing,
  Ashton G.; 676
  B.: 676
Russell (var. Russel),
  _____: 81
  David?: 178
  John P.: 306
  Mary (Mrs. William Glass): 298
  Robert H.: 132
  Samuel P., Dr.: 132, 173, 217, 345, 345 (bis), 350, 353-54, 394
  W. H.: 218
  William: 217
Russi?, Charles: 121
Ryan, Ann (Mrs. William Shelly): 533

Sac[k], Michel: 559
Sachell (Sackett?), S? (R?) P.: 359
Saide?, Carron?: 678
St. Amans (var. S. Amans, St. Amand),
  Amans B.: 529, 641
  Joseph Guillaume Bauvard de: 285, 499, 518, 520, 529
  Marie Amelie Eulodie (Mrs. Thomas Edward De Russy): 529
  Mathilde (Mme. J. B. Plauché): 308
St. André,
  André: 29, 145-46
  Felix: 53, 146
  Marië Adrienne (Mme. François St. Germaine): 368
  Marie Eloise (Mme. Louis Solastie Rachal): 143, 454, 527

St. André (cont'd),
Marie Louise (Mme. Pierre Moreau): A-681
Marie Victoire (Mme. François Baudry): 420, A-681
Marie Zeline, f.w.c.: (Mme. Jacques Le Court): 549
Onezime: 29

St. Germaine,
François: 368
Marie Hélène (Mrs. McKendrick Moses): 368

St. Vigne,
Antoine: 438, 453
Louis: 453

Saintville *[See J. B. Saint Ville Mariotte.]*

Saïs, Maria Bernarda (Dña. José Lasa? Sosa? Lasarino?): 672

Salcedo (var. Saucera),
Cayetan: 672
Desideria (Mrs. Leonard Rivers): 678
Desiderio: 665, 672
Jacoba (Dña. Juan Ximenes): 665

Salinas (var. Salenas),
Encarnacion (Dña. Mathias Bernea): 76
Joachim: 678

Salvado, Jeanne (Dña. Bazile Alvares): 432

Salvado *[See also Palvado.]*

Salvant,
Marie (Mme. Jean Pierre Cloutier): 21, 127
Marie Louise (Mme. Jean Chrisostomé Perot): 28, 67, 307, 463

Sn. _____a, Francisco: 30

Sanchez (var. Sanches, Sanctes),
Barbara (Dña. Raymondo Ximenes): 627
Candido: 570, 572
Ignatio: 627
Joseph: 14, 61
Joseph Aucle: 432
Joseph Maria: 61
Joseph (Jossé) Leander: 234
Joseph Manuel: 14
Manuela (Mme. Nicolas Deroque): 214
Maria Eulalia (Dña. Jossé Leander Sanchez; Dña. Pedro Del Rio): 234
Maria Feliciana: 512
Maria Louisa (Dña. Manuel Bustamente): 616

Sanchez (cont'd)
Maria Manuela (Dña. Joseph Cris. Cordova): 33, 347 (bis)
Maria Merced (Dña. Juan Bautista Chirino): 366
Mariano: 31

Sanders *[See Saunders.]*

Sandoval, Josefa (Dña. José Antonio Ocon): 90

Sanginette, S. H.: 274

Sanglier,
Etienne: 324, 351
Marie Felicité, f.w.c. (Mrs. George W. Duncan): 540

San Miguel,
Joseph: 295, 357, 493, 535
Maria Edouarda (Dña. Joseph Ramos): 357

Sansom,
André: 373
Theodore André: 373

Santa Cruz, Maria (Dña. Warline Guadalupe?) Cantona): 235
[See also Cruz.]

Santos,
José: 600
Manuel: 202
[See also de los Santos Coy.]

Sarnac *[See Jarnac.]*

Sarpy,
_____ (Sieur): 48
Jean Baptiste Lille: 181, 187, 197, 228, 233, 240, 286, 323, 327, 48?
Jerome I, f.m.c.: 43, 47-48, 74, 198, 334, 468, 497, 608
Jerome II, f.m.c.: 392, 497, 634
Marie Euphrosie, f.w.c. (Mme. J. Valcour Metoyer): 468
Marie Lilette, f.w.c. (Mme. Ambroise Azenor Metoyer): 608
Teresa (Mme. Graciano Noyrit): 12

Saucera *[See Salcedo.]*

Saucier (var. Socier, Sosier),
Felicité (Mme. André Chamard): 197, 518
François: 72
Louis: 16, 72
Marie Rose (Mme. Theodore Deterville): 404

Saunders,
John: 206
Julius C.: 206
Savaille, Maria Ramona (Dña. Gasinto Troquillio): 467
Saxon, Eugenia Rebecca (Mrs. Patrick James O'Doherty): 670
Saydeck (var. Saidec, Sidec),
Marie Cecile (Mrs. Thomas McDonald): 346
Marie Rose (Mrs. Stephen Grant): 461
Schamp,
George: 291
Marie An[n] Cynthia (Mrs. Obadiah D. Oaks): 291
Schifler, Magdeleine (Mme. Nicolas Kieffer II): 548
Schmitt, Louis: 617
Sciolli, Marie Celeste (Mme. Jean Antoine Soldini): 367
Scopini, François: 77
Scroggins, Jordan: 325
Segoure, Jacoba (Dña. Joachin Rodriguez): 95
Sepulvedo,
José Antonio: 14, 575
Maria Juana (Mme. Joseph Bébé): 575
Serda *[See de la Cerda.]*
Serpentini, François: 5, 16, 69-70, 270
Sers,
Abel Napoleon: 169, 194-95, 247, 382, 417
Abel II: 677
Charles: 333, 389, 417
Pierre Jean Abel: 169
Shattuck,
B. F.: 352
Rachel (Mrs. Samuel Hazelton): 11
Shelburne (var. Shelberun),
Marie Susanne (Mrs. Louis von Schonbrock): 642
Silas: 642
[See also Sherburne.]
Shelly (var. Shely),
John: 533
Patrick: 533
William: 533
Sherburne (Cherbourne), Felix B.: 127, 142, 550, 565, 669
[See also Shelburne.]
Sherdien, Mary (Mrs. James McGown): 564
Shirlitiff, Marie (Mrs. Raphaelle Morgan): 430
Shulman, P.: 640
Sibley,
H. H.: 547
Helena (Mrs. Peter French Kimball): 306, 345, 547
Henrietta (Mrs. Benjamin Franklin Chapman; Mrs. William Patrick Reyburn): 279, 345, 547
John, Dr.: 11, 275, 277, 305, 345, 345 (bis), 547
Margaret: 11
R. A.: 547
Sidec *[See Saydeck.]*
Sidre *[See Cedars.]*
Silvie, Louis: 113
Simon *dit* Larouille (var. Simeon),
Simon, ______: 287
Charles, I, f.m.c.: 126, 130, 216, 238, 410, 442
Charles II, f.m.c.: 130, 149, 179, 216, 238
Charles *[See also Joseph Chas.]*
Damassene *[See Jeanne Damasene]*
Eulalie, f.w.c. (Mme. Zenon Mézières): 130
Jean, f.m.c.: 442
Jeanne Damasene, f.w.c. (Mme. Simeon Trichel): 126
Joseph Charles, f.m.c.: 410
Marie Josephe, f.w.c. (Mme. Ls. Lamathe II): 216
Maria Rosalis (Dña. Luca McDonato): 262
Simmons (var. Simons),
Samuel S.: 519, 656
William: 519
Slocum,
Charles: 17, 31
Juliana Josepha (Mme. Firmin Poissot): 11, 17
Smith,
Elisabeth (Mrs. Asa Kimball): 345
James: 597, A-680
Joseph: 597
Socier *[See Saucier.]*
Soldini,
Jean Antoine: 367

Soldini (cont'd),
Joseph: 367
Soldoti, Anna (Mme. Pierre Balzaretti): 620
Soligny,
Catherine (Dña. Joseph Alphonse Dominingo): 116
Joseph: 100
Marie Rose (Mme. Edouard Lestan Roblo): 100
Solis,
Antonio: 16
Esteban: 16
Sompaÿrac,
Adeline (Mrs. J. G. Campbell): 567
Adolphe: 193, 239, 292, 541, 595, 618, 654
Ambrose: 13, 19, 46, 135, 140, 168, 181, 218, 285, 296, 313, 331, 359-60, 376, 382, 446, 465, 545, 567, 595, 618, 637-38
Ambrose Bernard Theophile: 350, 376, 382, 545, 595, 618, 654, 666
Charles Emile: 345 (bis), 354, 359, 372, 376, 382, 465, 618
Jules: 532, 595, 637?, 666, 675
Louis: 181, 228, A-679
Louise Victoire Desirée (Mme. Jules Victor Bossier; Mme. Ambroise Le Comte): 218, 618
Marc: 9, 21, 64, 162, 169, 181, 190, 194-95, 218, 225, 229, 231, 246, 252, 264-65, 287, 305, 360, 376, 382, 504, 532, 545, 567, 595
Marie Armeline (Mme. Ambrose Bernard Theophile Sompayrac): 382, 545
Marie Marzeline (Mme. Alexandre L. Deblieux II): 465
Paul Victor: 135, 181, 331, 382
Virginia (Mrs. Peabody Atkinson Morse); 359-60, 545, 567, 617
V. (*Veuve?* or widow?): 218, 360
Sorel (var. Sorelle),
Clarisse (Mme. J. B. Besson II): 205
Dominique: 5, 205, 321
Felicité (Mme. Vital Vascocu): 458
Geneviève (Mme. J. B. Grappe): 55
Marie Jeanne (Mme. Augustin Fredieu): 5, 19, 191, 507
Ursin: 321
Sosa (var. de Sosa),
Andeloisine (Dña. Francisco Himenes): 627
Sosa (cont'd),
Maria Juliana (Mme. Denis Caseneuve): 516
Miguel: 516
[See also Lasa, Soto, Suza.]
Soto (Sosa?),
Cristoval): 69
Maria Josefa del Refugia (Dña. Torivio? Darvon?): 69
Soto (var. de Soto),
Firmin: 182, 601
Francisco: 314
Getrudes (Dña. Martin Prado): 574
Gregorio: 314
José Maria: 314
Juan: 182, 601
Lorenzo: 182, 601
Maria Ignacia (Dña. Manuel Martinez); 366
Marie Incarnacion (Dña. Alexandre de la Garce): 342
[See also De Soto.]
Sou?, Marie Françoise (Dña. José de la Garze): 95
Southerland (var. Suderline, Sudderline),
Emelie, f.w.c.: 179, 540
Marguerite Adelaïde, f.w.c. (Mme. Emanuel Trichel): 179
Souvone (Louvone?), Magdalene (Mme. J. B. Choppin): 87
Stansburg?, William: 360
Stevens, Susanna (Mrs. Bryan Morse): 360
Stone,
Mary (Mrs. James B. Tucker), 654
Nancy (Mrs. John Marrs), 654
Stucchi, Adolfo: 501
Sturges, James?: 678
Sudderline *[See Southerland.]*
Symes, Maria l'Infans (Dña. Atanasio de la Cerda): 467
Sueyos, Marie (Mme. François Arcoit): 18
Suza, Maria Antonia (Dña. Lumin? Cruz): 119

Taber, David F.: 359
Talon, Julia, f.w.c.: 531
Tarby,
Eugenie: 312

Tarby (cont'd),
Josephine Madleine (Mrs. John Hardy): 312, 638
Taylor,
James, 643
T. N.: 641
Tauzin,
C. E.: 650
E. C.: 193, 197
Eugenie (Murphy): 264
F. C.: 356, 360, 499, 545
H.: 360
J. E.: 637-38
Joseph: 13, 49, 60, 72, 180, 193, 218, 264, 510, 637, 666
Lezin Eugene: 180, 193, 197
Louis Joseph: 140, 180, 264
Marcelin: 193, 336, 356, 446, 457, 637, 666
Marie Celeste Victoire (Mme. Benjamin Dranguet): 356, 422, 499, 641
Marie Euphrosine (Mme. Alexandre Louis Deblieux I): 465, 482, 545
Theophile E.: 264, 292, 356, 359, 422, 446, 465, 510, 545, 596, 618, 628, 631, 637, 656
Ternier (var. Ternié),
Louis: 54
Marie Arsise Odisse (Mme. Jean Louis Christomé Perot): 28, 464, 580
Marie Cephalide: 105, 332
Marie Odisse *[See Marie Arsise.]*
Pierre I *dit* Grenoble: 18, 28, 77, 105, 393, 415, 431
Pierre: 431, 437, 464, 580, 649
Terrell,
Bardet Ashton: 462
George Hunter: 462
Tessier,
J. M.: 615, 677
John (Jean): 615
Nativity (Mrs. Neill McClean): 615
Phelonise (Mme. Simon De Soto): 452
Pierre: 452
Thierry *[See Quierry.]*
Thomassie (var. Thomassi, Tomassi, Tomasin),
Agnes Aglaë (Mme. Charles Gallien): 622
Cezer: 24
Jerome: 208, 622
Thomassie (cont'd),
Louis I: 4, 8, 24, 208
Louis II; 4
Marie François (Mme. Louis Emanuel Gallien): 8, 424, 625
Marie Reine (Mme. Louis Julien Rachal): 274, 318-19, 624
Thompson (Thomson),
Marie (Mrs. Amos Donovan); 471
Thomas: 362
Tillebory, Catherine (Mrs. Joseph Jeremy Molone); 597
Titus,
Amos, 594
Lewis M.: 491, 555, 594
Tobal, Marie des Anges (Dña. Macedonio Carmona; Dña. Joseph Fecond Agustera): 474
Torbeyns (Torbayas?), Michel: 400, 408, 416
Torchson?, T.: 519
Toro?, José: 76
Torres (var. Toures),
Bernardo: 37
Felicité M. (Mrs. John O'Connor): 97
Joseph Andres: 37
Josep[h]a: 607
Miguel: 366, 537
Julienne (Mme. J. B. Vallery): 138
Patricio de: 1, 2
Tosson *[See Chauson.]*
Totin,
Leon: 83
Remy: 84-85, 399
Tournoir, Lucile (Mme. J. Jarreau): 305, 361b, 488
Trego, Serafina (Dña. Pedro de Luna): 202
Tremaux,
François Etienne: 617
Joseph Leon: 617
Trevino,
Antonio: 34
Francisco: 493
Trezzini (var. Trezinni),
Caroline (Mme. Jules Compaÿrac): 595
Jean Baptiste: 7, 13, 49, 264, 336, 356, 482, 499, 543, 595
Louis: 134
(Cont'd)

Trezzini (cont'd),
Marie Heloïse (Mme. Joseph Numa Deblieux): 482
Pier[re] Celestin: 13
Trichel (var. Triché, Trichele, Trichell, Trichelle),
Arsene (Mrs. Joseph T. Robinson): 160, 372
Athanase Pierre: 55, 67, 73, 144, 189
Celisie *[See Marie Ceizie.]*
Emanuel: 160, 245, 387, 498
Emanuel, f.m.c.: 179
Bertille François, f.m.c.: 157, 214, 216, 365, 391, 401, 478
François Henry: 245
Françoise "Fanchonette," 103, 189
H. T.: 484
Henry: 18, 54-55, 67
Henry F.: 283, 431
Jean Baptiste I: 133-34, 336, 505
Jean Baptiste II: 134, 193, 237, 285, 385, 402
L.: 498
Leonard: 498, 503
Marguerite, f.w.c. (Dña. Ramon del Rio): 652
Marie Celizie (Mme. Celestin Ely): 393, 580
Marie Celezie, f.w.c.: 179
Marie Celina (Dña. Chrisanto de Odiardi): 387
Marie Emelie (Mme. Raymond Durand; Mme. J. B. Derbanne; Mme. Jules Cesar Napoleon Luvini): 133, 336
Marie Felicité (Mme. J. B. Perot): 378, 530, 596
Marie Françoise (Mme. Jean François Le Vasseur): 193, 446
Marie Julienne, f.w.c. (Mme. François Grappe): 563
Marie Odise, f.w.c. (Mme. Noël de Mézières): 365
Marie Thérèze (Mme. Hypolite Bordelon I): 67, 503
Melanie (Mme. Louis Darmelin Pavot): 176, 283
P.: 191, 300, 320
Pierre: 104, 238, 266, 271-73, 283
Severin: 464, 469, 505, 507, 580, 589, 596, 629
Sylvain: 649, 654, 668
Simeon, f.m.c.: 126, 216, 272, 563

Troquillio,
Athanas: 433-35, 467
Gasinto: 467
Trotreau (var. Trotraut),
François: 504
Jules: 418, 504, 554
Trouvat, Louis: 316, 346 (bis), 504
Tucker,
James B.: 654
James M. B.: 654
John: 654
Tuomey,
Patrick O.: 643
William L.: 595, 643, 650

Ustry, Pauley (Mrs. James Ector); 436

Vaca (Vacca), Antonio: 365, 410, 609, 627
Vail, Daniel H.: 360
Valbois, Marie (Dña. Juan Bautista Aragon): 155
Valentin (var. Valentine),
Jean Andres: 50
Joseph: 50, 100, 514, 517, 591
Marie Louise (Mme. François Poirier): 514
Marie Magdelene (Mme. Ursin Poirier): 517
Thérèse (Mme. Pierre Gagnon I): 173
Victor: 591
Valery (var. Vallery),
François: 138
Jean Baptiste: 138
Vanier,
Jean Baptiste: 278
Louis Narcisse: 278
Van Melder, Pierre: 383
Van Schonbroeck *[See Von Schonbroeck.]*
Varela *[See Barela.]*
Vargas *[See Bargas.]*
Varrera, Juan: 33
Varrera *[See also Barrera.]*
Vascocu (var. Baccocu, Bacocu, Vacocu, Vaastcocu, Vaast coqu),
André: 78, 85, 144
[See also Martilien André.]

Vascocu (cont'd),
Celine (Mme. Pierre Mathieu Backen): 419
Chrisostomé *[See Jean Chrisostomé]*
Donatien: 99
Hélène (Mme. Isaac Gourinat): 443
J. B.: 658
Jean Baptiste: 63, 97, 384, 419
Jean Baptiste André: 438, 485
Jean Baptiste Xandre: 408
Jean Chrisostomé: 78, 84, 101, 102, 191, 270, 297, 384, 452, 658
Jean Louis: 63, 84-85, 97, 270, 384
Jean V.: 68, 84, 85, 101
Joseph: 63, 85
Louis: 191, 443 *[See also Jean Louis.]*
Madame: 102
Madeleine (Mme. Jean Victor L'Herisson): 438
Marie Aimée (Mme. Eusebe Hissoura): 78, 469, 588
Marie Aimée (Mme. Frederic Montier): 485
Marie Eulalye: 84
Marie Françoise (Mme. Jean Ris): 63, 84
Marie Lollete (Mme. Mathieu Leon Boudrige): 270
Marie Louise: 191
Marie Madelein (Mrs. William Walker II): 658
Marie Miramis (Mme. Joseph Vascocu): 85
Marie Therresse Andres: 88
Martilien André: 101, 318
Raimond: 144
S.: 658
Vital: 458
Vaughn,
Mathilda (Mrs. Theodore J. Moise): 614
Robert: 614
Vega (Bega): José Antonio: 50
Vega *[See also de la Bega.]*
Veiss, Anne (Mme. François Bollender): 548
Vercher (var. Verchere, Vergere *[not to be confused with Verger.]*,
A. Beloni: 209, 415
Celimen (Mrs. J. B. McTire): 209
Daunoye: 184
Vercher (cont'd),
Jacques: 162, 184, 268, 293, 309, 397, 418, 425, 506, 528
Jean Pierre: 290, 307, 315
Joseph: 29
Joseph *fils* Jacques: 528
Josephine (Mme. J. B. Le Noir); 397
Laiza (Mme. Silvestre Hernandez): 162
Louis: 506
Marie Adelaÿde (Mme. Jean La Lande): 76
Marie Catherine (Mme. Breville Perot): 307
Marie Emelia (Mme. Michel Lattier): 290
Marie Rosalie (Mme. Dominique Rachal): 38, 105, 108, 159, 332, 402
Marie Suzette (Mme. Athanase Denis): 293
Marcelin: 506
Maximin: 415
Maximin *[brother of above]*: 635
Valsin: 528
Zulma (Mme. Ozmin Pierre Derbanne): 418
Marie Celeste (Mme. Augustin Langlois); 22, 139, 282, 350
Veulemans (var. Veleumans, Veulement, Vulments),
D.: 366
Jeanne (Mme. Henri Von Scholbroeck): 383, 642
Peeter: 541
Vidal, _____: 75
Vienne,
Azenor, f.m.c.: 662
B.: 19
E.: 639, 644
F.: 604, 629, 666
François: 355, 639
Louis François Neuville: 355, 653
Marie Marianne Azoline (Mrs. William Penn Morrow): 638
Villareal (var. Biareal, Viareál),
Domingo: 535
Juan: 248
Marie Gertrude (Dña. Francisco Robles): 329

Villareal (cont'd),
   Ramon: 535
Villaret?, Calletano: 33
Villegar,
   Ignace: 472-73
   Maria Josefa (Dña. Joseph Guadaloupe Ferel); 98
Vimines *[See Ximenes.]*
Vicente (Bensan), Michel: 50
Vineda, José: 77
Von Schonbroeck,
   François: 383
   Henry: 383, 642
   Louis: 383, 642
Voorhies, Octave: 670

Walker,
   Benjamin: 269
   Diane (Mrs. John West-Cavert): 96
   Joal: 96
   William: 658
Wallace (var. Walas, Wallet *[not to be confused with Wallet, Ouallette]*),
   Delize (Mme. Marcel De Soto II): 256
   James I: 2, 256, 298-99
   James II: 298
   Maximilien: 299
   Pierre: 2, 379, 584
Wallet *[See Oualette.]*
Wals, W. S.: 540
Walter, Celeste (Dña. Ilario Carasco): 373
Warksmut, F?: 529
Waters:
   Gerry R.: 385
   Mastin: 385
Watkins, Anna (Mrs. Ebenezer Ash): 417
Watts, Charles: 358
Wayble, Celeste (Mme. Noel Roy): 187
Webster, Mary (Mrs. William Hickman): 236, 369, 490
Welche, James: 562
Werly, Ann (Mrs. Isaac Middleton): 491
West (Cavert), John *[See Cavert.]*
White,
   Andrew: 304
   Henry: 564
Whiteman, Paula (Mme. Guillaume Brevel): 220
Williams,
   Frederic: 306, 327, 345, 345 (bis), 356, 643, 675
Williams (cont'd),
   George F.: 345 (bis)
   Henry J.: 345, 345 (bis)
Willson, Rebecca (Mrs. Richard Woods I): 440
Winter,
   Caroline (Mrs. Jared Cable): 372
   Harriet Hogden (Mrs. Alexandre W. Pannell: Mrs. Robert D? Coombs: Mme. Peter Petrovick): 359, 519, 656
Wisby,
   Patrick: 310
   Youwell: 310
Woods, Richard: 424, 440
Woolf, Antoine: 510

Ximenes (var. Giminez, Hymenes, Zimenes),
   Domingo: 556
   Francisco: 627, 665
   Gertrude (Dña. Gregorio Soto): 314
   José: 556, 587, 672
   Juan: 69, 627, 665
   Maria (Dña. Polinario 495
   Raymondo: 627

y Barbo (var. Barbe, Barbo, Hevarvo, Ibarbe, Ibarbo, Ybarbe, Ybarbo, Yvarbo),
   Dionicio: 587
   Francisco: 352, 426, 556, 587
   Gregorio: 412-14, 558-59
   José: 347 (bis), 426
      [See also Joseph, Juan José]
   José Gregorio: 347 (bis)
   José Maria: 600
   José Polonio: 587
   Joseph: 32, 352
   Joseph Antonio: 426
   Joseph Miguel: [illegible]
   Juan: 286
   Juan José: 286, 558
   Manuel: 536, 573, 600
   Maria Antonia (Dña. Miguel Sosa); 516
   (Cont'd)

y Barbo (cont'd),
Maria Antonia (Dña. Juan Villareal): 248
Maria Brigida (Dña. Andres Bermella): 573
Marie Canuti (Dña. Jesus Flores); 399
Maria Jetrudis (Dña. ____tos Santos Procela): 79
Maria Josepha (Dña. Sanchez); 61
Maria Louisa (Mme. Jean Baptiste Prudhomme): 379, 413
Maria Pedra (Dña. Salustiano Vasquez); 667
Maria Tiburcia (Dña. Joseph Cordova): 33-34
Martin: 39
Miguel: 248
Pedro: 399
Remy: 399
Vicente: 587
Yong, Clara (Mme. Paul Aimé Fleury): 444

Zimenes *[See Ximenes.]*
Zoriche, *dit* Michel,
Marie Rose (Mme. Sylvestre Rachal): 348
Marie Suzette (Mme. Jean Benjamin Morantine): 542
Marie Zepherine (Mme. Pierre Adolphe Lafargue): 466
Pierre Michel I: 29, 348
Pierre Michel II: 348, 361, 466, 542
Zarnac *[See Jarnac.]*

www.ingramcontent.com/pod-product-compliance
Lightning Source LLC
Chambersburg PA
CBHW071949160426
43198CB00011B/1612

9781585499243